TO:

FROM:

EXPERIENCING

GOD

AT HOME

DAY-BY-DAY

EXPERIENCING
GOD
AT HOME
DAY-BY-DAY

A Family Devotional

TOM BLACKABY
& RICK OSBORNE

PUBLISHING GROUP
Nashville, Tennessee

978-1-4336-7984-1

Published by B&H Publishing Group
Nashville, Tennessee

Tom Blackaby is represented by the literary agency
of Wolgemuth & Associates, Inc.

Dewey Decimal Classification: 649
Subject Heading: FAMILY LIFE \ CHRISTIAN LIFE \
DEVOTIONAL LITERATURE

Unless otherwise noted, all Scripture is taken from the Holman Christian
Standard Bible® (HCSB), Copyright © 1999, 2000, 2002, 2003, by
Holman Bible Publishers. Used by permission. Holman Christian
Standard Bible®, Holman CSB® and HCSB® are federally registered trade-
marks of Holman Bible Publishers.

1 2 3 4 5 6 7 8 • 17 16 15 14 13

From Tom

To my family: Kim, Erin, Matt, and Conor, who have been such an inspiration and support to me in ministry.

From Rick

This book is dedicated to my amazing wife Luba who walks with me daily in God's presence, in prayer, and in His Word. Thank you, sweetness, for being my partner in life, in ministry, and in spiritual growth. It's a joy to experience God with you!

Experiencing God at Home Day-by-Day

THE IMPORTANCE OF FAMILY DEVOTION TIME AND BIBLE READING

The family is very important to God. He created it! So when families come together around the study of God's Word this allows them to be in harmony with the heart of God! All throughout the Bible God chose families to be a part of His activity. How crucially important it is for each family to seek and search for the heart of God together through a time of prayer and in the study of His Word.

God's Word has been integral to my life and to my family. Not just reading it, but listening to what God is saying to us through it. That is how I discovered the principles that became the Bible study called *Experiencing God: Knowing and Doing the Will of God.* Through this study millions of people around the world have come to know God more intimately and more personally. They have been able to join God in what He is doing in their life and through their family. They have seen the wonder of God changing lives and bringing hope to people who had never before heard the Good News. All five of my children have felt the hand of God on their lives and all five have been involved in full-time Christian service in one way or another.

It is a joy to talk as a family about God's Word and see the eyes of your children light up as they realize God wants to use them too in a significant way in His kingdom. It is not our desire that you read a devotion every day—we want you to experience God every day! We want you to see how He can transform your own heart, to mold and shape you after the image of His Son Jesus Christ, and to inspire you to be "salt" and "light" in your own community. Be careful not to skip over the Bible verses on each page when you read the devotional thought. Open God's Word together with your children and let the Spirit of God take the Word of God and apply it to your lives each day. A devotional book should never be a substitute for reading God's Word directly.

In addition, family devotionals will prepare the heart and mind for further thought and deeper times in God's Word. A devotional time is a pacesetter for a deeper study of God's Word. Take a nugget from a devotional thought and go deeper with God. Search Him out, study the people He was talking with, decipher the deeper meanings of the words and phrases you read, ask yourself whether or not God is truly speaking to you and guiding you in the way you should go in various areas of your life. Seek and you will find, knock and the door will be opened unto you, ask and it will be given unto you as you seek God's kingdom to be an integral part of your life and in your home.

Simply reading the Bible—especially out loud—impacts every person who hears it because it is the "tool" the Holy Spirit uses. Thus, reading the Word of God is always enriching and powerful. Reading to the family in the family setting is vital: as you begin each day, as you live out each day, and as you conclude each day. It is essential that you have Scriptures in your mind and heart throughout the night. David affirms this in the Psalms! It is also crucial to have Scriptures in your thoughts throughout the day for every planned and unplanned moment. You never know what or who you will meet where the Scriptures will be a vital factor and life-changing!

Deliberately spending time with God for a time of devotion is a wise practice and will impact each individual family member and beyond as you implement what the Lord shows you in His Word! Remember God thinks in terms of generations and beyond, not just individuals. What you do as a family today in obedience to your heavenly Father will impact those who follow in your footsteps. Children, grandchildren, and great-grandchildren will see how God has blessed your obedience to Him, and they will want to follow your example.

A family devotional time will also prepare your children to develop their own habit of seeking God in their own lives. This is so important for each believer to know God personally and intimately so that they will have a vibrant, authentic, and growing relationship with God. May God add His blessing to your family as together you seek and search for Him.

Dr. Henry T. Blackaby

INTRODUCTION AND INSTRUCTIONS

God's purpose and will for us is that we walk with Him, learn from Him, and be transformed by His Spirit who is at work within us daily. Therefore, every spiritual discipline and endeavor, whether it's prayer, Bible reading or study, church attendance and church involvement, or even family devotions, should achieve this same purpose—not merely "go through the motions" of doing them. We pray this book will increase your Bible knowledge, help you and your family draw closer to God, and experience Him more and more in your home.

Using This Devotional

This book begins in the book of Genesis and ends in the book of Revelation, so you will have a chance to go through the whole Bible together within a year, using:

- Fifty weeks of devotions, including a "Parent Connection" feature and five daily devotions
- Flexibility to accommodate church attendance; personal, special devotionals; and life's interruptions
- Undated devotions—begin any day of the year and not feel rushed

Each week begins with the **Parent Connection** to brief you on the week's devotions and help prepare you for the issues and questions that may arise. Set a special time each week to review in advance, along with the portions of the Bible that you'll be reading through for the week, and to pray for help and wisdom.

Each daily devotional includes several features:

- **Reading**—This Scripture passage is the key to the devotion. You may want to have your older children take turns reading with you. This will be the focus for the day's devotion—don't miss it!
- **Quick Start**—The conversation-starter. Try not to rush this; instead, use the time to make sure everyone is engaged. You may want to use the questions and conversation ideas provided or take things in your own direction. (You'll also find this feature will encourage less distraction and more listening for what's next.)
- **Quest**—Short devotional readings to encourage thought, application, and interaction. Consider sharing the reading responsibilities with other family members.

• **Quiet Family Prayer**—Suggested prayer topic, if it fits the conversation; if it doesn't, then pray about what you did discuss. Take this prayer opportunity to include additional items that are relevant to what's going on in everyone's life. Keep it short enough that everyone stays engaged. Remember, when you're praying as a family you should pray in a way that everyone can simply understand and agree to. This is an opportunity to encourage your children in public prayer—encourage but don't push. Start them off with one item to pray about (when they're ready) and praise them for their efforts. Prayer is conversation with God; there isn't a list of rules.

• **Quiet Times**—Bonus feature for each day, a chance for your children to reflect and pray on their own.

• **Children's Assignments**—Age-appropriate assignments for personal devotions. You can decide which one best suit each of your children. We encourage you to sit in on these until your children are old enough (and disciplined enough) to do devotions on their own. **One more very important** note on this topic—children learn by example; be sure to let them in on when you have your personal devotions and what God is taking you through—remember, you're on this journey together.

Special Occasions

The **Special Occasion** section includes devotionals for holidays and other important moments such as birthdays, baptisms, death in the family, and weddings. All of us learn better when life and lesson match, and this section will help you do that for your family.

How Not to Use this Book

This book is not intended as a substitute for discipling your children; rather, it should supplement what you are already doing to disciple them. This book should be one small component to a **larger discipleship** strategy; we want to help parents do everything possible to instill Christ in their children; our prayer is that this book will be a springboard to that end.

Your Children as Disciples

You cannot teach a child to walk with Jesus their Savior by sending them to church two hours a week; it's a 24/7 thing that must be taught in daily life, where kids can learn to follow their Lord in every thought, word, and deed.

We want to congratulate and encourage you for having this book in your hands. We live in a day and age where many feel that many parts of raising our own children are someone else's responsibility. Many parents erroneously think that the spiritual development of their children is the church's responsibility. The church certainly partners with parents in the spiritual development of their children, but the responsibility for it falls squarely on the shoulders of the parents.

The book of Genesis records what God called Abraham to do and how his call would affect us: "For I have chosen him (Abraham), *that he may command his children and his household after him to keep the way of the Lord* by doing righteousness and justice, so that the Lord may bring to Abraham what he has promised him" (Gen. 18:19, emphasis and parenthesis added). God called Abraham to be the first in a very long line of parents to trust and obey God and then to teach and train their children to do the same.

Years later before Abraham's descendants crossed the Jordan River and entered the Promised Land, God directed Moses to preach a very long sermon (Deut. 1–6). The heart of that sermon is contained in the sixth chapter. In that chapter Moses (for proper emphasis) tells the Israelites the same thing three times (but he said it a little differently each time). Moses explained that they absolutely must remember to teach and train their children how to trust and obey the Lord. If you read the history of the Israelites in the Old Testament, you'll find that whenever Israel's parents trusted and obeyed God, and then taught and trained their children to do the same, the next generation flourished. Whenever they didn't, the next generation walked away from God.

Fast-forward to the New Testament. God chose Mary and Joseph to continue the same trend that He had originally called Abraham to do. God didn't pick just anyone to parent Jesus; he chose two who would follow His command to bring up Jesus God's way. Granted, Jesus went to the synagogue to learn God's Word, but He practiced living what He had learned, and walked with and experienced God at home under the purposeful direction of His mother and adopted father. The Bible records that Mary and Joseph were righteous people who obediently followed God and His Word and they followed this important (and much repeated) imperative to bring up their children God's way.

The apostle Paul reiterates and therefore carries forward this parental responsibility into the New Testament church in his letter to the church at Ephesus: "*. . . bring them up in the discipline and instruction of the Lord*" (Eph. 6:4, emphasis added). Notice that there's no mention of Sunday school.

If you think about it, trusting, obeying, and walking with God is the foundation of who we are as God's children. It's what defines us and should influence and direct each of our thoughts, motives, words, and actions. Christianity isn't just something we believe; it's who we are inside and out. It's the foundation of our lives. You cannot teach a child to walk with Jesus their Savior by sending them to church two hours a week. They must be taught throughout their lives to follow their Lord in every thought, word, and deed. It's no wonder that there is not one place in the Bible that leaves the spiritual training of children to church workers (volunteer or professional). Every verse in the Bible clearly assigns the task to parents.

It's interesting to ponder what God said about Abraham in Genesis 18:19. As we've discussed, Abraham was to bring his children up to trust and obey the Lord and to do his best to make sure that this spiritual training continued in the succeeding generations. Then the Lord says, ". . . so that the Lord may bring to Abraham what he has promised him." God was clear that having each successive generation of parents intentionally focus on raising their children to know and serve God was essential to bringing about what God had promised to Abraham. God identifies the promise He's referring to in the previous verse: ". . . seeing that Abraham shall surely become a great and mighty nation, and all the nations of the earth shall be blessed by him." Wow! We know now that this promise is still being fulfilled on the earth today as the gospel message is shared to all nations. The promise continues to unfold and therefore so does one of its operating conditions—raising godly children. Thousands of years ago God showed us that parents continuing to raise generation after generation (then and today) to serve the Lord are essential to all the nations of the earth being blessed through and by Jesus.

It's the church's job according to the Great Commission (Matt. 28:18–20) to go and make disciples of the nations and to have those disciples multiply themselves by also going and making more disciples for Jesus (2 Tim. 2:2). Once those disciples become parents (or if they already are), it's essential to God's plan that they multiply themselves as well, by making disciples for Christ in their own home. That is and always has been God's plan for reaching the nations. This makes a ton of sense since God's plan stretches across the generations and each of us is only here for one.

The book of Acts records that salvation came to entire households or families at the same time (Acts 11:14; 16:15, 30–34; 18:8). We live for only one generation so we tend to think that salvation came to that family, in that house, at that time. God views all generations and therefore sees things differently. Throughout the Bible He often spoke to those who served Him (Abraham, David, etc.) about their successive generations and His desire to continue His blessing on their families. Although God desired this for these families, He knew that these promises could only be fulfilled in Christ. Today when God blesses a family with salvation, it is His desire and plan for that blessing to continue generation after generation, and now in Christ, that's possible. Amazing! We can trust God not only for our kids but also for the generations of our families.

Think of this from a gospel perspective: it would be wonderfully beneficial, saving much future pain, prayer, and effort, if each time salvation came to a household, that the family served God in each and every generation until Christ's return. That way, future evangelists wouldn't have to reach our families all over again. Instead, our children, grandchildren, great-grandchildren, etc., would join those evangelists reaching families that have not yet been reached.

So when salvation comes to our houses, we need to take the long-term view—the generational view—trust Him for help, roll up our sleeves, and get to work bringing up our children as disciples of Jesus Christ. It may seem like a small mission field now, but it truly includes MANY who are not yet born, who you will one day love in eternity. God already knows each of them for generations to come and He's calling you to start reaching them by starting with your kids now. So how do we do that?

The Bible tells us in the book of Ephesians (4:11–12) that it's the church's job to equip each Christian to do God's work. Since you are a parent, part of your work/ministry in Christ is to bring up your children in the instruction and training of the Lord. Therefore, it is the God-given task of the church (and each individual church) and the ministers of the church, to help equip you with that task. We as part of the church and as His ministers called to this purpose are here to help you, and that's why we've created resources like this family devotional, which are specifically designed to equip and encourage you in your task. You're about to embark on a ministry that will carry a blessing to your children, your grandchildren, and so on until Jesus returns. May the Lord bless you and your family and give you wisdom and strength through His Spirit who dwells in you, as you take this step of faith and obedience.

The Holy Spirit's Help

The number one stated reason why Christian parents have difficulty passing their faith on to their children is that they just don't know how and feel ill-equipped for the task. The fact is that Jesus called us all to go into the nations and make disciples for Him; teaching them all that He taught (God's Word); how to be His disciple and learn from Him, how to walk with Him and how to be transformed by His Spirit and become Christ like. Unfortunately, we progressively began to think that it was the leaders' of our churches responsibility to take care of all things spiritual in life for us—which of course excuses us from effort. Consequently, most Christian parents today don't fully grasp what it means to be a disciple of God and to have a personal, practical, daily, and loving relationship with the Father, the Son and the Holy Spirit. This of course, is usually no fault of theirs; how can you become a disciple when no one teaches you how or even tells you that it's the next step after salvation?

When we ask practical questions of Christians (many of whom have been Christians much of their lives), like, "Who took you aside and taught you how to pray? Who taught you how to read, understand, and live God's Word? Who taught you how to minister to others? Who taught you how to see God at work?" to name a few, the most common response is, "No one did," or "I just learned as I went." Yet these are the types of things Jesus taught His disciples, and commanded that they, in turn, teach others.

If this describes you (like it does the vast majority of Christian parents), we have some good news. It starts with the example of two generations of Israelites. God called the generation of Israelites who left Egypt stiff-necked, unbelieving, and rebellious. That generation didn't know God or how to trust and obey Him at all. Yet, their children grew up to be the generation who trusted God and followed Joshua and took the Promised Land. So how does a generation of stiff-necks raise a generation of God followers? Simple! The first generation didn't stay rebellious, they progressively started to learn, grow, and obey. The way they viewed things, thought and acted all began to change. In the meantime their kids were watching, learning, and growing with them.

Regardless of where you might be on that spectrum right now, the key is to get started and trust God along the way. Growing in Christ and learning to be His disciple isn't about getting it right all the time; it's about being open to learning, trusting His grace and power to help you grow and be transformed. The most powerful way to teach your children is to take them on the journey with you. Your kids will learn how to learn and grow as they watch you learn and grow.

When we try and appear perfect and rain down instructions on them from our lofty parental thrones, it just doesn't work. Despite your best efforts to hide it, your children know that you're not perfect. Growing in Christ as a family means walking the journey together. Talk to each other about being able to learn, grow, make mistakes, and grow past those mistakes with God's help. Then pray together and use this family devotional to help you experience God together.

God was present, creating each one of your children as they were conceived. He knows them better and loves them more than even you do. He is their third-parent, their heavenly Father, and He never meant for you to raise them alone—so ask for His help and wisdom as you go.

Devotions

God's Word has much to say about reading, meditating, knowing, and understanding the Bible. It also records many prayers and it repeatedly calls us into constant conversation (and also set aside time) with God. The words *devotions* or *quiet time* have become words that describe our time spent in response to these biblical teachings. Let's look at what Jesus, our example and teacher, did and taught about devotional time. When Jesus was twelve years of age, He astounded the Jewish leaders and teachers with His knowledge and understanding of God's Word. He didn't get that understanding auto-imparted because He was God's Son. The Bible says that He became like us in every way (but without sin) so that He could understand how we feel and what we go through. Jesus obeyed the Old Testament's many directives to God's people to read, meditate on, understand, and live God's Word and He had to do that the same as we.

When the devil tempted Jesus, He quoted from God's Word. One relevant verse that Jesus quoted is, "Man shall not live by bread alone, but by every word that comes from the mouth of God" (Matt. 4:4). We've all heard the old saying "You are what you eat" and from a mental and spiritual perspective that's basically what Jesus said. Jesus was a great Teacher. The vast majority of what He taught us about God, life, our behavior, and even about Himself all either came directly from God's Word or was built on the foundation of its teachings.

Jesus knew that God's Word is exactly that—"the words of God" given to us as an instruction book for life. He knew that in order to discover truth, live life God's way, know God and His will, and experience Him, He needed to know God's Word. Simply put, Jesus taught by word and example that life works according to the manufacturer's instructions and that our part is to read it. The New Testament writers (under the direction of the Holy Spirit) continued to teach the importance of God's Word. The apostle Paul wrote: "All Scripture is breathed out by God and profitable for teaching, for reproof, for correction, and for training in righteousness, that the man of God may be complete, equipped for every good work" (2 Tim. 3:16–17).

In ancient times, it was more difficult to read and study God's Word since printing presses and the Internet weren't invented. Today we have unprecedented personal access to God's Word and countless wonderful tools to help us learn and live by. We just need to make learning a priority because without studying and reading the Bible, you cannot (nor can our kids) mature as Christians (Eph. 4:13). For example, we all want our children to be protected from the temptations, deceptions, and works of the devil. Jesus our Lord and God needed to know, understand, and use God's Word in order to resist Satan. The apostle Paul called God's Word "The sword of the Spirit"—without it our children are unarmed (Eph. 6:17).

We need to spend time everyday plowing into God's Word and learning from it. Each day is a journey, not a destination. Remember the purpose. Paul wrote, "Do not be conformed to this world, but be transformed by the renewing of your mind, that by testing you may discern what is the will of God, what is good and acceptable and perfect" (Rom. 12:2). The point of this devotional is to help you and your family learn God's Word, change the way you think, and give God's Spirit (who is inside you) your hearts and minds so that He will transform you all.

Prayer

When the disciples asked Jesus to teach them how to pray, He immediately spoke what is now famously known as "The Lord's Prayer." However, if you read Luke 11:1–13, you'll find that Jesus gave them more than one example. In fact reading through the Gospels, you'll find that He never stopped teaching them how to pray. He was even trying to train them in prayer in the garden of Gethsemane right before His arrest.

As with any good teacher, Jesus taught by example and prayer was no exception. The Scripture records that Jesus went off on a regular basis to be alone so He could pray. He also prayed and kept an open communication going with the Father as He walked about, taught, and ministered. Jesus said that all He did and all He taught were His Father's works and His Father's words. You can't rightfully claim that you did God's very specific will in every instance unless you're having a constant running conversation with Him.

Since God uses His Word to speak to us, guide us, and change us, it needs to be part of our conversation with Him. And since He uses prayer to help us understand His Word and will, prayer needs to be part of our reading and study of God's Word. So it's best to marry the two together: reading the Bible prayerfully and praying with God's Word in your heart. Setting time aside for a consistent devotional life isn't easy; and Jesus knows that we can no more struggle our way to a wonderful, loving, growing relationship with the Father than we can pay the price for our own sin and overcome sin in our lives. These things are achieved by God's grace, power, promise, and love through the work of the cross. Everything that is available to us from God or required of us by God we can only receive or achieve because of Christ and by faith in God's grace.

We can't earn and struggle our way to any part of God's will for us—it's all a gift. The same Old Testament promises, that promise the New Covenant would wash us from sin, give us a new heart, and place God's Spirit inside us, also provided that we would know God—all by grace not by our struggle (Jer. 31:31–34; Ezek. 36:25–27). So please, stop struggling; lay your relationship with God and your devotions at the Lord's feet and ask Him, by His grace, to draw you near and help you know Him. Let Him produce a great relationship with you, that you can give Him the glory for, because He did it. Admit your inability to understand His Word, and get to know Him in prayer on your own. Then ask

Him to help you, teach you, and lead you in your time together by His grace—and then trust Him to do just that.

One last thing before we get to the last section of this introduction: Have you ever noticed that the Lord's Prayer uses the pronouns *our* and *us*? The Bible calls us to both public and personal worship, prayer, Bible reading, and study.

How do we accomplish this inside the home? Dinnertime prayers, family prayers, family Bible reading, family worship, and family devotions are all examples of public time with God. Our children need to learn both; an abundance of one does not make up for a near absence of the other. The public exercise of these spiritual disciplines is all about fellow Christians strengthening, encouraging, and supporting one another. This family devotional is designed to help you do that.

If you'd like more in-depth instruction about helping your kids develop a thriving personal prayer life, visit ChristianParentingDaily.com and purchase the eBook *Teaching Your Child How To Pray* by Rick Osborne.

You're about to embark on a ministry that will carry a blessing from now until Jesus returns. May the Lord bless you and your family, and may He give you wisdom and strength through His Spirit who dwells in you, as you take this step of faith and obedience.

Now, on to God's *big* story of the Bible . . .

Day 1: Parent Connection

This Week's Topic:
The Bible—God's Incredible Book

If we are truly convinced that the Bible's words are truly God's words and that they are life-changing, then it makes sense that we would spend time in them. In order for our children to share our passion for the Bible, they not only need to learn from the Bible but they also need to learn *about* their Bibles—how we know that it is God's Word, how it was put together, why we can trust it, and how we can experience God through it. This week's devotions will strengthen your children's understanding of the truth about God's Word.

Tips

The foundational truth is that the Bible is God's book; however, that foundation is meant to have a very real relationship with God built upon it. God's Word points us to God so we can experience Him in our lives; then, God points us back to His Word to learn more about Him and therefore, experience Him more deeply and profoundly.

The Bible and our relationship with God are inseparable. To help your children establish this connection, share stories from your own walk with God, showing them how things you've learned from God's Word have changed you and/or your life and helped you experience God. It's this life-changing connection that truly demonstrates that the Bible is God's book.

For a more thorough understanding of how to read the Bible with understanding, see *Encounters with God: Transforming Your Bible Study* by Drs. Henry, Melvin, and Norman Blackaby.

DAY 2: GOD'S BOOK

Read: 2 Timothy 3:13–17

Quick Start

The Bible is much more than a book, or a compilation of books; it is even more than words on a page. It is what God uses to speak to His people. What is your favorite Bible story?

Quest

The Bible is comprised of sixty-six different books; this is actually one of the most miraculous features of the Bible, as these books were written by approximately forty different writers over a period of 1,500 years. These writers were not only from different eras in history, but they were also from different places, spoke different languages, and were from different walks of life: kings, physicians, fishermen, tax collectors, priests, royal servants, slaves, military officers, scribes, etc. Some were rich and some were poor, some were in difficult circumstances while others were prosperous and secure. The Bible addresses topics like: God, love, marriage, family, faith, wisdom, money, religion, politics, education, war, crime, law, good versus evil, and much more . . . yet every book is in mutual agreement on every topic. There's only one way that could have happened—God planned each book from the beginning and managed the Bible project Himself, choosing each writer and helping them know what to write. And that's exactly what happened.

Quiet Family Prayer

God not only gave us His miraculous book so that we would know Him better and know His will—He also wants to help us love it and understand it. Ask God to help make you a family who loves His Word. Ask Him to help each family member understand, learn, and grow as you read it.

Quiet Times

Younger Kids: Read one of your favorite Bible stories. Prayerfully thank God for these true and wonderful stories about Him and ask Him to help you learn more from them.

Older Kids: Read 2 Timothy 3. As a young leader in the church, Timothy had to help people know the truth. After reading the first part of the chapter, can you see why Paul reminded Timothy why God's Word is important. Back up a bit and read 2 Timothy 2:14 and in your prayers ask God to help you follow that advice.

Day 3: God's Story

Read: Genesis 1:1–5; Revelation 21:1–7

Quick Start

If you want to know why you are here on the earth, how it all started, and what happens next, the Bible is the book that tells that story. Each book in the Bible shares a part of the bigger story. What do you think the bigger story is?

Quest

The God-inspired writers of the Bible tell the one *big* story of God's plan for humankind. The first book, Genesis, starts by telling us why and how He created us, and the last book, Revelation, tells us what God has planned for us when Jesus returns. The Bible is like a library, because it's made up of all different kinds of books: history, poetry, records, law, personal and public letters, songs, prophecy, sermons, eyewitness accounts, and more. Each book adds a little more to the big story; we see how God has worked in the past and how He will work in the future. It's mind-boggling to realize than none of the writers knew what the other writers were going to write, or even that there would one day be a single source containing all of their books—a book written over the course of 1,500 years, comprised of very different types of books, and woven together to reveal the one *big* story. God's book tells God's story.

Quiet Family Prayer

Ask God to help you see and love the beauty and creativity that He put in His Word and thank Him for giving us such an amazing book.

Quiet Times

Younger Kids: Ask your parents to read one of their favorite Bible stories. Why do they love it? Pray and ask God to help you love His Word.

Older Kids: Read Joshua 1:1–9. Have you ever taken a test that you couldn't answer, or been in a situation where you had no idea what to do? How confident did you feel in those situations? By knowing God's truth and His plan in our lives, we gain courage, strength, and confidence. That's why He told Joshua to know His Word and to be strong and coura-geous—they're linked together. Pray and ask God to help you make the "Joshua link."

DAY 4: JESUS IS GOD'S WORD

Read: Isaiah 53 (written 700 years before Jesus was born)

Quick Start

Historically, Jesus grew up and lived around Galilee, traveling with His disciples to many towns and villages sharing the Good News. Can you name some of those places?

Quest

The most important person in the Bible is Jesus. Centuries before His birth, the prophets knew God's Son would be born of a virgin in Bethlehem; would speak in parables; be whipped and beaten for us; would have His hands and feet pierced; would be buried in a rich man's tomb; would rise again from the dead on the third day; and much, much more. In fact, Jesus fulfilled more than three hundred biblical prophecies. The Old Testament told everyone that God's Savior was coming; the New Testament records the life and teachings of Jesus, as well as those who followed Him. Jesus asked God to remind His disciples of all the words that He spoke to them and He prayed for those who would hear those words (John 17:8, 17–21). This is why we have a Bible today—and Jesus is the connecting point of it all. No wonder the apostle John calls Jesus God's "Word" (John 1:1–14).

Quiet Family Prayer

Jesus did not come to fulfill the Bible's purpose; rather, the Bible's purpose reveals that of Jesus—to serve, suffer, and die for each one of us so that ultimately we could become God's children. Thank God for sending His dear Son to rescue us and ask God to help you live for Him.

Quiet Times

Younger Kids: Read the story of Jonah. Nineveh was rescued because they listened to God. Pray and ask God to help you listen, too, to the great things the Bible tells us about Jesus.

Older Kids: Read John 1:1–14; 17:8, 17–21. Can you picture the disciple John (who walked with Jesus before and after Jesus died and rose again) sitting down and writing these words? After reading them, do you think that John knew He was writing part of God's Word? Pray and ask God to help you to really know Jesus and that He'd use you to help others know Him as well.

DAY 5: GOD'S KEEPING

Read: 1 Peter 1:22–25

Quick Start

Because the Bible is God's Word, we can trust its account as truth: miracles, plagues, giants, visions of heaven, God speaking to people, angels, healings, miraculous births, and people raised from the dead, etc. Which things do you wish you could have been there to see?

Quest

Jewish people considered the books of the Old Testament as holy; they used extreme care to copy and preserve it accurately from generation to generation. Jesus quoted from and confirmed that the Jewish Scriptures (our Old Testament) were accurate. Ancient pieces of manuscripts found called the Dead Sea Scrolls confirmed that the Old Testament we have today and the one Jesus read are the same in every important detail. Church leaders who lived after Jesus carefully kept and copied the collection of books/letters now known as the New Testament. With much prayer, discussion, and care, those leaders gathered these works together into one collection. Each time one of these treasures is discovered, it reinforces that what we have today is an accurate copy of these books.

Quiet Family Prayer

God gave us His Word to reveal the truth about Himself, Jesus, life, etc. But He also gave it to us so that we'd know what kind of loving, godly people He wants to help us be. Ask God to help you live what you learn from His word.

Quiet Times

Younger Kids: Read the Bible story about the Holy Spirit's arrival on the day of Pentecost. When we become Christians, the Holy Spirit comes to be with us forever; He helps us live and understand the Bible. In your prayers, thank God for the Holy Spirit.

Older Kids: Read 1 Peter 1:22–25; 2 Peter 1:19–21; 3:14–18. Peter wrote that the point of the Old Testament was to tell us about Jesus; that Jesus' life and teachings were all God's Word; and that what Paul (himself and the other disciples) was writing about Jesus would also be part of God's Word. Paul emphasizes, however, that we not just believe in God's Word but that we let it change us. Ask God to help you to be changed by His Word.

DAY 6: GOD'S LOVE

Read: Psalm 119:97–105

Quick Start

What great things do you remember about God's Word so far?

Quest

What do you think God wants us to do with the Bible? First, God has clearly shown us that Jesus is the key to understanding the Bible—the ancient prophesies, the stories, the accounts, reveal Jesus' identity and purpose. From there, Jesus helps us understand that by knowing the Bible, we get to know God better. Unlike other storybooks, however, regular Bible reading strengthens and grows us as we walk with God. And our appetite for God increases, so we read more. Pray each time you open it. He'll help you learn and grow.

Quiet Family Prayer

When Jesus' lived on the earth, He changed people's lives for the better. He's still changing people's lives through the Bible, testified by millions of people alive today who tell amazing stories about how God used His Word to change their lives. Ask God to keep changing each family member as you get to know His Word.

Quiet Times

Younger Kids: Read a short picture book that you like. Stories are fun, but they're just stories. Talk with your parent about how Bible stories are different—they're true, God wrote them, and God uses them to show us His love and speak to us, even today. It's okay to love books, but pray and ask God to help you love His Book the best.

Older Kids: Prayer and Bible reading are meant to be a conversation with God; you can do both at once. Pray and ask God to help you learn His Word and how to pray. Then choose a place to read in your Bible. As you read, think and pray about what you're reading and how it could apply to you or others—then pray about that and keep reading. Say your prayers with your Bible still open. God's Spirit is in you so trust Him to help you.

DAY 1: PARENT CONNECTION

THIS WEEK'S TOPIC: CREATION

This week we're going to talk about how we can experience God through His creation; it speaks volumes about how much He loves us and cares for us, telling us much about what He's like.

Creation is orderly and precise, showing us that God plans well. Some of His creation is large and often displays great power, showing us how big, powerful, and capable our God is. The microscopic things that He's made demonstrate that God cares about everything, and no detail escapes His notice. The consistency of what God created speaks to His faithfulness. The fact that He created families and friends shows that He not only wants us to have great, loving relationships, but also that He is a relational God who wants loving relationships with each of us.

Before sin came into the world, God saw all that He created and said that it was good. While His creation reveals many of God's characteristics, it also reflects ourselves, whom He made in His image and likeness (Gen. 1:26). He loves beauty, so He created us to love beauty—and then surrounded us with it. This week talk to your children about everything God made for us and in us; discuss what that tells us about Him, our Creator.

Whether it's humor, joy, peace, art, music, food, etc., we sometimes take creation for granted. When we consider God's role and revelation through it, we actually enjoy it more—because we are experiencing Him more. Pray that God gives you more insight from His creation to pass on to your kids as you prepare for this week's devotions.

Tips

Children can come up with some pretty amazing questions about creation: Who made God? Did Adam have a belly button? Etc. It's important not to 'wing it' or guess; if you don't know the answer, praise the asker for their great question and admit that you're not sure of the answer. Then take time to find the answer together.

(The book *801 Questions Kids Ask about God and the Bible* [Heritage Builder Series, Tyndale House Publishers, 2000] is a great resource if you have children who love to ask questions.)

DAY 2: CREATION

Read: Genesis 1:1–28

Quick Start

Since God is love (1 John 4:7–8), everything He does is born from His great love for us. In what way was creation an act of love for those whom God would place on the earth?

Quest

Have you ever stared at a beautiful flower and heard God whisper, "I love you"? Have you ever gazed at majestic mountains, or watched a beautiful sunset, and sensed that God put these things here for you to enjoy? He did. It is such a shame when people do not take time to enjoy the wonderful, beautiful, exciting, and amazing things God has placed all around us. God didn't have to make rainbows colorful, or flowers smell nice, but He did. The Bible tells us (Rom. 1:20) that we can learn a lot about God from what He created, and that what God made clearly shows us how much He loves us. Planting nice flower gardens, taking care of our property, picking up trash while we are on nature walks, and not wasting the natural resources we have all show respect for God's creation. Taking time to "take in" what God made lets Him know you appreciate all His has done.

Quiet Family Prayer

Look out the window or sit outside. Point out any birds, trees, flowers, etc., you see. Take time to thank God for what He created around you and for what it says about His love for you.

Quiet Times

Younger Kids: Read the story of Creation in your own Bible. In your prayers tonight thank God for all the wonderful things that He's made.

Older Kids: Read Psalm 19. Notice that the psalmist begins with how God's creation speaks to us, testifying to His existence, His love, and His faithfulness; His creation is consistent, not random. If His creation speaks to us so clearly, how much more does His Word? What is our response? In your prayers tonight, thank God for communicating His character and His will to you and ask Him to help you respond well. Pray the last verse of Psalm 19 and make it your prayer.

DAY 3: LET US

Read: Genesis 1:26–31

Quick Start

The first five days of creation, God began with, "Let the . . ." or "Let there be . . ." but in verse 26, when it came time to create man, God said, "Let *us* make . . ." Even at the beginning of time we see the Father, the Son, and the Spirit working together for the good of mankind. Compare Isaiah 44:24 and Ephesians 3:9.

Quest

By design, God put everything exactly, perfectly where it needed to be before creating His masterpiece: the first people. People were a very special creation; different, because they were the only ones God created in His own image and this enabled them to have a personal relationship with God (see John 17:20–26). Throughout the Bible the Father, the Son, and the Spirit of God have worked together to show us just how much they love us and want to be in relationship with us. When we pray, they all listen; when we bring our problems and requests to God, they all work together to answer us, protect us, and guide us. It is great to know that we have such a wonderful team who stands with us all the time.

Quiet Family Prayer

Think about who is listening to your prayers. What do you want to thank Jesus for? Or the Spirit? Pray today asking God to help you reflect His image better to others throughout the day so that they may see Jesus in you.

Quiet Times

Younger Kids: Read the story of Adam and Eve in your own Bible. In the Garden of Eden, God visited them, walked and talked with them. Ask God to help you talk to Him like that, believing that He's right there with you.

Older Kids: Read Exodus 33:7–11. Can you imagine having your prayer experience like that? Maybe not with a tent or with millions of people watching, but God wants to meet with you in the same, very real way and develop a close relationship with you. Talk to God as though you are face-to-face and ask Him to help you have an awesome prayer life with Him.

DAY 4: ADAM

Read: Genesis 2:7–8; 1 Corinthians 15:22, 45–49

Quick Start

When God created Adam, He had so many great plans for him and quite a lot of work for him to do as well. Do you think that God has a purpose for everything He creates? Including you?

Quest

Being the very first man, Adam had a lot to learn about God, hard work, and how to take care of all the things God put under his care. Being the first person ever created was a huge responsibility; he didn't have a father to explain how to be a husband or father, or how to make tools and grow food. God had planned for Adam to play a very important role in his creation: it was going to be a lot of hard work to accomplish all that God had given Adam to do, but God would be there to guide and help him. Every person is born with amazing potential to know God and to be used by God—if we walk with God as Adam did, He will show us what He has planned for us along the way.

Quiet Family Prayer

Keep in mind God worked for six days before He rested from creating things (Gen. 2:2). Work is a blessing from God because it means we can contribute to our communities and provide for our family's needs. Pray for people who do not have jobs right now, and thank God for the work he provides for your family to do.

Quiet Times

Younger Kids: Using your own Bible, read the story about Samuel working in the temple. Samuel worked hard and completed his chores everyday for Eli. God is pleased when we do things well, even things that don't seem important. Ask God to help you be a good and willing worker.

Older Kids: Read Proverbs 21. See how many verses (or proverbs) give helpful wisdom about our attitude towards and our ideas about work. Ask God to show you ways in which you can prepare yourself now for the work He will give you in the future. Ask Him to guide you toward good work habits, developing important skills, and maintaining a good attitude about work.

DAY 5: GOD MAKES THE FIRST FAMILY

Read: Genesis 2:16–25

Quick Start

It was always God's plan to make families, friends, and communities—lots of people He could love and be loved by, and people who would love each other. Have you considered that when God created Adam and his family, that he already saw you and your family in the future?

Quest

This was a big day for Adam; up to this point, God had only created animals as his companions. Now he would have a woman—a partner that was like him. It was God's plan that a husband and a wife would work together and create a new family, separate from the ones they came from. They would create a home designed to raise the children that God would give them. A home is where you can be yourself and be loved for who you are. Every home might be a little different because each family is different—yet exactly what God wants them to be because He places them there. The most important ingredient to have in a home is God Himself; to include Him in family decisions, to talk with Him in prayer times, and to read His Bible together so they know what is on His heart. Allow God to be at the center of your home and in all your activities make His plan complete.

Quiet Family Prayer

Take a few moments for each person to pray and thank God for giving you the family you have. Then pray together and ask God to be a bigger part of your family. Invite Him into your home, your decisions, your fun, your conversations, and anything else you can think of.

Quiet Times

Younger Kids: Read the story of the first family from your own Bible. Ask God (since He's part of the family) to help you have the wisdom to be a good son/daughter and brother/sister.

Older Kids: Read Ephesians 5:22–6:4. Think and pray about what it says. Ask God to help your family grow spiritually so that you would all experience Him and His blessings.

DAY 6: THE GARDEN OF EDEN

Read: Genesis 2:5–15

Quick Start

When you think of God's design and plan to make the earth, you can also be thankful for how He created you, too. How you look, your talents, your interests, your abilities, are all a part of how God made you—and God does not make mistakes. What do you like best about each person in your family?

Quest

What God creates tells us about what He likes and what is important to Him. God did not just throw everything together randomly—His creation had a very clear design and order as He fashioned it together. Just the right air, just the right temperature, just the right amount of water and sunlight and food all work together to support the animals and people. Isn't God amazing? The wonderful variety of animals and plants; the amazing array of colors and textures; the way we get to enjoy the seasons; and even the way babies are born all say something about God's love.

Quiet Family Prayer

Each family member has a special gift and a special role within the family unit. Thank God now for placing each member in your family and for how each person contributes to making your family what it is.

Quiet Times

Younger Kids: Read a Bible story about your favorite Bible character. Think about what made that person special. Take some time to thank God for making you special and completely unique.

Older Kids: Read Psalm 139:1–18. Your birth was not a random act of fate; God had amazing plans for you before you were even conceived. He deliberately formed and shaped you with purpose. If He took the time to make a garden as amazing as Eden, He certainly would make sure that He made you just as amazing. Thank God for making you exactly the way you are. Thank Him for the things you like about yourself, and ask Him to help you learn, develop, and grow so you can become all that He created you to be.

DAY 1: PARENT CONNECTION

THIS WEEK'S TOPIC: SIN, DISOBEDIENCE, AND THE FALL

This week we will cover a few important topics that are repeated throughout the Bible: temptation, sin, justice, and consequences. What happened in the Garden of Eden profoundly affected all of God's creation, including our planet and all people (Rom. 8:18–23). Help your children understand the Fall of Man; it is key to helping them understand a whole lot about their lives presently and in the future.

Genesis talks about God creating good seeds and cycles—seeds that would produce after their own kind and cycles that would repeat themselves. Unfortunately some very destructive seeds and cycles were introduced when deception, lies, doubt, disobedience, and sin entered the picture. Let's call these weeds.

Read Genesis 3:17–19. The bad that corrupted the seeds and cycles of the earth reflected the bad that corrupted the good seeds and cycles in humankind's hearts. When we become Christians, God gives us a new heart and puts His Holy Spirit inside us. He then calls us to seek after Him, and learn His Word. And one day God will make a new earth that will be finally free from evil and sin. We all look forward to this future return to the Garden of Eden, but we also need to take care of and weed the Garden of Eden that God has already established in our hearts by learning to turn away from sin's seeds and cycles, letting God's Word and way of living produce (by His grace and Spirit) a fruitful garden in our lives.

Tips

By understanding the Fall of Man, children can see that the evil and corruption in people, society, and the world itself—and the resulting destruction—are all there because of the consequence of that first sin (and every sin that's come after it). Sin and evil, once planted, multiplied and expanded. The world/we reap the consequences of our actions. God is love. He is not inflicting evil. In fact, He sent His Son to rescue us from all that. (If you haven't yet read "Your Children as Disciples" within the introduction, with your kids, this may be a good week to supplement your readings with that.)

DAY 2: THE TWO TREES

Read: Genesis 2:9; Luke 6:46–49

Quick Start

God gave Adam and Eve absolutely everything they could have wanted to have a great life in the garden and everything was theirs for the taking with only one exception. Rather than enjoying everything else, they wanted the one thing they could not have. Have you had a similar experience, and it caused big trouble in the end?

Quest

Two special trees were placed in the middle of the garden: the tree of "Knowledge of Good and Evil" and the tree of "Life." The Bible says that all of the trees had very tasty fruit on them, even these two special trees. But God warned them that the fruit on the tree of "Knowledge of Good and Evil" was bad and they would die if they ate it. Adam and Eve had to choose whether they would obey God and follow His instructions or whether they would disobey Him and face the consequences. Sometimes we think we know better than God what is best for us. Sometimes we don't like people to tell us what we can't do. But God always knows what is best for us, even when we don't understand.

Quiet Family Prayer

Thank God for caring enough about us to warn us about dangerous things in life. Thank God for giving us good instructions in the Bible to follow so we can enjoy our life and live under His care and protection.

Quiet Times

Younger Kids: Read the Bible story where Jesus talked about building on sand or on the rock (parents, if it's not in their own Bible, tell them the story found in Luke 6:46–49 in your own words). God gives us instructions about how to live our lives because He loves us and wants us happy and He knows what will make us happy. Ask God to help you make right and happy choices.

Older Kids: Read James 1:12–25. God doesn't lead us into sin—we make that choice. So we can never blame Him for the consequences. Notice that through James, God teaches us a better way; learn God's Word and do things God's way. Think and pray about these verses in James.

DAY 3: THE SERPENT

Read: Genesis 2:17; 3:1–5

Quick Start

When we start to listen to people who tell us things that are different from what God tells us, we are heading down a very dangerous pathway. What lies have people told you about God or His Word that you know are not true?

Quest

God's enemy, the devil, used a serpent to tell lies to Adam and Eve. The devil lied to Eve, and lied about what God had said the consequences would be for eating the forbidden fruit. He changed God's warning, and made Eve question God's instruction. If we do not train our minds to only think about what pleases God, we will walk through doors that lead us down the wrong path and into trouble. The devil cannot cause us to disobey God; we do that all on our own. He is aware of our weaknesses and only encourages us to submit to them. The Bible says "Therefore, submit to God. But resist the Devil, and he will flee from you" (James 4:7). Eve didn't ignore the devil and she didn't put up much of a fight; instead, she chose to ignore God's warnings and believe the lies.

Quiet Family Prayer

Thank God for giving us the Bible so we can know the truth. Thank Him for putting the "Spirit of truth" in us as His children to guide us and teach us His ways (John 14:17, 26). Ask Him to guide you to know when you are thinking about things that are not pleasing to Him, and helping your mind to think about the things that please Him.

Quiet Times

Younger Kids: Read the story about Jesus and the Pharisees (Matt. 23:24–26). Parents, explain what Jesus taught about cleaning a cup. God doesn't want us just to please Him with what we do, but with the way we think as well. Ask God to help you to always think good and loving thoughts—He will help you.

Older Kids: Read Romans 8:1–9. One of the reasons that it's so important that we read and understand God's Word is so we can know His will in everything and therefore set our minds on thinking and doing what is right. Read and pray about setting your mind on God and on His way of doing things, with the Holy Spirit's help.

DAY 4: WRONG CHOICES

Read: Genesis 3:6–8

Quick Start

Wrong choices always have bad consequences. We cannot undo the consequences of our sins, but God promises to forgive us and help us through them so that we can learn from them and choose differently next time. What bad choice have you made recently?

Quest

When Eve chose to disobey God, it broke God's heart. He saw her trying to decide what to do; He saw her pick the fruit from the tree, and He saw her eat it with her husband. He knew that His friendship with them was forever changed. Sin always has consequences and in this case, the consequence was that Adam and Eve would no longer be able to live in His garden, and now they were going to die. They made a choice to hurt God. No wonder they felt they needed to hide from Him; when we sin, we are embarrassed and ashamed. But in the midst of the dire consequences, God still loved Adam and Eve and gave them protection and guidance. He also set in motion His wonderful plan to bring a Savior who would undo the penalty for Adam's sin and make a way for us to live with God for eternity once again.

Quiet Family Prayer

Acknowledge that we all will make bad choices at different times, but that we do not have to hide from God. We can approach Him, ask for forgiveness, and ask Him to walk with us through the consequences of our sin.

Quiet Times

Younger Kids: Read the story of Zaccheaus (Luke 19:1–10). Just like Zaccheaus, we've all made mistakes and sinned. God wants to forgive us—if we ask. Then as we try and do what's right, Jesus helps us learn and grow. Thank God that He's helping you learn, and that He always forgives you and helps you get it right.

Older Kids: Read 1 John 1:1–1 and John 2:5. As Christians, we have chosen to live God's way and trust Him to help us learn and grow. God knows that this is a process, however, and we'll make mistakes. These verses tell us what to do when we blow it. If you've made any mistakes that you haven't talked to God about, go ahead and do it now.

DAY 5: SENT OUT

Read: Genesis 3:8–24

Quick Start

Sending out Adam and Eve from the garden was not God's punishment for them; it was actually God's protection. He prevented them from making another serious mistake. God is always thinking about what is best for us, even when we sin against Him. Have you ever found good things coming out of bad situations?

Quest

When God sent Adam and Eve out of the garden they learned many important lessons. First, they learned that God means what He says. When God told them there were serious consequences for eating the forbidden fruit, He wasn't joking with them. Next, they learned that sin hurts more than just ourselves—it hurts others around us. The relationship Adam and Eve enjoyed with God had been damaged. Also, they learned that God placed an angel to prevent them from re-entering the Garden to stop them from eating from the Tree of Life, which would have caused them to live in their sin for eternity with no way out. God was able to use the penalty of death for good in the end—so when a person dies, if they have put their faith in Christ, they will have another chance to live with God for eternity. Had Adam and Even eaten from the Tree of Life after they sinned, God might have had to start all over again as He did in the days of Noah.

Quiet Family Prayer

Don't forget that God is love, and the consequences we face when we sin are meant for correction and instruction, not punishment. Thank God for caring enough to walk with us as we learn from our mistakes.

Quiet Times

Younger Kids: Read the story in your own Bible about Jesus' return to the earth and the New Jerusalem. (Parents, you may also describe to them Revelation 21:1–22:5.) Thank Jesus tonight for dying for you so that you can live in paradise with God forever.

Older Kids: Read Revelation 21:1–22. Notice that verse 22 talks about the Tree of Life—we'll be back living in paradise like Adam and Eve were before they sinned. Thank Jesus for what He suffered so that we can be with God forever.

DAY 6: HARD LIFE

Read: Genesis 3:16–19

Quick Start

Learning from the past can make a good future in the end. What is the hardest job you have ever had to do?

Quest

It was as if the ground was fighting with Adam to grow anything. Every time he planted a seed, weeds sprouted up too. Whether he was checking their progress or harvesting the results, Adam was always fighting something else that shouldn't have been there. Providing food for his family was a lot of hard work. When Adam worked, something worked against him. God still provided the rain, good soil, sunshine, and made the plants grow and bear fruit for them to eat; but sin caused everything Adam and Eve did to be much more difficult. Instead of our lives working the way God intended, sin adds weeds and thorns or problems and troubles to our lives. Our sins can also put weeds in other people's lives and their sins can make trouble for us. Work was never meant to be a penalty or a punishment; but when sin came into the world, it caused everything to break. Through Jesus, God starts to pull the weeds out of our lives and things work out much better.

Quiet Family Prayer

Following Jesus and living God's way cuts life's weeds, thorns, and thistles in our life down significantly. Thank God for His love for you and your family and ask for His help and direction so that you can live life His way and avoid what sin produces.

Quiet Times

Younger Kids: Read the story about Adam and Eve being sent out of the Garden of Eden. Thank God that Jesus made a way for you to live with God again today, and one day in heaven.

Older Kids: Read Matthew 4:1–11. Jesus knows the mess that sin causes. Satan tempted Adam and Eve and they fell for it. When he tried the same thing with Jesus, Jesus wouldn't fall for His lies! Notice what Jesus did—He battled Satan's lies with God's Word and used it to guide Him always. Pray while you read these verses and ask God to help you know His Word and to help you use it against all temptation.

DAY 1: PARENT CONNECTION

THIS WEEK'S TOPIC: OUTSIDE THE GARDEN

Once Adam and Eve were outside of the garden, we start to see the darkness in humankind making their hearts harder and harder. We also start to see the pain and trouble caused by sin and hard-heartedness. This week we'll talk first about hardened hearts and God's plan for giving us new soft ones. Of course, this week's story deals with hardened people and the misery that comes from sin, but we still need to pay attention. Christians have been given new hearts and have God's Spirit in them to guide, help, and transform them, but they can still learn many lessons from these stories. We still live in a fallen (sometimes sad and hurtful) world, we are still tempted to do the wrong thing, and we still must choose to leave our hard-heartedness behind. Instead, we must allow God to have His way in our hearts, minds, and lives. So this week we'll talk about seemingly diverse topics that really fall under the bigger topic of "walking with God through a fallen, broken world."

Tips

When you're discussing important, practical topics like anger, take the opportunity to get everyone to agree on a new way of moving forward. Do this before you pray as a family. So if, for example, angry outbursts are a problem in your household, then while you're reading that devotional, talk through changing that behavior and what that would look like in your family. Get everyone to agree that this isn't what you all want your family to look like, and decide together that with God's help (and reminders and support from one another) you will actively pursue changing it. Then pray together and ask for God's wisdom and help to transform this part of your family. In the following days and weeks, use reminders when necessary and help your kids apply the new way they've learned.

DAY 2: HARD HEARTS

Read: Genesis 3:20–24; Ezekiel 36:25–27

Quick Start

Ever been happy when your enemies got into trouble, or not felt sorry for difficult people when they were hurting? Have you ever wanted to do the wrong thing, even though you knew it was wrong? How pleasing do you think this is to God?

Quest

The Bible tells us that God is a God of compassion (Gen. 19:16; Exod. 33:19) and that He is merciful, long-suffering, gracious, and abundant in goodness (Exod. 34:6). When we rejoice in other people's suffering, or wish certain people harm because of how they have treated us, we are not reflecting God's heart; we are showing a heart of stone. Sometimes it is not those who have offended us who are the real problem; sometimes we ourselves need the attitude adjustment so that God can bring healing to some of our relationships. A hard heart will not feel compassion for those who are hurting, or will refuse to show God's love to those in need. God took away our hearts of stone and gave us new, soft hearts by sending Jesus. We can trust Jesus to soften our hearts, help us to love, and help us to do the right thing. Unfortunately for the first family, the darkness was making it much harder for them to listen and do things God's way, and it cost them dearly.

Quiet Family Prayer

Read Ezekiel 36:25–27 again. Pray these verses together, asking God to show you how to use your new loving heart and thanking Him for these amazing promises.

Quiet Times

Younger Children: Read the story about God sending Adam and Eve out of the garden again. Aren't you glad that Jesus helps us have a soft, loving, happy heart? Watch this week to see if you can help someone in need.

Older Children: Read Ephesians 4:17–32. Pray as you read that the Holy Spirit will help you understand, grow in, and live the life described here.

DAY 3: CAIN AND ABEL

Read: Genesis 4:1–4

Quick Start

The differences we have as family members is God's way of making our family exciting and helping us learn about love. What has each of your family members taught you about love?

Quest

God gave Adam and Eve two sons—Cain and Abel—and their interests were quite different. These two brothers had a lot to learn about hard work and about getting along with one another. Sometimes it is hard to get along with your brother or sister when you don't seem to have a lot in common—but you are still family, and God put you in your family on purpose. Each person in your family has something special to offer; each person has strengths and weaknesses intended to depend on and appreciate one another. It's also great when you have a lot of different interests in your family because then your home won't be so boring when you all get together.

Quiet Family Prayer

Thank God for your sibling(s) and the differences you have. Ask God to teach you to get along with each other. Jesus commanded us to love one another, and He helps us learn and do everything He asks us to do.

Quiet Times

Younger Kids: Read the story of Jesus and the Two Greatest Commandments and The Good Samaritan in your own Bible (Luke 11:25–37). We don't just love others with our feelings, but also with our words and actions. The Good Samaritan loved a stranger in trouble by being kind and helping him. How much more should we love, be kind to, and help our own family? Ask God to help you do this.

Older Kids: Read 1 John 3:11–18 and 4:7–21. The most important person who ever lived is Jesus Christ. The most important decision anyone will ever make is to follow Him. And He said the most important thing in life is love—not the feeling, but the commitment. He wants us to love others by putting them and their needs ahead of ours. Ask God to help you really live a life of loving others, starting with your siblings and your parents.

32 DAY 4: CAIN KILLS HIS BROTHER

Read: Genesis 4:3–12

Quick Start

Anger can be one of the most destructive emotions; we must guard against giving into it and falling into sin. Have you ever been so angry that you did something you were sorry for later?

Quest

Sometimes anger causes us to hurt people by hitting them, throwing something, or just with the words we say. Anger is a dangerous thing in a family because it can cause you to do things and say things that you will regret later. Cain was angry enough that he killed his own brother and then lied about it to God. In verse 7, God warned Cain ahead of time to control his anger instead of letting it control him—and of course, he didn't. This led to some very harsh penalties for Cain that affected him for the rest of his life. God knows that we will become angry at times. He gave us anger so that we would respond against injustice and wrong behavior. Cain's anger was the anger of a hard and selfish heart; God wants us to have soft hearts that love others. When something bothers you, stop and ask God to help you think of others first and love them instead. If someone is really treating you or others badly or unfairly, stay calm and pray for help and wisdom to solve the problem with love.

Quiet Family Prayer

Make a decision as a family to not ever use hard-hearted anger. Ask God and your family members to forgive you for your angry times. Ask God to help each one of you to have soft, loving hearts towards each other and to help you work out problems accordingly.

Quiet Times

Younger Kids: Read the story of Cain and Abel in your own Bible. Ask God to help you to have a soft heart that has love, not anger. Talk to a parent about ways you can love your siblings.

Older Kids: Read 1 Samuel 17. David was angry for the right reasons, at the right things, and it caused him to do the right thing. Ask God to help you use the gift of anger correctly to help others and honor God.

DAY 5: SETH

Read: Genesis 4:25–26

Quick Start

God loves us and cares about us when we are sad or hurting; He can mend our broken hearts. Have you every been so sad or disappointed that you didn't feel like talking to God?

Quest

Adam and Eve didn't like it when their children fought with one another; they probably knew Cain had a bad temper, but now one son was dead and the other one was banished because of it. But God felt compassion for Adam and Eve, and gave them another son named Seth. They would have many other children, but Seth was a special blessing to Eve; when she looked at him, she remembered God's goodness to her. Sometimes when we are sad about losing something or someone who is special to us, we forget that God cares deeply and begins to do what He can to bring healing to our sad hearts. We don't always get back what we lost, but we do have a God who can replace our pain with joy . . . if we let Him.

Quiet Family Prayer

Ask God to help you trust Him and turn to Him in sad times. Pray for anyone you know who is going through hard times. Ask God to help them and to bring healing to their hearts.

Quiet Times

Younger Kids: Memorize a part of 1 John 4:8: God is love. That means He really cares for you and wants to be with you and help you. Talk to Him right now about anything you care about; if you care about it, so does He.

Older Kids: Read Philippians 4, paying particular attention to verses 6 and 7. Talk to God about whatever is bothering you or is unresolved in your life. Ask Him for the peace that comes from knowing that God cares and is taking care of what you've talked to Him about.

DAY 6: THE WORLD GETS DARK

Read: Genesis 6:1–6

Quick Start

In those days, men were giants, warriors, and very powerful; they did whatever they wanted without any regard for God or what was right. But God would not permit His creation to ignore Him nor His instruction. What changes would there be in our world if everyone always followed the rules and the laws?

Quest

Some people (because of their dark and hard hearts) love to be bad. They love to break the rules. Our jails and prisons contain many people who have made bad choices and who chose to disregard the laws. God still loves them, but if they don't turn to Jesus, repent, and let Him change them, they will face God's judgment upon them one day. When we honor Him in our actions, He blesses us. When we choose to disregard God's ways and the laws of the land, consequences always follow.

Quiet Family Prayer

Thank God for giving us rules, commandments, and laws to help protect us from evil people. Ask God to help you live a life that pleases and helps others. If you know anyone who is disobeying the laws of God and man, pray for them to meet Jesus, have their sins forgiven, and find a new life.

Quiet Times

Younger Kids: Choose a story about Jesus and read it with your parent. Jesus obeyed God in everything and cooperated with the laws of the land. Doing things the right way keeps us (and people around us) safe and happy. Ask God to help you live an obedient life like Jesus did.

Older Kids: Read Romans 13:1–10. God gave humankind the ideas for government, laws, police, judges, soldiers, etc. While humankind's hearts are still dark, right and wrong need to be defined by law and the laws need to be enforced. Christians (with their new soft, Spirit-filled hearts) should have no problem obeying the authorities. Pray and ask God to help you have a good attitude towards—and to cooperate with—the authorities.

DAY 1: PARENT CONNECTION

THIS WEEK'S TOPIC: NOAH'S ARK—GOD'S MESSAGE

God's plan was set from before the beginning: He was going to send His Son to die for fallen humankind so that our sins could be forgiven and we could be His children again. In the end, He will make the heavens and the earth new and live with redeemed humankind here for eternity; in essence, a return to the Garden of Eden through Christ our Savior.

But God also knew that thousands of years would pass before He would send His Son; humankind was already so corrupt and violent that God's heart was grieved by all the sin and pain. He needed to start over, but knowing the time that still needed to pass, He needed to send a *really* strong message: sin comes with consequences, will be judged, and will be punished. God made sure that the people who were spared would pass the message on to their children, and the rainbow would serve as a reminder till the end.

Tips

It's important that we help our children understand who God really is. Some see Him as a big angry God in the sky who casts lightning bolts at anyone who displeases Him, but that's not who God is. Even during the flood, God was extremely compassionate; by flooding the earth, He stopped all of the pain and violence that sin was causing then, and kept it in check going forward. God's purpose was to keep His plan on track; a plan that would have God the Son Himself taking the penalty for our sins— past, present, and future. Yes, it's important that we understand that there are consequences to our sins; but it's also important to know that He is love and that everything He does has the purpose of warning us, keeping us safe, and getting us to heaven.

36 Day 2: God Calls Noah

Read: Genesis 6:5–14

Quick Start

Choosing God's ways leads to God's blessings. Do you think you could do the right thing in God's eyes even if others around you might make fun of you?

Quest

When God looked at Noah, he was living a life that was pleasing to God. He was a man of good character and integrity; he was a person who kept his promises and honored his commitments. God chose Noah because of how he lived and He knew Noah would obey Him when He gave him specific instructions on how to build the ark. We never know who is watching us throughout the day, nor do we always know what our reputation is among other people. Noah tried to live a life that was pleasing to God, regardless of what other people thought of him—and he was chosen to complete an extraordinary task. It is always more important to honor God than to try to please people around us. People around us may not understand what drives our decisions, but it will make sense when they see God blessing us!

Quiet Family Prayer

Ask God to help you love Him so much that you would be willing to obey Him no matter what anyone else thought of you or said about you.

Quiet Times

Younger Kids: Read the first story about Noah in your own Bible. God chose Noah because Noah did what was right and because God knew he'd obey Him, no matter what. Talk with your parent and to God about being part of God's plan.

Older Kids: Read Matthew 6:33 and 16:24–27. We can't see our future, so it's easy to get caught up in all the world's distractions instead of seeking God with all our hearts. However, Jesus knows all of that; He also knows that God's plan for us is so awesome, He was willing to die to get it for us. Read the verses again and ask God to help you put Him and His awesome will for you ahead of everything else. He knows we need His help—He just wants us to ask.

Day 3: Noah's Family Builds an Ark 37

Read: Genesis 6:14–22

Quick Start

It is always best to follow God's instructions, because He knows past, present, and future—and we don't. Can you remember a time when you avoided getting hurt because you listened to your parents' instructions?

Quest

Build a big boat? It was a very odd request that God made of Noah's family. Thankfully God brought all the animals—that would have been pretty much impossible for them to do that on their own! No one else in Noah's day believed in God, and they thought Noah's family was crazy for building such a huge boat. God's ways don't always make sense to us at the time, but we trust that God knows what He is doing. When we follow His instructions, we get to see His plans come together in a way we never imagined. And it wasn't just about building the boat—Noah had to follow God's specifications or the boat would have sunk in the flood. It was very hard work, and Noah's family was subjected to ridicule, but their obedience saved their lives in the end. When we know the One who knows the future, we can be confident what He tells us and instructs us to do.

Quiet Family Prayer

God's warnings to us are never to keep us from fun; they are given to keep us from harm. Thank God for this; tell Him you are grateful that you can trust your life into His loving hands.

Quiet Times

Younger Kids: Tell your parent a Bible story that you remember or ask them to read it to you. Whether the person did right or wrong, do you notice that God's stories keep telling us the same thing—that God's way is always best? Ask God to help you make wise decisions.

Older Kids: Read Proverbs 3. The rest of the chapter tells us the difference between right and wrong and instructs us to do the right thing; verses 5 and 6, however, tell us what to do when we have a personal decision to make that isn't about right and wrong. Ask and trust God to direct you in all your decisions.

DAY 4: NOAH THE PREACHER

Read: Hebrews 11:7; 2 Peter 2:5

Quick Start

Proverbs 22:1 says that a good name or reputation is better than great riches. Do you know what your reputation is among your friends or neighbors? Do you wonder what your reputation is with God?

Quest

Earlier this week we learned why Noah was chosen by God. Noah's pursuit of God persisted in spite of the world's criticism; he wouldn't have stopped if his wife had wanted him to, or if his three sons quit. Noah's actions showed everyone around him that God's instructions were his top priority; he must have warned as many people as possible about the coming judgment of God, but no one cared. They all thought he was crazy. Sometimes the right thing to do isn't always the easiest; the Bible says, however, that what we do says more about what we believe than what we say (John 13:35; James 2:14–20). Noah preached to the people, not just with his words, but with his actions.

Quiet Family Prayer

Our non-Christian friends and neighbors may not understand our faith, but when they see us consistently acting out what we believe, it helps them see that it's real. Ask God to help your family send a helpful message about Him to your friends and neighbors.

Quiet Times

Younger Kids: Count and name the animals in the picture of the ark in your own Bible. Which animals are your favorites? Aren't you glad that Noah was obedient and didn't leave them behind? When we do things God's way, it works out better for others and us. God cares for animals too; pray for the animals that you know.

Older Kids: Read about the "Heroes of Faith" in Hebrews 11. Which heroes on the list are your favorites? Ask God to help you join in His work and be a hero of the faith.

DAY 5: THE FLOOD

Read: Genesis 7:11–24

Quick Start

God is patient and loving, but He is also just and righteous. When people refuse to listen to God's warnings time and time again, and refuse to follow His commands, they will face His judgment rather than His blessings. How do you feel when you have to start all over again at something?

Quest

It only rained for forty days and forty nights, but Noah, his family, and all the animals had to live in the ark for over 200 days! That's as many days as most children have to go to school in a whole year. Noah probably wondered if God had forgotten about him, and what they would find when God finally opened the door to the ark. It must have been pretty overwhelming to know that God was going to depend on their family to start mankind all over again; things hadn't worked out so well with Adam and Eve or Cain and Abel, but God was going to take another chance with Noah and his wife, their three sons, and their wives. It was going to be hard work to rebuild houses, find food to eat, and start tilling the ground to plant crops. But they would be free to worship God and follow His instructions for them without any fear of evil people around them anymore. God finally had people on the earth who would love Him and appreciate all that He had done for them.

Quiet Family Prayer

Since God already knows the future, everything will work out for our best. Thank God for being a God of new beginnings.

Quiet Times

Younger Kids: Read about the flood in your own Bible again. Talk to your parent about what that would be like if your family was on the ark instead of Noah's. Thank God for the life you have—God has different plans for you.

Older Kids: Read Lamentations 3:22–26. Because of what Jesus did for you, God lets us start new again everyday. When you talk to Him, ask for His forgiveness, wisdom, and help. If you need a fresh start just ask—God has an endless supply.

DAY 6: THE RAINBOW

Read: Genesis 9:1–17

Quick Start

God keeps His promises. The rainbow was put in place as a reminder of God's promise to not wipe mankind out with a flood. How many reminders can you think of that God has designed to help us remember His love, His righteousness, or His faithfulness?

Quest

It is interesting how something so beautiful could remind us of something so tragic. Rainbows are more than a reminder of His promise to not destroy mankind with a flood; they remind us of His presence, and that He was watching over mankind. The first peoples forgot about God and lived without any regard for Him. When new generations saw the rainbow, they would *have* to think about God and remember all the evil people who died in the flood. They would also remember God's power and that He will not tolerate evil people. God is great at making good things come out of sad times. When God makes a promise to us, He always has our best interests in mind. There are many other reminders God has designed to symbolize about His goodness, His holiness, His protection, and His great love for us. We should never be too busy to appreciate the reminders of God.

Quiet Family Prayer

Thank God for His rainbows. Thank Him for watching over us and for His faithfulness to keep His promises. Ask Him to help us keep our promises that we make to Him as well.

Quiet Times

Younger Kids: Is there a certain Bible story that reminds you about something you love about God or Jesus? Read that story. Do you have anything in your room or house that reminds you of God? The biggest reminder we have is God's Holy Spirit inside of us. Ask the Holy Spirit (He's God too) to help you think about God even more.

Older Kids: Read Romans 8:28. God has a wonderful way of turning even the most difficult things around so that they work out for us when we trust Him. Talk to God about any situations that you might be in the middle of; ask Him to please work it out each one for good, granting you wisdom where needed.

DAY 1: PARENT CONNECTION

THIS WEEK'S TOPIC: ABRAHAM—BLESSED TO BE A BLESSING

In Christ, we are the children of Abraham. God wants us to experience His love as He guides us, protects us, gives us wisdom, teaches us, and blesses us, just as He did with Abraham. We must also walk with God by faith and trust, just as Abraham did, even when we don't understand. God is love and everything He asks us to do is truly in *our* best interest—not His. God called Abraham to be blessed and to be a blessing—God has called us to the same.

This week, help your children see Abraham's obedience to God as something that resulted in Abraham and his family being blessed and being a blessing. Today many think that as long as they don't hurt anyone else it doesn't matter what they do. That is one of Satan's lies; when we do what God wants, we and many others get blessed; when we don't, then everyone is worse off because of our selfishness.

Further Reading and Review

- Proverbs 13:20–21
- Isaiah 6:1–8
- John 6:4–14
- Jeremiah 29:1–14; John 15:1–11

Tips

We can be so easily distracted by the shiny distractions of this world and what we think will be the best plan for our lives—but unfortunately we don't know everything—we don't even know what will happen tomorrow, never mind what will happen next year or what God has planned for us in eternity. So we need to, like Abraham, walk in faith not understanding all the details but trusting that we are in the hands of love. This is the same principle that God wants us to teach our children: He asks them to honor and obey their parents. Help your children understand that by learning to trust that you may know something they don't and that you really do have their best interest in mind, they learn a bigger lesson—how to walk with and trust God. Also, a great way to show your children that obeying and honoring you is best is to let them see you doing the same thing with God.

DAY 2: TOWER OF BABEL

Read: Genesis 11:1–9

Quick Start

People with hard hearts never seem to change; it seems they make the same mistakes over and over again without learning from them. In what ways do you depend on God? In what areas do you prefer to do your "own thing"?

Quest

The story of the Tower of Babel is sometimes confusing. On one hand, it looks like God should be proud of just how creative and ingenious mankind had become; they built a huge tower that could be seen for miles. The problem, however, was with the purpose of the tower: trying to show God and everyone else how strong and proud they were. You see, God had commanded the people to scatter around the earth, to be fruitful, and multiply—not to stay in one large city and build a large tower. These people thought they knew better than God, however, and one morning they discovered they could no longer understand the language of other families around them. This would have been frightening; families who understood one another left to find other places to live. The tower was abandoned; instead of serving as a symbol of power, it served as a reminder of their arrogance and pride.

Quiet Family Prayer

God knows everything. He made us and knows what He has planned. It's completely silly to ignore Him and do our own thing. Pray and tell God that you want to live and enjoy His plan, now and in the future.

Quiet Times

Younger Kids: Read the Tower of Babel story. Have you ever seen a baby get a great present and then play with the wrapping instead? We're like that when we get distracted from God's plan for us. Pray that God will help you stay focused on Him and His great plan and gifts for you.

Older Kids: Read John 15:1–11. In verse 5, Jesus says that apart from Him we can do nothing. What do you think this means? Talk to God about what these verses say.

Day 3: God Calls Abraham

Read: Genesis 12:1–5

Quick Start

When we give our lives to God, we also give Him the right to take us wherever He wants to go and to do whatever He feels is best. A life with God is exciting and fulfilling. What is the scariest change you have had to make in your life so far? How did it turn out?

Quest

When God called Abram, God had huge plans for his family. God had started mankind all over again with Noah's family; now He wanted to create a special people on all the earth to demonstrate to the whole world who He was. In fact, God changed Abram's name to Abraham to reflect the changes God would make in his life. Abraham's descendants would include important people such as Jacob, Jesse, David, Boaz, Joseph, and Jesus. But it all started with Abram accepting God's offer—and leaving his homeland, his relatives, and everything that was familiar to him. It meant traveling to a foreign land, facing new challenges, new enemies, and trusting that God would keep His promises. This was a huge decision; fortunately Abram trusted God. He and his family made major adjustments, but sometimes that is required in order to obey God. Sometimes what we give up may actually be keeping us from experiencing God's blessings in the first place. We can be assured that what is "sacrificed" is small in comparison to what God will provide for us. God always knows best.

Quiet Family Prayer

Ask God to help you be a family that He can use to bless others. Ask Him to help you have the courage and trust in Him to obey Him whatever the cost may be. Remember that God loves to reward obedience with blessings.

Quiet Times

Younger Kids: Read the first story about Abram (Abraham) in your own Bible. Thank your heavenly Father for loving you so much that He has great plans for you.

Older Kids: Read Jeremiah 29:1–14. God's people had been taken away to Babylon. False prophets told them God wanted them back home; Jeremiah disagreed. It's important to understand that God's plans for us are always best, even when they don't seem like they are.

DAY 4: GOD'S PROMISE

Read: Genesis 12:1–9

Quick Start

God promised Abraham and Sarah they would be the founders of an entirely new, chosen nation that would show the world who God is. How would you like to be the founder of a country? What would you name it?

Quest

Much like when God created Adam and Eve, God planned to create a whole new nation from one family to be special to Him. Through this nation God would demonstrate His power, protection, generosity, grace, and love. He would show all the other nations that their gods were false, whereas He was the Living God, all-powerful and mighty. When this new nation honored Him, there was no nation or army that could defeat them. But when they did not follow God or His ways, He allowed their enemies to have victory as a reminder of how small they were without His help. The land that God promised to Abraham in this passage is the same land that the nation of Israel occupies today. Just as it was fought over many times in Abraham's day, so it continues to be disputed today. But God's ways always prevail when His people call upon Him and honor Him with their lives. It is amazing to think about what God can do through one family who obeys Him.

Quiet Family Prayer

Ask God to show you the plans He has for your family—to help you recognize and respond to opportunities that He opens up for you to serve and bless others.

Quiet Times

Younger Kids: Read the story about Jesus feeding a crowd with a boy's lunch (John 6:4–14). The boy in this story was willing to give up his lunch for Jesus, and Jesus blessed thousands with it. Ask God to help you find ways to help bless others.

Older Kids: Read Isaiah 6:1–8. God gave Isaiah an incredible experience! When God reveals Himself to us, He does it because He loves us but also because He wants us to show that love to others. Pray Isaiah's words from verse 8.

DAY 5: LOT

Read: Genesis 13:1–18

Quick Start

Selfish choices can lead us too close to dangerous temptations. Lot did not mean to get his family into trouble, but it is easy to become like the people you hang around. What everyday decisions can you make that steer you towards God and away from potential trouble?

Quest

When Abraham gave Lot a choice of where he could live, Lot did not give the best land to his uncle out of respect, he selfishly took it for himself. Then he eventually moved to Sodom and lived among wicked people, needlessly placing his family in harm's way. They were even taken captive (14:12) by the enemies of the king of Sodom. Fortunately his uncle Abraham had a strong army himself and rescued Lot and his family from being forced into slavery. There is no record of Lot worshipping God or making any altars to God, as did Abraham. Lot's choices were unwise and placed his family in dangerous situations. In the end Lot lost everything he had except his two daughters; he is remembered as a man who squandered great wealth and influence on things not worth chasing after.

Quiet Family Prayer

Ask God to help you be more consistent with making decisions that move you towards Him, His plan, and His blessings. If you need to, ask God to forgive you for making wrong choices.

Quiet Times

Younger Kids: Read the story of Lot in your own Bible. The Bible says that God wants children to listen to and obey their godly parents—it helps keep us safe and learning not only from them, but from Him. Ask God to help you listen, learn, and make right choices.

Older Kids: Read Proverbs 13:20–21 and Psalm 1. Think and pray about this: Eve was the first person to fall for Satan's lie that she knew better than God what was best for her. You may think Eve was stupid for what she did, but when you listen to your friends and start to think you know better than your parents, counselors, and even God, you've fallen for the exact same lie. Choose whom you hang out with and listen to wisely.

DAY 6: SODOM AND GOMORRAH

Read: Genesis 18:20–19:1; 19:12–17, 24–29

Quick Start

The wages of sin are *always* death—closed doors, lost opportunities, broken relationships, painful consequences—if we choose not to turn from our sin and ask forgiveness. But God is patient and merciful with those who do. Name two people you know that you think are good examples to follow, and say why.

Quest

Many times God sends prophets to warn people of His coming judgment; when God's messengers went to Sodom, the people only wanted to hurt them. That was when God knew it was no use; the only family in the city that would listen to God was Abraham's nephew, Lot. But even he was reluctant to leave the city before its destruction. His daughters had boyfriends there, and he and his wife were comfortable. God's messengers had to take them by the hands and lead them out of the city, leaving all their possessions behind. That day Lot finally realized that he had been living among people who hated God, who refused to listen to God, and that he and his family were very close to becoming just like them. It is important for us to have good friends around us who will encourage us to act in ways that are pleasing to God and avoid potential trouble.

Quiet Family Prayer

Thank God for giving us Jesus, a great example to follow. Ask Him to give you good discernment with regard to friends and associates. Pray for people you know who need God's grace and salvation.

Quiet Times

Younger Kids: Read Jesus' parable about the Good Samaritan. Jesus loved, helped, and prayed for everyone, but He spent most of His time with the disciples. Ask God to help you be like Jesus—kind and giving to everyone, but able to choose friends wisely.

Older Kids: Read Psalm 1. Abraham stayed closest to God, His family, and those who honored God. He was friendly towards and tried to help people like Lot who wanted to serve God, but didn't get it right. Abraham was *not* close to those who chose to be wicked. He loved, was kind to, and prayed for all three groups—but was careful who was influencing whom in his life. Pray and ask God for this kind of wisdom.

DAY 1: PARENT CONNECTION

THIS WEEK'S TOPIC: ISAAC—TRUSTING GOD WITH OUR LIVES

This week we'll talk about God's will for our lives: how we can receive His wisdom and direction; how we are tested along the way as we trust, follow, and wait; how God helps us with difficult decisions; why short-cuts aren't short-cuts at all; and how God is faithful to wonderfully care for all the details of our lives as we follow Him. In short, you'll be talking to your family about trusting God with your lives.

God asks us to give Him our lives and turn to Him for wisdom and direction. Why? Because He loves us and really wants to guide us as our loving heavenly Father. It's important that we help our children understand that. God is not far off and stingy with His wisdom and direction; He is waiting on the edge of His seat (metaphorically) for us to ask and trust. Trusting God for His direction, receiving it, and following it is something we continually grow in with God's help. Ask Him to help move you and your family on from where you are and learn more.

Tips

Following God's will and direction for our lives starts with a willingness to obey what we already know. God kindly helps walk us through the easy stuff first and as we learn to trust and follow Him, He moves us forward and deeper. Your younger children may have difficulty seeing beyond the activity they're involved in and their next meal; your young teens will see further, but may not be able to focus on much outside of their teenage years. That's okay—the timing is up to God. Your role is to help them see God giving them wisdom and direction at their point of need—when they see that working, they'll press in further. If you make the lessons about their way-off future, it may not register—ask God to help you take them from where they are.

DAY 2: ISAAC IS BORN

Read: Genesis 21:1–7

Quick Start

Baby Isaac was the result of Abraham's obedience and God's promise. Can you think of times when God has surprised you when you obeyed Him?

Quest

How would you like to have a father that was more than 100 years old? That was how old Abraham was when his son Isaac was born. Isaac was the son God promised to Abraham and Sarah; even though his parents were quite old compared to everyone else's, they were specially chosen by God. Isaac grew up with the favor of the Lord and learned a lot about worshipping God from his dad. Abraham would have told him stories about the land of Ur where he had come from, about defeating the army that captured his great uncle Lot, and about when he spoke with God. He would have heard about visiting angels and the fiery storm that wiped out two cities. All of those stories depended upon Abraham's obedience; had he never obeyed God, there would have never been any stories—and Abraham would never have been mentioned in the Bible. We never know how our obedience to God will affect the future, but God does.

Quiet Family Prayer

Thank God that following Him is never boring! Thank Him for having exciting plans for our lives and for going to all the work to plan things in advance for us to enjoy and experience as we follow Him (Eph. 2:10).

Quiet Times

Younger Kids: Read about an adventure of one of your favorite characters in the Bible and how he or she experienced God because of their obedience. Let God know that you'd like to have faith adventures with Him.

Older Kids: Read Samuel 23:8–23. These men were soldiers; their job was to rescue and keep God's people safe. They were called mighty men because they did things that no man could do without faith and God's help. Today God's mighty men and women rescue people with love, the truth, and the power of God, but the results are no less amazing and impossible without His help. Let God know that you want to be a mighty person of faith who follows Him and does the impossible.

Day 3: Abraham and Isaac
on the Mountain

Read: Genesis 22:1–18; Hebrews 11:17–19

Quick Start

If God already knows how we'll do in every test, why do we need to be tested?

Quest

This was going to be the greatest test Abraham ever faced in his life. God had asked him to do the unimaginable, but Abraham knew God well enough to know that He had a purpose in everything He asks. When God asked Abraham to offer his only son as a sacrifice, God did not intend for Abraham to kill his own son. He intended to see if Abraham was worthy of the great honor God was about to bestow upon him. As the father of a nation, Abraham needed to be a good example. He needed to be trustworthy, faithful, and godly in what he did so that subsequent generations could see that the founder of their nation was a man who did whatever God told him to do. There is no doubt that this event left a huge impact upon Abraham's son Isaac as well. When he finally realized what his father was about to do, he must have been very scared. But it was important for Isaac to see that nothing was more important to his dad than obeying God, no matter what the cost.

Quiet Family Prayer

The purpose of every test is for us to get better at trusting. Ask God to help you count it as joy and to grow stronger in each test.

Quiet Times

Younger Kids: Read the story of Abraham and Isaac on the mountain. Whether it's a math test, a test in friendship, a test of our patience, or a test of our faith, they all help us get better. Pray and ask God to help you like every test in life and do well at each one with His help.

Older Kids: Read Daniel 3. Jesus died in our place because we couldn't come to God on our own, but also because we can't get to know God on our own, either. Jesus was there with these three men, just like He's always with us. Talk to God about this story and ask Him for the same faith and courage for facing your tests.

DAY 4: ABRAHAM'S SERVANT

Read: Genesis 21:5–13

Quick Start

When we get impatient and try to do God's will our way instead of His way, we can get into serious trouble; but even then, when we ask, God can take our mistakes and make something good out of them. Have you ever tried to accomplish the plans of God with your own wisdom and strength?

Quest

Abraham and Sarah were impatient with God and took matters into their own hands to try to get a son for Abraham—but things did not turn out at all like Sarah had thought it would. In fact, in the end, she regretted her decision. She soon became so upset that she told Abraham to send them far, far away never to return. This was not fair to Hagar and her son Ishmael, but God would protect them and keep them safe. Ishmael was not the son that God had promised to Abraham, but God loved him too. And since he was Abraham's son, God would pass the blessings on to him and create a nation from him as well. Sometimes we become impatient with God and we think He needs our help. We need to be sure to check back with God often when we are following Him to be sure what we are doing is pleasing to Him.

Quiet Family Prayer

A great prayer response to Isaiah 55:8–9 comes from Psalm 25:4–5. Ask God to show you His ways, help you follow His paths, and to guide you into His truth.

Quiet Times

Younger Kids: Can you think of a time when you had to get your parents to help fix something you broke, or to solve a problem you did not understand? Ask God for any help you may need and/or thank Him for loving you so much.

Older Kids: Read Daniel 4. How could the king have avoided what happened to him? When we seek God and search the Bible trusting God to teach us and then live it, we've chosen the easy way to learn. Life and learning gets harder when we do things our own way. Pray and ask God to help you apply yourself to learning the easy way.

DAY 5: ISAAC AND REBEKAH

Read: Genesis 24:1–26, 61–67

Quick Start

We always have to wait for something, because everything can't happen at the same time; waiting helps us enjoy today for what it is and to look forward to our tomorrows. What are you waiting for now?

Quest

Abraham sent his servant on a long quest to Mesopotamia in search of a young woman to be a bride to Isaac. The telltale sign that she was the right one was if she would draw water from a well and give to the servant and their camels. Sure enough, when Rebekah came upon the servant, she did exactly what Abraham had foretold; this woman was not only beautiful, but she was even from the same people as Isaac's family. Rebekah would be the mother of twin boys to carry on the family name. God rewards patience and trust. He is never in a hurry, and never without a plan in mind. When we trust in Him with all of our heart, He is faithful and will reward us when we wait upon Him. Waiting is not sitting still; it is moving forward with the calm assurance that God will do just as He says He will if we will trust in Him.

Quiet Family Prayer

Thank God that He is never early and never late, but right on time every time. Ask God to help you know how to enjoy each day while you're waiting for all the wonderful things He has planned for all your tomorrows.

Quiet Times

Younger Kids: Read the story about Abraham's servant going to find Rebekah. When we trust Him, pray about everything, and obey Him, He takes care of us. Talk to God and ask Him to take care of all of your tomorrows.

Older Kids: Read the long version of this story in Genesis 24. Notice how God orchestrated things and made everything work out wonderfully. When we don't trust God, we miss out today because we're too busy trying to shape our own tomorrows. Give your life and all your tomorrows to God right now; ask for His help.

52 DAY 6: THE LORD APPEARS TO ISAAC

Read: Genesis 26:1–6

Quick Start

God always hears our prayers, but sometimes we don't hear His answers. When has your family asked God for direction and followed God's answers?

Quest

Sometimes we are faced with very tough decisions to make—a move to a new city, changing schools, etc. It is not always a very easy choice to make. When we pray and ask God's help, He is ready to give us guidance. But we have to be on the lookout for His answer and direction. He may use something we read in the Bible; something we hear at church; the answer may come while we are praying and listening to Him; or it may become very clear in the circumstances we see in the coming days. The key is to expect an answer from God when we pray to Him. Isaac could have gone with others down to Egypt to find food during the famine, but God wanted him to stay where he was. That day was coming—generations later—but God was not ready for that to happen yet.

Quiet Family Prayer

God has told us to submit our decisions to Him and to trust Him for direction, so obviously He is ready and willing to give us His help. Are there things you could ask God's direction for right now? Ask, trusting Him; then listen and watch for His answer together.

Quiet Times

Younger Kids: Read and talk about Proverbs 3:5–6 with your parents. If you're hurt or have a need, do your parents answer you when you ask for help? God is always listening for when we call to Him too. When you pray, know that God hears every word and answers.

Older Kids: Read Psalm 37. Think about these verses: 4–7, 23, 31, 34, and 37. We don't always think of prayer as God speaking to us, but prayer can be a conversation if we stop and listen. Take time to listen to God when you pray; it will take practice, but it is worth the effort.

DAY 1: PARENT CONNECTION

THIS WEEK'S TOPIC: JACOB—FAMILY MATTERS

Every family is different, and God loves each one uniquely; so this week we talk about a somewhat dysfunctional family that God used. Our kids need to know that no matter who their family is and what their family dynamics are, God still loves them and wants to work in them. Obviously, we'll talk about kindness and forgiveness in sibling relationships, but also how God can use everything that happens in our lives for good, and to prepare us for what He has planned. He does, however, call us to obey Him in our family relationships; doing otherwise makes our journey to where God wants to take us much more difficult. God will often put dreams or desires about our future into our hearts as a guideline to navigate us through every circumstance as we trust Him. As we pray, trust, and obey, God will forgive, help, guide, and work. No situation, family or otherwise, is too difficult for God to turn around and use for our good.

Tips

Kids often compare their family situations to those of their friends; they have a bigger television, a nicer house, a father who lives at home, and/or their parents let them do. . . . It's important that our kids know that each family is unique and has their unique set of both blessings and challenges—comparing isn't helpful because there is no such thing as the perfect family situation that will work for everyone. What's important is that we love each other, that we're thankful for our blessings, and that we trust God to help us through our challenges. As our children trust Him and live His way, He'll get them to where He needs them to be—no matter where they start.

DAY 2: JACOB AND ESAU

Read: Genesis 25:27–34; 27

Quick Start

We should treat others graciously today so that we don't have to apologize tomorrow. Is there anything you can think of you have done for which you might need to apologize?

Quest

Brothers and sisters don't always treat each other very well. Sometimes they tease one another or play tricks on one another. Sometimes they take things or make fun of each other. Jacob was a deceiver and a trickster; he schemed to take his older brother's special privileges (birthright) and then he tricked his own father into giving him the special blessing that belonged to his brother Esau as well. Understandably, Esau was extremely angry. Jacob left home and eventually was deceived and tricked by his new father-in-law; he finally understood what his brother must have felt like. It would be twenty-five years before the two brothers would meet again, and this time there was no more trickery or deceit—only love and forgiveness. Just as Jacob had learned that treating others as you would like to be treated is best, so Esau had somehow learned that forgiving those that hurt us is also best.

Quiet Family Prayer

Thank God for your family members. Ask God to help you love them and treat them in a way that would please Him. Ask God to help you apologize for anything you have done to harm them and ask them for forgiveness so there will be peace and unity in your home.

Quiet Times

Younger Kids: Read the story of Jacob and Esau in your own Bible. What are two nice things you can do for your brother(s) or sister(s) this week that would show them you care about them?

Older Kids: Read James 3:1–12. Did you know James was one of Jesus' brothers? As he wrote these verses, he may have remembered that Jesus always spoke to Him kindly and treated Him well. If you are an older brother or sister, think and pray about the kind of example you need to be for your younger siblings in how you treat and speak to them. If you are a younger brother or sister, think and pray about how you can support your older siblings and encourage them in what they are doing.

DAY 3: ISAAC BLESSES JACOB

Read: Genesis 27:1–47

Quick Start

Say one encouraging thing to each person around the room that you think they would like to hear about themselves.

Quest

Esau knew that one day his father Isaac would give him a very special blessing over his life and his future. This was a very important time between the father and his children. It was a time where a father called God's favor upon his children and God's guidance for the future they will have. Esau was excited and quickly ran off to fix the special meal his father had requested. Isaac was old and frail now and had very poor eyesight. When Esau finally arrived for his blessing, however, it was gone—stolen by his younger brother who was assisted by his own mother. He must have felt very angry, but after Jacob ran off, he was the only one left to run the family's estate. Eventually his anger subsided and he lived a very prosperous life.

Quiet Family Prayer

Even though Isaac's family got it all wrong, God used them in a special way. Ask God to help you understand how He can do good things through your family and enable you to be a blessing to one another and to others. Thank God for the soft hearts you have because of what Jesus did, and ask God for His help to always treat each other with soft and loving hearts.

Quiet Times

Younger Kids: Read the Bible story of Jacob stealing his brother's blessing. When we ignore God's instructions for families and do things the wrong way, life can be frustrating. Pray for you and your family to love and be kind to each other according to God's instructions.

Older Kids: Read Ephesians 4:17–32. Can you imagine what life would be like if we all followed these instructions? Thanks to Jesus, we no longer have hard hearts but we still have to choose to, with God's help, decide to live our lives God's way. Pray verses 31–32 and ask God to help you live every moment (starting with your family) according to what they say.

56 DAY 4: JACOB'S DREAM

Read: Genesis 28:10–22

Quick Start

Have you ever had a dream about something that later came true?

Quest

Jacob was exhausted from his traveling and found a safe place to rest. As he slept, his dream was so real and so amazing that it gave him great courage; he had been running for so long, fearful his brother was going to kill him. Now he knew that God had a plan for his life—even his running away was part of God's blessing for his life. Jacob had much to learn, but God's hand of protection and guidance was on him. Sometimes God puts a dream or a vision in our mind and heart; we should consider if it's a goal we have to accomplish one day. Many times God will put His hand upon a child and guide them throughout their lives to accomplish great things when they grow up—as long as that child pays attention. Don't dismiss your good dreams and desires as foolishness; God may be putting something in your mind for a reason.

Quiet Family Prayer

Thank God for what He has planned for you as a family and for each one of you. Ask Him to reveal His plan for you either in a dream, the desires He puts in you, or even by opening up opportunities. Ask Him to help prepare you to do His will.

Quiet Times

Younger Kids: Read the story of Jacob's dream in your own Bible. God created us to have dreams. Most of them have no special message and don't involve God talking to us. Pray and ask God to help your regular dreams be good and let Him know that you're willing to have Him speak to you in a dream as well if He wants to.

Older Kids: Read Acts 2:1–18. The people who heard this first sermon were amazed; the Holy Spirit was meant for people like Moses, Elijah, David, and Ezekiel. But now Peter was quoting the prophet Joel and saying that the Holy Spirit was for every Christian—even children, servants, and the elderly. Pray and let God know that you'd like to have the Holy Spirit guide your life as well.

DAY 5: LEAH AND RACHEL

Read: Genesis 29

Quick Start

Have you ever been tricked by someone? Do you have a favorite magic trick or is there a trick you just can't figure out?

Quest

It is easy to understand why people think God has a sense of humor. The woman Jacob fell in love with took care of sheep—just like Esau. He was also hired by Laban to do the same type of work as Esau had done. Then, when Jacob thought he was marrying one of Laban's daughters, he found he had married the wrong one! Jacob was learning a hard lesson, being treated just like he had treated others; his own father-in-law tricked him over and over again. But God still blessed Jacob just as He had promised. Jacob grew wealthy, influential, and prosperous. Eventually Jacob's confidence and character grew out of this experience as a shepherd and he knew it was time to go back home to his father's land.

Quiet Family Prayer

Ask God to forgive your sins, to keep helping you, and changing you so that the seeds you plant are all His good seeds rather than weeds that come from our sins. You can also pray that God helps you pull weeds out of your life—it's not always easy, but He'll help you through.

Quiet Times

Younger Kids: Read the Bible story about Jacob and his two wives. Can you see that whenever we do something unkind to others, we are being unkind to ourselves as well? The way we treat others is the way we'll end up being treated. Pray and ask God to help you plant kind and loving seeds.

Older Kids: Read Galatians 6:7–10. When we think a little sin and compromise doesn't matter or that it won't hurt us, we are being deceived and actually attempting to mock or challenge God. God's not waiting eagerly to punish you; He loves you and He's eager to bless you. He knows how He created everything to work and He gave you His Word and His Spirit to help you live according to His instructions so that you can be blessed.

DAY 6: TWELVE SONS

Read: Genesis 35:23–26

Quick Start

What do you think the perfect number of children would be for a family? Can you imagine having to share a house with twelve siblings?

Quest

Jacob had thirteen children, but unfortunately he did not learn an important lesson from his own parents. Just like his mother, he showed favoritism to one of his own sons, Joseph. This caused a great deal of jealousy among the other brothers, particularly the older ones. This set into motion an amazing plan that no one could have imagined possible in the years to come. Every child has a special role to play and is important to the family no matter if they are first, last, or somewhere in the middle. God can use the things we have to endure in our homes and with our families—it shapes and molds us into the person God wants us to become. When we stay faithful to Him, it is encouraging to know that whatever we face, whatever we must endure, God is greater and His love will guide us through to His blessings on the other side.

Quiet Family Prayer

Pray together and ask God to help you face your challenges with wisdom, love, and strength. Ask Him to use it all for your benefit and His glory.

Quiet Times

Younger Kids: Talk with your parents about one of your favorite fairytale stories—why do you like it? Probably because you know that there is a happy ending. Ask God to help you love your life like you love your favorite stories—because you know that God will always work things out for you when you trust Him.

Older Kids: Read Genesis 30:1–22. In the midst of their challenges, some of Jacob's family must have thought that nothing in life was bigger than the issues they faced. We know now that God was building a nation and unfolding a plan that would bring Jesus into the world. No matter how crazy your life gets, when you trust and obey God, He can take you through and show you His bigger plan for your life. Talk to God about your issues and ask Him to help you trust that He's working.

DAY 1: PARENT CONNECTION

THIS WEEK'S TOPIC: JOSEPH—A HERO

This week we'll learn what it means to be a hero from Joseph's example. Heroes are servants, are empathetic, have integrity and strong character, and are faithful. They put God and others ahead of themselves. Joseph was a picture of Jesus, who is the ultimate hero. Jesus came as a servant; He was compassionate and empathetic; and His character and integrity were and are unquestionably perfect. He was faithful to God, to all those He came for, and to His difficult task. Everything He did, He did because He loves the Father and loves us—He put us first and laid down His life so that we could live. As Christians, we are called to be the disciples of Jesus, to be taught by Him and to be transformed into His image. Since Joseph is such a wonderful picture of Christ, his example is a great one to learn and grow from. (Plus, the story is awesome.)

Tips

Grace! When serving up the idea to your kids that God wants them to be heroes, to follow Joseph's example, and to be like Christ, they may choke a bit on the serving—especially the older ones who may have already experienced some sin and failure. This is where the message of grace comes in; Jesus didn't just die to get us forgiven and to set us up as children of the Father. His work was complete in that He set it up so that we could become the true and righteous children of God. Jesus paid the price for our transformation into His image, and we get there by His grace and God's promise—not by our own efforts. Help your kids understand that we don't just get into God's kingdom by grace—we also grow by that same grace. Our children can be heroes, they can follow Joseph's example, and they can be transformed (one step at a time) into Christ's image (2 Cor. 3:18), because Jesus is helping them and teaching them. God's Spirit is also in them, transforming them from the inside out. Praise them for feeling like they can't on their own—they're right—but they can, because Jesus is with them every day.

DAY 2: JOSEPH'S DREAM

Read: Genesis 37:1–11

Quick Start

Have you ever had a dream where you were the hero who saved the world from destruction?

Quest

Joseph's dreams made his family look pretty silly while he came out looking like the hero! The Bible tells us that his father Jacob "kept the matter in mind" when he heard of the dreams—given that God had also spoken to him the same way—but even Jacob thought his son was getting "big-headed." Joseph was young and inexperienced and had a lot of growing up to do. Even his own brothers didn't want to hang out with him—and these crazy dreams weren't helping. God wasn't planning on putting Joseph in an important position so that Joseph could be more important than others; rather, so he could give his life to serve others. Joseph would have to go through a very difficult and lonely time away from family, away from friends, in a foreign land where he would even have to learn a new language—all to help him learn to serve. Many years later Joseph had become a gracious, godly, and powerful ruler who wanted to help others—because heroes are servants.

Quiet Family Prayer

Jesus was the ultimate example of a servant, even though He was God. Ask God to help your family enjoy serving others and to show you how you can use your time and lives to help others in need.

Quiet Times

Younger Kids: Read the story of Joseph and his dreams in your own Bible. Even though God had big plans for Joseph, he started by teaching him to obey his father and willingly do things for him. Ask God to help you learn by being helpful to your parents.

Older Kids: Read Matthew 20:20–28. There's nothing wrong with working hard, getting ahead, and occupying a place of importance if that's what God has planned for you; however, our reason for wanting that should always be so that we can better help and serve others. Pray about that and your future. Ask God to help you learn how to serve others now, within your family, at school, etc.

DAY 3: JOSEPH A SLAVE

Read: Genesis 37:17–36

Quick Start

What is the worst thing your brothers or sisters (or friends) have done to you? How did it make you feel? Did you ask God to help you forgive them so that you did not resent them anymore?

Quest

It seems like there are a lot of stories about brothers hating brothers in the Bible, aren't there? Cain killed his brother Abel, Esau wanted to kill Jacob, now Joseph's ten brothers wanted to get rid of him once and for all. But God was with Joseph, and his life was spared for a very important purpose. In the end, it would be Joseph that would spare the lives of his brothers, but today was one of several times in his life where he felt completely alone, abandoned, wrongfully treated, and afraid. He had no one left on his side but God. But one person together with God can do anything God can do; so Joseph prayed to God for help. In the end, God's amazing plans came together for Joseph and he was a better leader because of what he had gone through. He wanted to do things that would prevent people from hurting and bring comfort to those who were hungry—because he knew how it felt. But it was his trust in God that brought him to that place.

Quiet Family Prayer

God used Joseph's hurtful experiences to help him grow. Heroes are empathetic. Pray for people you know who are hurting right now. Ask God to help you be more empathetic.

Quiet Times

Younger Kids: It's important that we always remember how it feels when others hurt us or treat us mean—that way, we will never want to do things that make others feel that way. Ask God to help you do and say things that help make others feel good.

Older Kids: We need to always forgive those who hurt us, because we also need to be forgiven for hurting others. We need to always care for those who are hurting, because we also need to be cared for when we are hurting. Read Romans 12:14–21 and talk to God about each verse.

DAY 4: JOSEPH A PRISONER

Read: Genesis 39:1–23

Quick Start

What does "the best defense against a false accusation is a good reputation" mean?

Quest

It seemed like Joseph's life went from bad to worse. His brothers sold him into slavery; now he found himself in jail because he stood up for what was right. Even his reputation was tarnished by false accusations—and he might be executed for a crime he didn't commit. Joseph felt very alone, but he still had God, and he remembered the dreams God had given him as a teenager. If there was one man who had integrity and good character after all he'd been through, it was Joseph. This was a young man God could certainly trust with more important things. God had him right where He wanted him—next to two fellows who knew Pharaoh. One of them would be the key to Joseph's next adventure, but it would be two more years before that would come about. God's timing is always perfect; Joseph's reputation for being a godly and trustworthy man was growing among all those who knew him. It wouldn't be long before the dreams God gave Joseph started to come true.

Quiet Family Prayer

When you really love God, your character is the same no matter where you are or whom you're with, because the One you love most is always with you. Ask God to help you be just like Joseph in this way.

Quiet Times

Younger Kids: Read the story of Joseph and Potiphar in your own Bible. Joseph did the right thing even when no one was watching because he wanted to please God. Ask God to help you always do the right thing, regardless of who might be watching.

Older Kids: Read Proverbs 1:7–33. If God is going to put you in a place of leadership, influence, and power, He needs to prepare and strengthen you so people, fear, money, power, or temptation will not change you. Ask God to help you be true to Him, no matter your situation. Ask Him to help you grow stronger with each choice, large or small.

DAY 5: JOSEPH A RULER

Read: Genesis 41

Quick Start

Who do you know who is there for you no matter what, and always does what they say they will do? A person who acts like that is faithful.

Quest

Now God was speaking in the dreams of important people, but they couldn't understand and were troubled by them. God had prepared Joseph for this opportunity of a lifetime; a slave, a prisoner, a foreigner, brought before the ruler of all Egypt to give counsel and wisdom regarding his dreams. Once Pharaoh saw that Joseph had the wisdom of God in him, he was put second in command over Egypt. From the prison to the palace—that's what God can do. But just as it was with Noah, Abraham, and Jacob before him, Joseph had to remain faithful to God in the midst of confusing and troubling times. He proved himself worthy of the very important task God had planned for him to do. He had governed faithfully over sheep, over a household, over a prison, and now he would govern over a nation. What we do is not nearly as important to God as who we are—but who we are is shown by what we do.

Quiet Family Prayer

When we realize how faithful God is to us and how great it is to always be able to rely on Him, it should make us want to be faithful as well. Pray and ask God to help you always be faithful to Him, to others, and in all you do.

Quiet Times

Younger Kids: Read the story of Joseph and the Pharaoh's dream. Have you noticed that no matter what Joseph was tasked with, he always did a great job without complaining? Ask God to help you be a willing helper.

Older Kids: Read Matthew 25:14–30. A person who is faithful is also consistent and reliable; they always do what they commit to do, and do their best to never let people down. The core of faithfulness is caring—about what we do, the people for whom we do it, and the difference our efforts make. Talk to God about being faithful—He's already committed to help you get there.

DAY 6: JOSEPH'S FAMILY REUNION

Read: Genesis 42–45

Quick Start

Has anyone in your family ever gone on a very long trip where you didn't see them for several weeks? Even though you missed them, did you understand that it was important for them to be gone?

Quest

Joseph must have been very surprised when he first saw his brothers coming to buy food in Egypt? It seemed like an entire lifetime since he had seen them, and he didn't even know if his father Jacob was even still alive. He could have thrown them in jail for how they treated him or refused to give them any grain to take home. But because he knew everything was a part of God's plan, he chose instead to be kind to them. He knew God used what they did to accomplish His will, and now he was in a position of authority that could save the life of his family and their families. He was happy to be able to be a blessing to his brothers, even though they had been a curse to him. Joseph knew how to put the past into the past because he knew how to put the needs of others ahead of his own.

Quiet Family Prayer

Can you imagine what a family would be like if everyone acted like Joseph—willing to do whatever it took to help everyone else? Read Philippians 2:3–4. Ask God to help you live these verses—heroes put others first.

Quiet Times

Younger Kids: Read the story of Joseph's family reunion in your own Bible. Jesus taught that the two most important things are to love God and love others. Ask God to help you love Him and others like Joseph did.

Older Kids: Read Philippians 2:1–8. Jesus always put others first. He took on the role of a servant and laid down His life so that we could live. He put God the Father and everyone else ahead of Himself. The Bible says that we are to be like Jesus and God gave us His Spirit so that we would have the power to change and become like Him. Ask God to help you always put Him and others first.

DAY 1: PARENT CONNECTION

THIS WEEK'S TOPIC: MOSES

The story of Moses' birth, early life, and calling is full of wonderful lessons for all of us. God's special plan for Moses is shown in every event—even his birth. Our children need to know that they are no less special; God knew them before they were conceived, and He has a wonderful plan, in Christ, for each one of them that stretches into eternity.

Moses made mistakes along the way, but God kept loving him and just as with Joseph, God used everything Moses went through to equip and prepare Him for that plan. Moses didn't understand or even realize all of what God was doing, and only through getting to know God better did he learn to fully trust Him. God is working in this same way as we pray in our children's lives: in the foreground, in the background, and in every detail.

Ultimately, Moses realized that knowing, trusting, and following God and His plan for his life were better than anything this world has to offer—and that's God's goal for each of us.

Tips

The Bible is full of fantastic stories that feature men and women who accomplished some amazing things for God. As Christians, God has called each one of us to be part of His plan; He wants us to share in the adventure of reaching and changing this world. The amazing stories of the Bible feature very ordinary people who were willing to trust and obey God to do amazing things. Hopefully, you are inspired by them; encourage your children to gain inspiration from these stories by thinking about how this could happen in their own lives. God still does the amazing and accomplishes the impossible with regular people like us.

Day 2: Moses' Birth

Read: Exodus 1:1–2:10

Quick Start

Everybody loves it when a new baby is born; people celebrate with parties and gifts, passing the new baby around for everyone to welcome and love. Can you imagine having to be quiet and secretive about a baby's arrival?

Quest

Ever since the new Pharaoh had arrived, there was nothing but misery for the Hebrew people. Instead of living in peace with the Egyptians, they were forced into slavery. To make matters worse, the Egyptians feared that their slaves would rise up against them and rebel, so they ordered every baby boy to be killed. When Jochabed gave birth to a boy, she and her husband Amram decided to hide him—so they turned to God for a plan. Jochabed sent her baby down the river in a tiny basket where God knew Pharaoh's daughter would see it. While this young woman didn't know this was God's plan, she did take the baby Moses to raise as her own. No one would have guessed that Moses would be raised in the very house of the man who ordered every Hebrew baby boy to be killed!

Quiet Family Prayer

Moses parents did their best to love and protect him. Children learn to love each other in the family as they watch their parents. Pray asking God to help each one of you know how to show love to one another this week.

Quiet Times

Younger Kids: Read the story of baby Moses. You are just as special to God. Talk to your parents about your birth and imagine how God celebrated it. Let God know that you would like to know His love and live His plan for you.

Older Kids: Read Exodus 1—2:10 again. God blessed the two midwives because they did what was right. Moses' sister Miriam didn't realize until much later that by helping her mother, she was helping herself, her family, and all her people be freed from slavery. Every time we do the right thing and help others—even in small ways—we help God build the future. Ask God to help you do this with every opportunity.

DAY 3: MOSES GROWING UP

Read: Exodus 2:10–11; Hebrews 11:23–26

Quick Start

Can you remember a time when you felt like you didn't belong or felt you were out of place when you were with certain people? What felt different?

Quest

It is likely that as the adopted son of Pharaoh's daughter, little Moses was raised just like the other royal children—the same schools, the same lessons, same wardrobe—on the inside, however, Moses knew he was not an Egyptian. He was a boy caught between two worlds. He knew his people were being afflicted and mistreated by the Egyptian rulers, yet he lived with those rulers and ate his meals with them. How confusing it must have been for him! God had arranged for Moses to be looked after by his own mother until he was probably around four years old. His mother knew where he was going to live and would have spent a lot of time teaching him about God and Abraham, Isaac, Jacob, and Joseph. He probably grew up remembering what he had learned from his parents and wondered what his future was going to be like living between two worlds. Some of these questions and feelings were probably what caused him to get into so much trouble as he grew into a young man.

Quiet Family Prayer

Read Hebrews 11:24–25 again and thank God that you live in a Christian home. Ask Him to help you choose wisely when seeking the advice and counsel of others.

Quiet Times

Younger Kids: Read the story of Jesus and the Rich Young Ruler (Luke 18:18–30). The young ruler had a great foundation—but still needed to *decide* to follow Jesus. Ask God to help you to always follow and obey Jesus, no matter your circumstances.

Older Kids: Read Luke 18:18–30. Moses grew up with special privileges yet didn't want any of it. He wanted to serve God and help his family and his people. The young ruler was in a similar position. God isn't against us having things; He's against us making our lives all about things instead of loving Him and helping others. Pray about this.

DAY 4: MOSES FLEES

Read: Exodus 2:11–15

Quick Start

What do you do when you are in trouble and you want to feel safe? What if you're in trouble because of your own mistake?

Quest

As Moses grew older and stronger, the differences he saw and felt between himself and the Egyptians became more prominent internally and externally. He was probably treated differently from Egyptian boys because of his looks, and the Hebrew people became increasingly important to him. He wanted to somehow let them know he sympathized with them, even cared about them. When Moses decided to slay an Egyptian who was beating a Hebrew slave, the Hebrews only saw another rich and powerful Egyptian when they looked at Moses. They did not know God's plan and weren't interested in anything he had to say. But now Moses was in trouble; the king of Egypt put out an order to kill him. So Moses fled. He ran away never to return . . . or so he thought.

Quiet Family Prayer

God creates us with the talents and personality we need, takes us through life's experiences, and teaches us from His Word to prepare us for His plans. Ask God to show you His plans and help you be patient for His timing.

Quiet Times

Younger Kids: Read the story of the Lost (prodigal) Son in your own Bible. God never stops loving us, even when we make mistakes. Even though Moses and the Lost Son made wrong choices, God loved them. Ask Him to help you make fewer mistakes to show your love for Him.

Older Kids: Read Proverbs 4. One of the most important ways God will guide you is with right choices. Ask God to help you with each choice in life you face—He's always right there with you.

DAY 5: MOSES' NEW START

Read: Exodus 2:15–25

Quick Start

Have you ever felt all alone? Have you ever had to do something all over again because something went wrong?

Quest

Moses was lost. No home. No family. No job. He didn't realize that he was right where God wanted him to be—in the desert. He was closer to finding out what God's purposes were for him, but God wasn't quite ready to show him yet. Moses was going to have to make a new life for himself as a foreigner living in a new land. First he had to learn about how to care for sheep and goats and learn how to survive in the wilderness. Moses may have felt lost and alone, but God was still with him. He found a woman to be his wife, had children, and became a shepherd for his father-in-law Jethro, the priest of Midian. God was watching him and helping him start over in a new place. God also heard the cries and groans of the Hebrew people back in Egypt; very soon God would invite Moses to become a part of His great plan to free His people from slavery and take them to the land He had promised Abraham in Canaan.

Quiet Family Prayer

Sometimes starting something big can seem tough, but God will make it purposeful. When we trust God with our lives and ask Him to guide and teach us, He doesn't waste a thing. Pray about what each family member is experiencing and working through right now.

Quiet Times

Younger Kids: Talk to your parents about Jesus. Did you know that he said he'd always be with you (Matt. 28:20)? Ask Him to help you hear and understand the things He teaches you each day.

Older Kids: Read and pray about 2 Peter 1:1–11. God used Moses' experiences to help him develop skills that he'd need, but that's not all; when we learn something new, God can and will use those skills. He also uses our experiences to help us grow in relationship with Him and develop godly character. Ask Him to help you grow in the things that Peter wrote about.

DAY 6: THE BURNING BUSH

Read: Exodus 3:1–22

Quick Start

What would you say the difference is between *knowing* a person and knowing *about* a person? Reading about a celebrity in a magazine is far different than going to the same celebrity's home and having dinner with them. It is the same in our relationship with God.

Quest

After forty years of looking after sheep in the wilderness, God reveals His plans to Moses. God knows he's ready, but all Moses could think about was Pharaoh's order to kill him and the Hebrews who disrespected him. After all, he was settled now with a new home and a new family. We sometimes forget that our lives are in God's hands and that we are a part of a much larger plan that God has designed. Moses did not really know God yet; he would come to know God more closely than just about anyone else in the Bible. But at this moment, he didn't know what God could do and how weak the mighty Egyptian army would seem in comparison to what the Lord God could do. Moses was not only on a journey to discover who God had made him to be; he was on a journey to know God.

Quiet Family Prayer

The first step to getting closer to God and knowing Him is learning that He can be trusted. Ask Him to help you know and trust Him more with your family decisions and directions.

Quiet Times

Younger Kids: Read the story of Moses and the burning bush in your own Bible. God likes us to ask questions—but the important thing is that we always trust Him whether we understand or not. Ask God to help you understand when you can, but to trust Him always.

Older Kids: Read Exodus 4:1–17. Sometimes what God wants us to do doesn't make sense to us and we may think God's way isn't the best way. He welcomes our questions and will help us understand when we can, but we will always need to trust Him and His love because we cannot possibly know and understand everything He does. Talk to God about this in your prayers.

DAY 1: PARENT CONNECTION

THIS WEEK'S TOPIC: THE PLAGUES

This week we'll read about the plagues and learn some valuable life lessons. God teamed up Moses with his brother Aaron because of their different (but complementary) personalities, gifts, and strengths. Digging into this with your children will help them learn that our differences are a blessing, and not an annoyance. You'll also have the opportunity to discuss how God wants to demonstrate His power in us, through us, and with our lives so others can see how much He loves us. Families will also learn how to take opposition and persecution in stride. The Scripture references give valuable insight that will bring more peace into your home, strengthen your children's character and faith, and help everyone metaphorically avoid plagues.

Tips

Keep a notepad handy as you prayerfully prepare for this week; study the Bible readings and contemplate the devotionals. One of the amazing things about God's Word is that He has layered each story and section of Scripture with a multitude of lessons and life applications. We've spent time praying into each devotional in this book, but not every lesson we've presented is always going to be the best or most timely one for your family that day, so pray as you read and prepare; ask the Lord to reveal relevant lessons for your family. When a life application or something new is revealed to you, jot it down and add it to your discussion on the appropriate day. Do this each week to help you make this devotional a tailor-made resource for your family.

DAY 2: MOSES AND AARON

Read: Exodus 4:13–17, 27–31

Quick Start

Many families not only live together—they work together. What kind of business would you love to have with your family?

Quest

Moses was feeling overwhelmed, so God instructed his brother Aaron to help out. Aaron was a good communicator; Moses was not. Aaron knew the elders among his people; Moses did not. Aaron had grown up among his people; Moses had not. Moses, however, knew the Egyptian culture and way of thinking; Aaron didn't. Moses had grown up among the Egyptians and knew their language, their war strategies, and their strengths and weaknesses; Aaron didn't. Aaron knew God had spared his brother's life for a special purpose and an important assignment; he would do everything he could to help his brother.

Working with someone you love and trust gives you great strength. Many times in the Bible, God called family members to work together: James and John; Peter and Andrew; Judas and James (Jesus' half-brothers); Philip and his daughters; Noah's family; and others. Moses, together with Aaron and sister Miriam, would be a great leadership team to guide their people back to the land promised to their forefather Abraham.

Quiet Family Prayer

Talk about how your family works better when everyone does their part. God can help you with that; He created the family and placed each one of you in it. Ask God to show you what your family can be doing together with Him.

Quiet Times

Younger Kids: Read the story in your Bible of Moses meeting with his brother Aaron. What things can you do to help your family work better? What things do you like to do? Talk to your parents about it and ask God to help you be a good worker in your family.

Older Kids: Read 1 Corinthians 12:14–26. God has given us different gifts, talents, personalities—even different desires and passions—so we can all work together and get things done better. Sometimes we let our differences separate us instead of seeing them as something that helps us live and work together. This applies in the church, the workplace, in our social circles, and in our families. Talk to God about using your strengths and about recognizing and appreciating the strengths of others.

DAY 3: SIGNS TO PHARAOH

Read: Exodus 4:1–9

Quick Start

There is one all-powerful individual who is above all others. Can you guess who that is?

Quest

A staff that turns into a poisonous snake? A healthy hand that is suddenly disease-ridden, and then healthy again? Putting river water into a cup and pouring it out as blood? These were not tricks; they were signs from God to prove that Moses was God's messenger. People could not see God, but they could see what God could do. When God used ordinary items for His purposes, they became extraordinary instruments in His hands.

When we give our lives to God for His use, we do not become magical; we become God's instrument that He works through. We don't have the power—God does. We don't tell God what to do—He tells us what He is going to do. When we obey Him, we experience Him working through us to impact lives around us. What a privilege, what an honor!

Quiet Family Prayer

God wants to do amazing things in our lives and through us—and we really can't do amazing things on our own. When others see or hear about what happened, they will know it was God. Ask God to use your family in ways that show His love and power.

Quiet Times

Younger Kids: Read a story about Jesus healing a child in your own Bible. He wants you to ask Him for whatever you need and trust Him to do what's best. Talk to your parents about what you'd like to pray for and then pray together for those things.

Older Kids: Read about Philip in Acts 8:4–40. Simon the magician impressed people until they saw the amazing works God was doing through Philip. Simon thought He could buy God's power; he missed the point of the gospel. We cannot buy or earn or control God's love or power. Everything God gives us or does for us, in us, or through us, are all gifts—we can never be "good enough" or "do enough" to earn God's love. That is the essence of God's grace. Thank Jesus for what He did for you, and ask God to help you receive and share His grace.

DAY 4: BRICKS AND TROUBLE

Read: Exodus 5:1–6:1

Quick Start

Have you ever done something that turned out to be a lot harder than you thought it would be?

Quest

Homemade bricks are made by digging up clay and placing it into rectangular metal molds, which are placed into rows on the ground for the sun to bake them until they are hard. To make them dry evenly and quickly, however, people add straw or grasses to the clay. Too much straw is not good, but not enough means the brick will not dry quickly enough with the fine compact clay.

When the order was given to no longer provide any straw to the Hebrew slaves, it meant they could not meet their quota for the day. The only one to blame was Moses. Things were not getting better for them, but were getting worse. He had to go back to God to find out what to do next. Ten times Moses went back to Pharaoh, and each time God's message was more serious than the time before. Pharaoh would learn who the real God was, and would pay a very heavy price for mocking Him.

Quiet Family Prayer

Throughout the Bible we see story after story with a repeated pattern: (1) God's people obey Him. (2) Then they encounter opposition and things go wrong. (3) But they continue to obey and trust God anyway and He protects and rescues them. Pray and ask God to help you recognize and understand this pattern. When you trust and follow God and something goes wrong, smile big because you know what's coming next.

Quiet Times

Younger Kids: Read about Moses and Aaron visiting the Pharaoh for the first time in your own Bible. When something goes wrong, what do you do? Talk to God about the things you'd like help with and thank Him that He helps us in every trouble.

Older Kids: Read Matthew 13:1–23. Jesus warned us that the enemy will come to steal the truth we learn. Pray and ask God to help you always recognize the tricks of the enemy in your life and for the strength to stay on course with the truth.

Day 5: The Plagues

Read: Exodus 7:19; 8:2–4, 16, 21–24; 9:3, 8, 18; 10:4, 21; 11:4

Quick Start

Has anyone ever noticed something different about you that they thought was great?

Quest

Water into blood; frogs, gnats, or lice; flies; diseased livestock; boils; thunder and hail; locusts, darkness, and the death of the firstborn. Each of the plagues was a clear contrast between the power of the God of Israel and the gods of Egypt who were supposed to protect the Egyptians. The plagues progress from annoying and inconvenient to terrifying and devastating. The Egyptian people were happy to see their slaves go if it meant an end to the plagues.

During this time, the people of Israel were also getting to know just how powerful their God was. The Israelites lived in Egypt where all this devastation took place. Beginning with the flies, God made sure that the plagues did not touch them or their property to make clear who was serving the true God.

Quiet Family Prayer

As Christians, God is our God and our heavenly Father; He wants to care for us. He also wants those around us to see His goodness in our lives so that they'll be drawn to Him. Ask God how He wants to draw others to Himself through your family.

Quiet Times

Younger Kids: Read the story of the plagues in your own Bible. God cares for all people; He was helping the Egyptians and the Israelites know who He is. Ask God to help you know Him better and better each day.

Older Kids: Read Exodus 7:19–11:4. If you were an Egyptian during this time, what would you have said to Pharaoh? If you were an Israelite, what would you have said to those who were complaining about the bricks a few days before this? If a godly person was reading about what you're going through right now, what advice would they give you? It's always easier to give advice than to follow it; but if we seek God, He promises to guide us through each situation we face. Thank Him for that now.

DAY 6: PHARAOH REFUSES

Read: Exodus 10:16–20

Quick Start

Have you ever made a decision and later wanted to change your mind? Have you ever made a decision to do something and then not followed through?

Quest

Over and over Pharaoh was moved by each new plague and would have released the Israelites from slavery—but in the end, he just couldn't let them go. The Bible says that God hardened his heart.

God did not make Pharaoh do anything he didn't want to do already, but this means God was always in control of the situation. There is no one who can stand up to His might and power, no matter how strong they think they are. Pharaoh did not know that he was going to have to pay a very heavy price for refusing to grant Moses' requests. His stubbornness would lead to the death of his firstborn son, the devastation of his people, and the collapse of the entire economy of Egypt.

Standing against God is never wise. Whether we're running a great nation or our own lives, the quicker we submit ourselves to Him and His care, the better it will be.

Quiet Family Prayer

It's great to admit your mistakes or shortcomings and apologize, but that's not quite enough—we need to willingly change our ways (with God's help). Talk about mistakes you've made over and over again and decide to break the habit—then pray together and ask God to help you change.

Quiet Times

Younger Kids: Read the story of the plagues in your own Bible. Pharaoh kept turning back on his promises. When your parents ask you to do something—or even *not* do something—do you try to honor their instruction the next time? Ask God for help with this.

Older Kids: Read James 1:19–26. Anyone can listen, admit they are wrong, and say they'll change—but what makes it authentic is following through with God's help. A better life doesn't come from learning, but from learning *and* doing. Ask God to help you learn, change, and do.

DAY 1: PARENT CONNECTION

THIS WEEK'S TOPIC: LEAVING EGYPT

This week we walk alongside the Israelites as they: celebrate the first Passover; triumphantly walk out of slavery and into their new future; encounter the first impossible obstacles of their new lives; experience God's miraculous deliverance; and respond by composing and singing their first song of praise. All a perfect platform for talking to our children about communion (also known as the Lord's Supper or mass), walking in our new lives as Christians, how to pray instead of complaining, what the Bible's miracles mean to us, what the word *impossible* means to God, and how thankfulness and praise encourage our faith.

Tips

God is completely unselfish—not prideful or arrogant. Pure and holy in everything, He's very secure in Himself. So why does He ask us to thank, praise, and worship Him? Well to begin with, God is very worthy of those offerings, and by doing so, we are wonderfully reminded of that. It's also an amazing reminder of God's grace. We need to be reminded regularly that everything we receive from God is because of His great love for us and is given freely in Christ—we cannot earn anything from Him. This reminder and purpose is also to our benefit. Thirdly, thankfulness leads to telling the giver how great He is (praise), and praise helps us realize how much we want to draw closer to Him and trust Him more (worship). God calls us to thankfulness, praise, and worship because He simply wants to draw us into His love. Help your kids understand this and spend a little time in each family prayer time beginning with thankfulness, moving to praise, and ending in worship, drawing your kids into God's love. (For example, "Lord, thank You for all You've given and done for us [be specific]; You are so incredibly kind and loving. Lord, we trust You with our whole lives and want to trust and obey You in everything—please draw us into Your love.")

DAY 2: PASSOVER

Read: Exodus 12:1–28

Quick Start

Thinking back over the years, how many Christmas celebrations can you remember? What was special about each one?

Quest

To the Israelites, the Passover was another interesting story they could tell to their children and grandchildren as a reminder of how God rescued them. To God, however, it symbolized something much greater: the coming of Jesus. The Bible says that Jesus is the Lamb of God (1 Cor. 1:7); He died so that we could have eternal life.

Each year the Israelites would hold a special celebration to commemorate the Passover. We do the same thing now when we observe communion, the Lords' Supper, or mass, but we remember the death of Jesus, our Passover Lamb. If you recall from the story, those who did not put the blood around their doorposts were not protected from the angel of death. Today many people do not believe in the Lamb of God who takes away the sins of the world.

Moses had told the Israelite leaders about the pending Passover; from there, word spread until the head of every household knew about the Passover Lamb. Jesus has called us to do the same thing—to tell others about the true Lamb of God who died to give us eternal life.

Quiet Family Prayer

Do you celebrate communion, the Lord's Supper, or mass (different names for the same celebration) at church? Talk about what it means to each family member. Pray together and thank the Lord for dying in our place as our Passover Lamb.

Quiet Times

Younger Kids: Read the story of the first Passover in your own Bible. Ask God to help you remember to be thankful each day for what Jesus did for you.

Older Kids: Read Matthew 26:17–29 and 1 Corinthians 1:7; 11:23–28. Think about these verses and ask God to help you better understand what you are doing at church when you commemorate the Lord's death with the cup and the bread.

DAY 3: THE EXODUS

Read: Exodus 12:30–40; 13:17–22

Quick Start

What does it feel like when you are going home on the last day of school for your summer vacation? Do you have a big party or celebration? Do you do something special?

Quest

Four hundred and thirty years is a long, long time to be away from home. It all began with Joseph's brothers selling him into slavery. Eight generations later, they were finally returning to the land God promised to Abraham, Isaac, and Jacob so many years before. The Egyptians were so happy to be rid of them, that they actually gave them precious jewelry, gold, and other gifts, hoping that God would no longer wreak devastation upon them. Not only was it "freedom" day, there was great celebration with gifts, dancing, and singing along the way. There was still much to learn, however, about becoming a nation, about how to be God's people, and about not complaining (complaining would turn out to be a hard habit to break). Now that they were free, they had to stop thinking like slaves of cruel taskmasters and start trusting and serving an awesome God who loved them.

Quiet Family Prayer

When we become Christians, God makes us new (2 Cor. 5:17), and we learn a different way of thinking, acting, talking, and living. We have a great advantage over the Israelites with the Holy Spirit living inside of us—He's there to help us love and serve God. Thank God for the Holy Spirit and ask for His help every day.

Quiet Times

Younger Kids: Read the story about the Israelites leaving Egypt in your Bible. The Israelites were starting a new and wonderful adventure with God. He has an adventure for you as well; talk to God about your adventure with Him.

Older Kids: Read John 14:15–27 and 16:5–15. Jesus told the disciples that His leaving would be better. Better because the Holy Spirit would come and live inside Christians. Leaving Egypt with Moses or being one of the twelve disciples would have been great, but having God's Spirit inside of us is best. Ask God to help you learn to walk with Jesus through His Spirit inside you.

DAY 4: PHARAOH CHANGES HIS MIND

Read: Exodus 14:1–12

Quick Start

How do you act when something goes wrong?

Quest

The Israelites must have been quite confused; while they were singing and celebrating their new freedom, they saw the cloud of dust rising in the distance; a clamoring of horse's hooves and chariots was just behind them—the Egyptian army! They found themselves stuck between the Red Sea and people wanting to kill them. Moses had a lot of frightened and worried people on his hands; but as usual, God had a plan. And here was another opportunity for them to trust in God and to listen carefully for His instructions when faced with difficult situations.

God is our Father in heaven. He cares for each and every one of His children and already has a plan in mind for every situation we are going to face. Turning to Him quickly in a time of crisis can help us avoid a lot of worry and fear.

Quiet Family Prayer

It's easy to read this story and say that we would have trusted God; but we may have found it difficult as well. God's Spirit can bring us peace, give us strength, help our faith, and give us wisdom when things don't go like we expected. Ask God for the Holy Spirit's help and then pray together about your family's needs.

Quiet Times

Younger Kids: Read the story of Jehoshaphat's prayer (2 Chron. 20) in your Bible. Jehoshaphat knew what to do when he was in trouble; he knew God was on their side, and he prayed and asked for help. No matter what happens, remember God loves you and is on your side—thank God for that when you start praying.

Older Kids: Read 2 Chronicles 20:1–30. Jehoshaphat knew what to do when trouble showed up and when it looked like what God had promised was being opposed. When the Egyptian army came after the Israelites, they acted like God and Moses were against them. Jehoshaphat went to prayer knowing that God was on their side, and would keep His promises. Ask God to help you learn to react and pray like Jehoshaphat.

Day 5: The Red Sea

Read: Exodus 14:13–31

Quick Start

If you could accomplish one thing in your life that is considered impossible, what would it be (no limits)?

Quest

Most people underestimate what God can and will do. So far, God's people had only seen Him send plagues on the Egyptians; they still knew very little about Him. God demonstrated His mighty power by holding back the waters to allow His people to cross on dry ground and then unleashing the torrent over the army that had wanted to kill and enslave them. But what was important was that His people needed to see the kind of God that was leading them. He wasn't a statue sitting on a pillar or in a palace holding a scepter. He was all around them, protecting them, guiding them, and caring for them. Over the next few years, God's people would witness and learn a lot more about the God they prayed to, but never really knew. The parting of the Red Sea was the assurance to God's people that there was nothing and no one who would stand in the way of God accomplishing what was on His heart to do.

Quiet Family Prayer

God showed the Israelites what He was like by showing them His miraculous power, so they would know that they could come to Him and pray and trust Him with everything. Pray and ask our Father in Heaven to help you trust Him with everything.

Quiet Times

Younger Kids: Read the story about the Israelites crossing the Red Sea. God is always ready and willing to help you and rescue you when you're in trouble—just call out to Him! Trust that He's heard and answered you. Talk to your parent about this and then thank God for His love.

Older Kids: Read Mark 9:14–27. Even when we're convinced that God *can* do something, it still may be difficult to believe that He *will*. Read verse 23 again. The boy's father wondered if the miracle he needed was possible. Jesus let him know that "possible" wasn't the issue; "believing" was. Talk to God about this story and as you're praying, follow this father's example.

DAY 6: THE SONG OF MOSES

Read: Exodus 15:1–20

Quick Start

If Moses, Aaron, and Miriam formed a band, what name could they give to it? Passover? Red Cs? M and Ms? What do *you* think?

Quest

There must not have been much entertainment out in the wilderness. No television, no movies, no prerecorded music, no place to plug in your games. So Moses taught everyone a song to sing. Moses had complained to God that he was not a good *speaker*; hopefully he was a better *singer*. However they came up with it, it was a song of celebration and commemoration recalling the amazing feats God performed to protect them from their enemies. It was the first hymn of praise God's people would learn together to praise God. We don't know if the former slaves could read or write, but they could remember the words to a song. This was the way they would teach future generations about God's amazing deeds as well.

Music has always been a part of worshipping God; in fact, He was about to give certain people the job of helping His people sing and make praise music just for Him. God gives us great abilities and we can always use them to honor Him.

Quiet Family Prayer

Talk about the wonderful things that God has done for your family, and thank God for them all. If your family or anyone in your family is musical, sing your favorite praise song together.

Quiet Times

Younger Kids: Sing your favorite praise or Bible songs with your parent or listen to some worship music together. Thank God for making you, for His Son Jesus, for eternal life, for your family, for everyone you love, and for everything you like in your life that He's given you.

Older Kids: When it comes to God, thankfulness leads to praise and praise leads to worship; once you thank Him for all He's done for you, it leads to telling Him how awesome He is, which leads to telling Him that you want to get closer to Him. In an effort to trust and serve Him more (worship). Spend your quiet time moving from thankfulness, to praise, and then to worship.

DAY 1: PARENT CONNECTION   83

THIS WEEK'S TOPIC: MEETING WITH GOD

Grumble, complain, and grumble some more! This week we'll see the Israelites grumble, complain, and sin their way into trouble—but then experience God's glory because of Moses' intercession. Taking lessons from the Israelites' history, children will have biblical examples of why it is better to be appreciative and thankful instead of grumbling and complaining; they will also better understand that God's rules are for our own good and intended to keep us happy and safe. Putting anything besides God in our hearts and lives doesn't work; as humans, we are prone to do that. Thanks to Jesus' intercession, however, we can experience His transforming glory.

Tips

While reading this week's overview, you may have thought, "How can my kids learn and understand all this?" Read what Jesus says in Matthew 11:25–30. God has hidden truth in Christ, so there is only one way to really "get it"—by grace found in Christ. Jesus said that the wise and learned couldn't understand (in their own strength), no matter how hard they try—but in Christ, it's a level playing field. Through grace, Jesus reveals the Father and teaches all who come to Him and trust—yes, even little children. Pray and ask the Teacher to help your family learn, understand, and live the truth; go into each devotional time trusting Him to attend and teach. You'll be amazed at what He will help your children understand.

DAY 2: BREAD AND WATER

Read: Exodus 16:1–31

Quick Start

Do you know anyone who is ungrateful or always complaining? How would you feel if you were always doing special things for them and then when you asked for something small they said, "No!"

Quest

What if free bags of groceries simply appeared at your front door every-day—imagine how many other things you could buy with the money you saved! God miraculously delivered the Israelites from slavery, caused the Egyptians to give them riches, defeated an army that wanted to kill and capture them, and now He said He'd drop off food every morning. They could bake it and boil it (yum, dumplings!); fry it into cakes; and combine it with meat and dairy from their flocks and herds that Pharaoh had given them (as God willed). God even provided the quail to go along with the first manna meal; imagine roasted quail with fresh-baked manna-bread, or quail stew with manna dumplings, and maybe honey-manna doughnuts for dessert. God did all of this for free; were the Israelites were willing to do what God asked them to do?

Quiet Family Prayer

One way children can show their appreciation for all their parents do is by happily doing the simple things that they are asked to do. We show God our appreciation in the same way. Ask God to help your family with this principle of appreciation.

Quiet Times

Younger Kids: Read the story of manna in your own Bible. All of the things your parent does to meet your needs—like food and clean laun-dry—are kind of like manna. Thank your parent for caring for you and pray that God will bless them *big* for loving you so *big*.

Older Kids: Read Exodus 15:22–17:7. Remember how thankfulness leads to praise, and praise to worship? Thank*less*ness leads to complaining, which leads to bitterness. Think about the "manna" your parents provide—everything you need (like food and clean laundry) just shows up! Pray that you always take the way of love by being thankful, giving compliments, and willingly serving in every way that you can.

DAY 3: THE TEN COMMANDMENTS

Read: Exodus 20:1–17

Quick Start

Do not touch the hot stove! Do not put gasoline in the campfire! Do not back up your car until you check behind it! Do not eat food until you wash your hands! Why do we have rules like these?

Quest

The truth is, God's rules keep us from going through a lot of pain and suffering. So far in the Bible almost all of these commands had already been broken at some point: murder, coveting, stealing, dishonoring parents, creating idols to worship, adultery, and lying. These were all destructive things that brought conflict between people and nations.

God's rules are not meant to keep people from enjoying life; rather, they were designed to prevent them from experiencing the pain sin brings. If you jumped over a fence at the edge of a dangerous cliff, the thrill of the jump would be exhilarating, short-lived, and have a painfully fatal result. That fence was there for a reason. God's rules protect people from harming themselves and others and help them honor God. His commandments, by design, help His people get along with Him and one another in perfect harmony.

Quiet Family Prayer

Jesus talked about the two greatest commandments (Matt. 22:34–40). If we, with all our motives, thoughts, words, and actions, love God and others by always putting them first, we'll be pleasing God in every way. Talk with your family about this; affirm that you can't do this on your own—Jesus sent His Holy Spirit to help us all.

Quiet Times

Younger Kids: Read about the Ten Commandments in your Bible. Talk to your parent about ways you can keep the greatest commands by loving God and others. Pray and ask God for help with those things.

Older Kids: Read Matthew 22:34–40 and Ezekiel 36:25–27. Did Jesus really narrow down the commandments? Or did He expand our responsibility? The commandments required you to honor and obey your parents; that includes any unloving thought, word, action toward them. Who is always present to teach us and cause us to love and live God's way? Think and pray about the Ezekiel verse and ask for God's help to grow in love daily.

DAY 4: THE GOLDEN CALF

Read: Exodus 32

Quick Start

God's people wanted to worship a god they could see. Is it hard to pray to God or trust Him just because you can't see Him?

Quest

When Satan deceived Eve, he lied and convinced her that she'd have more fun figuring things out for herself and doing what she wanted to do; the Israelites were now listening to the same lie. They didn't mind letting God do cool stuff for them, but they wanted to do as they pleased—and idols will let you do that. Whenever we love and run after something else that we think will make us happy—money, partying, power, achievement, knowledge, even ourselves—we put something in God's place. It is an idol, just like the calf and Eve's fruit—and it never works. Only God can truly make us happy and provide the abundant life He always intended for us to have.

Quiet Family Prayer

There's nothing wrong with money, parties, fun, romance, knowledge, and achievement; God invented them all! But we need to put Him first and trust Him to bless us and keep His blessings in their proper balance. Ask God to help you with this.

Quiet Times

Younger Kids: Have your parent read you one of the Bible's shortest stories (Matt. 13:45–46). When we truly know how much Jesus loves us and wants to care for us, He is like this man's great pearl to us—more important than anything else in our lives. Thank Jesus for being your pearl. (Extra: Jesus is the way, and Revelation 21:21 tells us that each gate of the New Jerusalem is made of a single pearl.)

Older Kids: Read Colossians 3:5 and 1 Timothy 6:17. Paul realized that idolatry wasn't just limited to bowing down to idols; we live in a culture that believes being rich is the ultimate key to the good life. Many people have ruined their lives and families by chasing after this idol, and yet we never seem to learn our lesson. Pray and ask God to help you put Him first and ask Him to bless you richly with what you need as you do.

DAY 5: MOSES INTERCEDES

Read: Exodus 32:7–14

Quick Start

Have you ever been so frustrated with some project or activity that you just wanted to throw up your hands and walk away from it?

Quest

We've already encountered a couple of "do-overs" in the Bible with Noah and Abraham. Now God wanted to use Moses' family to start all over again because of the evil activities of His own people. Would they never learn? He created them, He blessed them, He freed them from slavery, He performed miracles for them, and He fed them, and kept them safe. Now they just turned their backs on Him and made a new god of metal to worship instead. How frustrating that must have been for God and Moses! God's anger was justified, but Moses called upon God's love, grace, and compassion—and asked for God's mercy.

We need to learn from this how merciful He could be in the midst of our own sin. Even when we disappoint Him, He is willing to accept our apology and forgive us. We all have sinned and deserve to die just like the Israelites; but God sent Jesus to take our punishment for us.

Moses asked God to spare the Israelites; we have the same opportunity through Jesus. Thanks to Him, our sins are forgiven; through Him, God loves us and works in our hearts to help us actually be obedient.

Quiet Family Prayer

Ask God to show you any areas in your life where you have replaced Him with something else. Thank God for Jesus and ask Him to help you grow as His obedient children.

Quiet Times

Younger Kids: Have you ever had someone get really angry with you? How did you feel? Because of Jesus, God is always patient with us. Thank God that even when you don't deserve it, He gives you a loving hug and helps you learn.

Older Kids: Read Isaiah 54:9–10. Thank God that Jesus took His anger upon Himself and we no longer have to fear God; instead, we come to Him as a loving Father.

DAY 6: THE TABERNACLE

Read: Exodus 33:7–11; 34:29–35; 40:1–16, 33–38

Quick Start

Have you ever slept in a tent outdoors? Were you excited or scared?

Quest

When Moses spent time with God, he went to his special prayer tent. When he did, the Israelites would see God's presence (in the cloud) cover the tent. After God listened to Moses' requests to spare the Israelites, He called him up the mountain again to talk. When Moses came back down, his face literally glowed because it was reflecting the glory of Holy God! It was evidence that proved God was with Moses and that being in His presence was incredibly amazing.

God's people had no church or temple or place to worship Him, so the Tabernacle would serve as a very special and holy place where God's presence would reside and His people could meet with Him and worship Him together.

Quiet Family Prayer

Read 1 Corinthians 6:19–20. When you spend time with God, a cloud may not fill your house, but His Spirit can fill your heart as you spend time with Him. Ask God to help you experience His presence today.

Quiet Times

Younger Kids: Read the story of the tabernacle in your own Bible. Jesus said that He'd be with you forever. He's with you right now. Close your eyes and just be still, thinking about God and Jesus being right there with you, for a little bit before you pray.

Older Kids: Read 2 Corinthians 3:7–18. God gave the law so that the Israelites could understand what God is like and be like Him. They struggled because they were separated from God in their hearts; God's presence (glory) was outside of them. Jesus died to fix that. Now God's presence is in us and as we follow Jesus, His Holy Spirit transforms us from the inside out—making us more and more like Him. Talk to God about Him transforming you and taking you from one level of displaying His glory to the next, and the next . . .

Day 1: Parent Connection

This Week's Topic: Spies and Other Troubles

This week we go on a forty-year journey with the Israelites and learn how to walk with God. The first step in our journey with God is choosing to trust Him. If we don't trust and obey God, He can't teach, lead, care for, and bless us. Grumbling about our lives and complaining in prayer is often the fruit of not trusting and not wanting to obey. Even as we start to trust and obey, we are often tempted to compromise, thinking that God will understand a little alteration here and there to His commands—but that is just mistrust. God loves us and wants us to obey Him because He knows what's best and He wants to help us. Yes, He wants us to spend time with Him and have a loving relationship, but He wants us to obey Him and love others because we are the ones He loves. Ask God to help you and your family trust and obey Him without alterations.

Tips

You've probably noticed by now that there's a very tight parallel between children trusting and obeying their parents and our relationship with God. God invented kids and parents, and then called Himself our Father in heaven; He wants us to see and use the parallel. He wants us to learn from His loving parenting, and He wants our children to understand that learning to trust and obey us is practice for a lifelong and wonderful journey with God. Use the parallel often with your children, moving back and forth from their relationship with you to the relationship you all have with God. The drawback to this approach is that your parenting needs to truly be selfless or it may come under your children's scrutiny. Remind them that you're growing in Christ as well.

Day 2: Twelve Spies

Read: Numbers 13:1–3, 17–33

Quick Start

Have you ever had to play against a bigger and stronger team than yours? Did you listen to teammates who were discouraged, or teammates who said, "We can beat them if we play our best."

Quest

Many times the opportunities God gives us come with great challenges. God finally brought His people to the Promised Land, and all they had to do was trust Him. God had already shown them how powerful He could be against their enemies, having demonstrated miraculous feats of strength in the face of danger. Now they were put into the position of having to trust Him again.

Yes, the land "flowed with milk and honey," and there were amazing vineyards and orchards to behold. But there were also big, scary men there who knew how to fight! The people let their fears conquer their faith and did not believe God could win the battle. Instead they ran away, blaming Moses for everything and threatening to kill God's leaders (Num. 14:2, 10).

Fear can cause us to do things we normally would not do—so will faith. Faith enables us to overcome our fears and follow God, regardless of what we see.

Quiet Family Prayer

Ask God to help you be a family that chooses to trust and follow God.

Quiet Times

Younger Kids: Read the story of the twelve spies in your own Bible. Ask God to help you have faith like Joshua and Caleb.

Older Kids: Read and think about Hebrews 11:6. Eve believed God existed but failed the second part. We need to believe He exists and that He can be trusted. Everything He asks us to do leads to rewards or our best possible life. Ask God to help you always trust Him (in good times and through tough times) and therefore, respond in faith, obedience, and perseverance.

Day 3: Joshua and Caleb

Read: Numbers 13:30–33; 14:1–11

Quick Start

Have you ever been around someone who decided not to do the right thing, even though the consequences could be severe?

Quest

It is never easy to stand up for what you believe when everyone else is going the other direction. Even when you know the truth and know the right way to go, it is sometimes very hard to convince others to follow you.

It was a very sad day for Joshua and Caleb. They knew that God would not be pleased with their friends and neighbors—none of them were willing to trust God. They knew that they should trust God and do what He said to do; no one else agreed with them. Read Numbers 14:11 again to see what God found upsetting.

Quiet Family Prayer

God was really trying to bless the Israelites, but they just kept refusing to trust Him. He gets upset with us when we don't trust Him; if we don't trust Him He can't teach us, help us, and bless us. Ask God to help you always trust Him so that you can receive His love and experience His blessings rather than face the consequences of our lack of faith.

Quiet Times

Younger Kids: Talk to your parent about Joshua and Caleb—and about how loving and trusting God leads to obeying God. Ask God to help you always trust Him, because He knows best.

Older Kids: Read John 14:15–26. The Israelites disobedience showed that they didn't trust God. Jesus said if we love Him, we would obey Him but almost in the same breath, He told us the Holy Spirit would help. Decide to trust and obey God and love Jesus by obeying them and then ask the Holy Spirit to help you—not just now, but when you have choices to make.

DAY 4: ACCORDING TO YOUR WORDS

Read: Numbers 14:17–38

Quick Start

Can you remember a time when you stood up for a friend, or when you had to come to protect someone who was going to get hurt?

Quest

There was a time when Moses did not know his own people very well, but now he had come to love them. As their leader, he wanted to protect them. He was even willing to stand up for them to God when God was ready to destroy them once again. God listened carefully to what Moses had to say and decided that He would once again show mercy. It is a wonderful thing to see such a devoted leader stand up for the people under his care.

They had not had an easy life as slaves and did not know God very well yet—nor did they know where Moses was taking them. God honored Moses' heart for his people and was willing to give them another chance to follow Him and serve Him. But there would still be consequences for those who had not, and their children would have to learn the lessons that their parents had missed. Fortunately they had Moses, Caleb, and Joshua to teach them how to love and serve God.

Quiet Family Prayer

Trust that as you follow God, He will guide and care for you, and lead you into a good future. Commit to no grumbling about your life or your future. Pray about this together.

Quiet Times

Younger Kids: Have your parent read and explain to you Psalm 139:14 and Jeremiah 29:11. Pray and thank God for wonderfully making you and planning a good future for you. He really loves you!

Older Kids: Read Hebrews 3. Remember, God is doing the same for us; Jesus died for us and sent His Spirit to live in us—we have the help we need. Ask God to remind you to ask for help each time you're confronted with the need to trust and obey.

DAY 5: MOSES STRIKES THE ROCK

Read: Numbers 20:1–12

Quick Start

What do you do when you are putting together a puzzle and one piece almost fits, but not quite? Do we often encounter something similar with God's instructions?

Quest

This is certainly a strange story. The last time Moses got water out of a rock, he took his staff and struck the rock and out poured tasty, refreshing drinking water. So the next time there was no water, Moses took his staff and struck the rock again; the only problem was, God didn't ask him to *strike* the rock this time—He asked Moses to *speak* to the rock.

God always says what He means to say and gives us specific instructions. As God's servant, Moses could not be excused for his disobedience any more than the people who listened to the evil report of the other ten spies. And God only allowed those people who were obedient to Him to enter the Promised Land.

Moses knew God was just and he had completed his assignment by bringing the people from Egypt to Canaan. This was a very important time for God's people, and it was time for another leader to guide the people the rest of the way.

Quiet Family Prayer

God had a reason for wanting Moses to speak to the rock and Moses needed to trust God and be careful to obey. Following the exact way God tells us to do things is always the best. Ask God to help each family member follow Him carefully without compromises and excuses.

Quiet Times

Younger Kids: Read the story of water from the rock in your own Bible. Just like obeying your parents, doing things God's way is even more important for the same reason: it keeps us from harm. Thank God for wanting to keep you safe.

Older Kids: Read Matthew 12:1–8 and James 1:26–27. In Jesus' time, the religious leaders refused to budge on religious, ceremonial exercises, but they compromised when it came to the important things like love and mercy. Ask God to help you stay uncompromising in the things that matter.

DAY 6: MOSES READS THE LAW

Read: Deuteronomy 6:1–9

Quick Start

What do you think would happen if people decided to only obey every *other* stop sign as they drove around?

Quest

When Jesus was asked which of all the commandments was the most important one to remember, he quoted these verses from the Old Testament. First John 4:16 tell us that God is love, so when He commands His people to love Him, He is telling us that He wants a loving relationship with us. Loving God includes respect, honor, and adoration. We sing praises to Him because we love Him. And we treat others around us with care because He created them. In short, we show our love for God by being obedient to Him. Just like a loving parent teaches their children how to love and respect them, and how to love others, God's commands teach us how to show our love to Him and others.

Quiet Family Prayer

Spend some time tonight as a family thanking God for all His blessings and telling Him how much you love and appreciate Him. Finish up by asking Him to help you show Him your love for Him each day by obeying Him in everything.

Quiet Times

Younger Kids: Read the parable of the sheep and goats from your own Bible. Jesus let us know that one of the biggest ways that we can show our love to Him is by loving and caring for those around us. Ask God to help you be a sheep and never a goat.

Older Kids: Read Matthew 25:31–46. God wants us to spend time with Him and let Him know how much we love Him . . . but other than that, He doesn't really *need* anything from us for Himself. So He asks that we show our love for Him by loving and caring for those who need it. Talk to God about this and ask Him to help you not just have "sheep *moments*" in your life, but to live a *"sheep life"*—always loving and caring for others.

DAY 1: PARENT CONNECTION

THIS WEEK'S TOPIC: JOSHUA AND THE PROMISED LAND

Joshua was a faithful assistant to Moses from his youth, learning from him and his example. He was a man of prayer and great faith, being one of the few who believed that God could and would give them the Promised Land. He was a great military leader and was chosen to take Moses' place. His famous line, "As for me and my house, we will serve the Lord" shows that he was also a wonderful leader in his own family. Joshua knew to stay in God's presence—and to seek and trust God in everything. But the true secret to Joshua's success is shown in Joshua 1:5, 9, and 24:19. He knew that we cannot succeed at loving and serving God in our own strength—we do not stand because we hold His hand, but because He can be trusted to hold ours.

Tips

Joshua's secret is the same secret to success in parenting God's way. We can read books, make resolutions, announce our commitments, and still find ourselves falling short. All the while the Third-parent, the One who created our children and knows them best, is standing by patiently to lovingly help us be the parents He knows we can be.

If you read Deuteronomy 6, you'll see that one of God's most insistent commands to them was to teach their children to love and serve God. Yet Judges 2:8–10 shows that the Promised Land generation grew up without knowing the Lord. God never meant for you to raise His children without His help; in fact, He wants to lead, not just help. Pray now and ask the Lord (by and through His Holy Spirit who is in you) to take hold of your hand and help you in this task. Whether you feel confident or insufficient, yield to Him in each moment, and He will fill any void to overflow with confidence and strength!

DAY 2: JOSHUA

Read: Joshua 1:1–9

Quick Start

What do you think people would say about what you are like? What are you known for?

Quest

We are introduced to Joshua as young man when he served as Moses' assistant. The Bible tells us that Joshua would wait for Moses when he went into his prayer tent, and even stay there in God's presence after Moses left (Exod. 33:11). He was also one of the twelve spies; it was he and Caleb who believed God, and encouraged the people to go into the Promised Land right away.

He had proven to be a faithful servant and a gifted leader; when Moses needed a commander of the army, Joshua was chosen. He was a faithful, godly man the people respected; but more importantly, he loved, obeyed, and wanted to serve God. Moses had brought the people from Egypt to the boundary of the Promised Land, but God chose Joshua to lead the people into the land to claim their inheritance. Joshua was a good man and a strong leader because he was a faithful servant to God.

Quiet Family Prayer

Joshua challenged the Israelites (Josh. 24:15) to choose to serve God and then reinforced that he and his household would serve the one living God. Talk about this and ask God to help you be a Joshua 24:15 family.

Quiet Times

Younger Kids: Joshua loved God, loved to spend time with God, and helped Moses. He believed that God would deliver them to the Promised Land. Ask God to help you love and trust God like Joshua did.

Older Kids: Read Joshua 1:1–9 again, then Hebrews 13:5. The writer of Hebrews quoted here from God's instructions to Joshua (Josh. 1:5). Joshua was to be strong and courageous in obeying God because God was with Him—we are to do the same. Read all of Hebrews 13 and ask God to help you be like Joshua in obeying everything He asks you to do with strength and courage.

DAY 3: RAHAB AND THE SPIES

Read: Joshua 2

Quick Start

Have you ever had to keep a secret that was really hard to keep?

Quest

Rahab had heard the rumors of a strong people who had a mighty God, and they were headed toward her city. Everyone, including their king, was quite worried about what was going to happen. But they were pretty confident the walls of their protected city would stand against such a vast army. But when the two men from the Israelites came to her house, she understood they were blessed people and that she would do well to protect them and assist them. She saved their lives and in return they promised to spare her life and the lives of those whom she had in her home when the battle against Jericho started.

Rahab's wise actions preserved her family and guaranteed her a place in history. But her actions also gave her a place in the lineage of God's son as the great-great-grandmother to King David who was called a "man after God's own heart."

Quiet Family Prayer

Whenever we face a problem, we can ask God for wisdom and He'll help us make the right decision. Do you need wisdom for anything now? Pray. Also ask God to remind you to pray for wisdom whenever it's needed.

Quiet Times

Younger Kids: Read the story of Rahab and the spies in your own Bible. Rahab lived in a wicked city, but she chose to believe in God and help His people. God wants us to help the people who do His work. Pray for the people you know that do God's work that God would protect them and help them.

Older Kids: Read Joshua 2:8–15 again. It's important to remember that Rahab's people were very wicked and were being judged by God. Rahab wasn't just trying to save her skin; she believed God and changed, and then shared her faith with her family. It may not always be evident to us, but when we courageously trust and follow God, our actions help others. Talk to God about your choices and actions.

DAY 4: RIVER CROSSING

Read: Joshua 3:5–17

Quick Start

Do you know your record for skipping rocks on water so far? What does the perfect skipping rock look like?

Quest

A whole new generation had been born in the wilderness since God parted the Red Sea. Now they could see the same kind of amazing miracle. The Jordan River was at flood stage; it would have been deep, very wide, and very fast flowing—too dangerous to cross. Instead of Moses stretching out his staff to part the water, the priests took the Ark of the Covenant and stepped into the water before God parted it. God rarely does anything exactly the same way twice in the Bible; He is always doing new things in new ways. This helps His people experience Him in ways they may not have ever considered before.

This wonderful miracle gave courage to God's people just before they were about to have one of the most important battles in their lives. But they would never have guessed what God had planned next— God is so creative, walking with Him is like an exciting adventure.

Quiet Family Prayer

Seeking and trusting God is always the right thing to do; we can be confident in the next steps and be surprised by His grace. Pray and ask for God's direction in decisions you need to make.

Quiet Times

Younger Kids: Read the story of the Israelites crossing the Jordan in your own Bible. Was it easy for the Israelites to figure out what God wanted them to do when the river disappeared? You can always trust God to help you know what He wants you to do—just ask Him. Ask God to guide you in His plan, throughout your entire life.

Older Kids: Read Joshua 4. As you trust and follow God, you will experience Him. This new generation of Israelites just experienced God in a *big* way and God told them to stack stones so they'd always remember. Find a way to mark and remember the things God does for you—it can be a great encouragement as you continue to trust Him. Talk to God about your "stack of stones."

DAY 5: JERICHO

99

Read: Joshua 6:10–20

Quick Start

If you had huge amounts of treasure, how would you turn your home into a fortress to protect it against robbers?

Quest

Jericho was one of the most fortified cities in the country. It was located on a hill, so attacking forces were always at a disadvantage. Its walls were thick and its gates were strong, so when they heard about potential attacking armies approaching, they just needed to stock up on food and water inside the walls and hope they could outlast their enemy.

They were aware of the approaching Israelites' and how all the nations had fallen in battle to them; they were quite nervous and didn't know what to expect. But it wasn't the people that worried them as much as their God who protected them. Relatively speaking, the Israelites alone were not very impressive—but the people of Jericho had never heard of a God who could do what their Yahweh God could do. That's what worried them.

Quiet Family Prayer

Is there any area of your life where you are trusting in your own wisdom and strength instead of trusting in God? Ask God to be your fortress and strength today so you can stand strong against the attacks of the enemy.

Quiet Times

Younger Kids: Read the story of Jericho. God doesn't want us to be fearful of how big and powerful He is; He wants us to be excited about it, because He loves us. Thank God for His greatness and His great love for you.

Older Kids: Read James 2:14–26. James uses Rahab as an example of someone who believed in God and then followed through with actions. Being a Christian is not just believing in God and going to church—like James pointed out, even demons believe in God. Being a Christian is receiving Jesus as Savior *and* Master, then letting Him live in us, teach and guide us, and transform us into His image. Talk to God about this.

DAY 6: THE PROMISED LAND

Read: Joshua 24:1–15

Quick Start

Have you ever tried to give instructions to someone who wasn't listening to you?

Quest

If getting to the Promised Land was no easy task, conquering the inhabitants was even more difficult. Having fought more battles than he could remember, Joshua was now old; he wanted to rest and live in peace. He knew God had won the battles for them and he reminded the Israelites that it was God who brought them to the Promised Land and gave them all they had. He reminded them that the new generation needed to understand that God honors those who honor Him and God blesses those who serve Him; but if they turn their backs on God, He is only patient for a while. The Israelites told Joshua that they would serve the Lord.

Quiet Family Prayer

God isn't good to us because we deserve it—He does good things for us because He loves us. Tell God that you trust His love and ask Him to help you show Him how much you love Him by how you live.

Quiet Times

Younger Kids: Talk about Joshua with your parent. Which "Joshua story" did you like best? People say Joshua was a great army commander and a great leader, but the truth is he just kept close to God and courageously did what God showed him to do. You can do that, too; talk to God about it.

Older Kids: Read Joshua 24:14–28. Joshua had been around since Egypt and seen it all. He had learned the secret of how to successfully serve the Lord. It's sad that the Israelites didn't ask Joshua what he meant when he told them that they couldn't serve God; Joshua knew that confidence in yourself and your own efforts never worked when it came to serving God—you had to ask for God's help and trust Him. You're not safe in your faith because you hold God's hand, but because you trust Him to hold yours. Talk to God about this and make it a daily prayer—He will keep you (1 Thess. 5:23–24).

DAY 1: PARENT CONNECTION

THIS WEEK'S TOPIC: THE JUDGES

This week we will discuss God's plan for passing faith from generation to generation and about four remarkable people: Deborah, Gideon, Samson, and Ruth. From what Scripture records about these lives, we can learn some equally remarkable and helpful truths: God uses people who apply themselves to learning and living godly wisdom to help others who need it; He shows Himself strong on our behalf when we are weak; He works in our lives best when we do our part; and everything works better with love and kindness.

Tips

It may seem a bit early to start discussing the idea of passing the Christian faith on to your grandchildren, particularly if your own children aren't even in middle school; the Bible is clear, however, that it's God's plan for faith to be transferred from generation to generation in families. Also, servant leadership (especially parenting) works best when those being served are included in and understand the process. Our kids need to know that the reason we are making an effort to teach them the faith is so they can joyfully love and serve God—and they'll know how to and will do the same. Consequently, our families will serve God and help expand His kingdom until Jesus returns. If your children grow up experiencing and knowing that this is an important part of parenting, it's something they'll naturally continue when they bring your grandkids into the world. By doing this, you're already grand-parenting.

DAY 2: THE PEOPLE FORGET

Read: Judges 2:7–16; Deuteronomy 6:6–7

Quick Start

Have you ever had to search for a pet or a brother or sister that got lost?

Quest

Do you see a pattern here? Think back to Cain and Abel; the people in Noah's day; the city of Sodom; the golden calf; and God's people refusing to go into the Promised Land. And now we see the next generation of Israelites doing the same thing! The Bible talks about people being like sheep that wander off from the shepherd into dangerous places. God warned His people many times about this, and they always promise to do better. But then they would forget and the cycle would continue. Parents were not teaching their children as God had commanded. God told the Israelites who conquered the Promised Land to teach their children about Him so that He could continue to bless each generation; the Israelite parents didn't listen, and the next generation grew up not knowing God. How sad for God to have to start all over yet again.

Quiet Family Prayer

Ask God to help you never neglect His Word or His commands so that you don't grow apart from Him in your love for Him.

Quiet Times

Younger Kids: Talk to your parent about all the things they do to help you learn about God and His love and how to follow Him. What will you do with your kids one day to help them know God? Ask God to help you learn well so that one day you can help your kids learn to love and serve God too.

Older Kids: Read Deuteronomy 6. God told the Israelites to teach their kids about God and how to follow Him. He knew that if they didn't, the next generation would be in trouble. The Israelites loved their children yet they caused them a lot of pain by not obeying God this way. God doesn't just want to love, bless, and guide you and your parents—He wants to do this for generations. Remember your life isn't just about you; it may seem early, but start thinking and praying for your children now and thank your parent for teaching you.

DAY 3: DEBORAH

Read: Judges 4:1–8

Quick Start

If you had a very difficult decision to make, whom would you call for advice? Why?

Quest

God knows people often get themselves into trouble, so He provides godly people that can pray and give godly counsel. During this time in Israel, God's leaders were judges. When God's people got tired of being harassed by their enemies, they cried out to God for help; God would raise up a judge to help them follow Him again and to protect them from their enemies. Deborah was one of God's judges. She was a very strong and godly woman that people respected and came to for help. When she saw that her people were not following God's commands, she would point it out and encourage them to do so immediately. Because Barak, the commander of the army, listened to Deborah's godly counsel, God helped the Israelites defeat their enemies and they were able to live in peace for forty years. God can speak through anyone He chooses to speak through—king, servant, woman, man, boy, or girl. Whoever seeks Him will find Him and He can use them as a blessing to others all around. When we learn to live according to God's wisdom, He'll take care of the rest.

Quiet Family Prayer

Ask God to help make your family wise in His eyes so that you can be a positive influence on those around you.

Quiet Times

Younger Kids: Read the story about Deborah in your own Bible. One of the judge's responsibilities was to pray for people. Pray for those you know could use God's help and wisdom right now.

Older Kids: Read all of Judges 4. Without God's help, Deborah had no way of knowing what would happen or what to do. The people in the Bible who gave godly advice always trusted God for help with what they should say. Ask God to give you the wisdom to help others, but also the wisdom to pray for His help before you give advice.

DAY 4: GIDEON

Read: Judges 6:11–16; 7:1–21

Quick Start

What stories can you think of where a small person or weak team defeated someone much larger and stronger?

Quest

What kind of amazing strategy would you think would help three hundred men defeat 135,000 soldiers? Well, it would take more than a great strategy to defeat them; it would have to be a great God.

There are many stories of God using reluctant leaders to accomplish great feats or win military battles with the odds stacked against them. But God loves to show Himself strong on behalf of the weak. That is why he wanted only three hundred men to use against 135,000—He wanted His people and the enemies of His people to see what kind of God they served. When the battles were over, there was peace again for another forty years (8:28). As long as the people followed God, He gave them good rulers and peace all around. But as soon as they began following and serving other gods, there was always trouble.

Quiet Family Prayer

Thank God that still today, He loves us and wants to show Himself strong on our behalf. Ask God for help doing things you've been trying to do on your own.

Quiet Times

Younger Kids: Read the story of Gideon in your own Bible. When we obey God—even in little things—He can give us *big* results. Let God know that you'd like Him to use you to do His will, in the little and *big things*.

Older Kids: Read the whole story Judges 6:1–7:25. Gideon would never have been heard of had he not said *yes* to God's invitation to join Him on an amazing journey. God invites each of us to join Him in what He is doing so that people will know He is God and that He loves them. Pray about your journey with God. Gideon didn't have anything to start with, not even courage—God just needed him to trust and follow.

DAY 5: SAMSON

Read: Judges 13:1–6; 5:4–16; 16:4–9, 16–31

Quick Start

Can you remember a time when you did something that everyone else thought was awesome or really cool?

Quest

Samson is one of the most tragic figures in the Bible. He had so much potential to be an amazing leader, but he made bad choices that led to a very sad life. No other person in the Bible was physically as strong as Samson; the Bible says that he killed a thousand enemy soldiers using only the jaw-bone of a donkey. He was so strong that he ripped the gates of a city wall off and carried them to the hilltop!

But his bad choices led to the loss of his strength and his imprisonment. Samson liked being blessed with God's strength, but he didn't want to follow God's instructions for his life. He went from being feared and respected by everyone to being a prisoner who was laughed at by his enemies. At the lowest point in his life, he finally turned back to God asking to be used one last time. The Bible tells us that the enemies he destroyed at his death were more than all he had destroyed during his lifetime. God does His best in our lives when we do our best to obey Him.

Quiet Family Prayer

Ask God to show you if there is any area in your life where you are no longer doing your best to honor Him.

Quiet Times

Younger Kids: Read the story of Samson in your Bible. God gives everyone gifts; you may not be strong like Samson, but you have special gifts. Ask God to help you discover and practice your gifts—and to use them to help others.

Older Kids: Read all about Samson in Judges chapters 13–16. God called and gifted Samson so that he could help His people, but Samson spent a lot of time taking care of himself and doing his own thing. Pray and ask God to help you use the things He's given you to serve Him and help others. Samson didn't get it, but that's one of the keys to a happy, rewarding life.

Read: The book of Ruth (If your children are young, you may want to read the story from a Bible Storybook.)

Quick Start

Who can you name that has shown kindness to you recently?

Quest

Ruth did not know if she would ever remarry or have any children at all. She was a loyal friend and a wonderful daughter-in-law, but Naomi was worried about her because everything Ruth did was for Naomi, and that Ruth was not considering her own happiness. What Naomi was forgetting, is that when we trust God and take care of others, He looks after us. God was watching Ruth's kindness as she traveled with Naomi to a foreign land, as she worked hard, and as she did whatever Naomi asked her to do. God rewarded Ruth's kindness by showing kindness to her in return: Ruth was chosen by God to play a part in His plan to bring His own Son into the world one day. We never know what will happen next in our life, but we can know that God is watching over us, that He has a plan for each one of us, and that He rewards our obedience in the simple things.

Quiet Family Prayer

Naomi and Ruth were family, and people noticed how kind they were to one another. Ask God to help you be more loving and kind to your own family and to others that God puts in your path; watch to see how it will return to you along the way.

Quiet Times

Younger Kids: Read the story of Ruth in your own Bible. Do you notice how kind Naomi, Ruth, and Boaz were? Life is better with kindness. Ask God to help you think of more ways that you can be kind to others.

Older Kids: Read Galatians 5:16–26. In verse 25, Paul gives us the secret to staying away from the works of the flesh and walking in the fruit of the Spirit: we need to keep in step with God's Spirit inside of us—praying for help, wisdom, and strength in each situation. Ask God to help you learn how to keep in step with His Spirit.

DAY 1: PARENT CONNECTION

THIS WEEK'S TOPIC: SAMUEL

Samuel was an amazing man of God, and this week is packed with some awesome lessons from God's Word for your family. As a family, you will discuss parents dedicating their children to God and the way kids should respond; about how each choice we make is a small step in that direction; and how a lot of similar choices will take us where we do or don't want to go. You'll also be talking about bullies and what Jesus taught about them, how God speaks to us today, and how we can have God's peace. Pray ahead for this week and ask God to orchestrate some equally awesome devotional times.

Tips

Read Proverbs 22:6. This verse (like all others) needs to be understood in its context. Proverbs is a book of principles, not a book of promises. For example, it teaches that hard workers will do well financially and lazy people won't; while that is generally true as a principle, we have all seen exceptions. Principles, not promises.

If you teach and help your child to pray for wisdom in every circumstance, for help in every problem, and they see it working, they'll likely continue in the habit. When trouble hits, their automatic response will be to pray. It's true that if we make one wrong choice, we can easily reassess and retreat; however, a string of similar choices start to define us and our life's direction—the longer the string, the more entrenched we become. Proverbs 22:6 shows us that our task as parents is to teach, discipline, and direct our children so that their long string of choices (in every area of life) takes them in the right direction. That's why it's important for us to stay on top of our children's choices, teaching and training them in everything. In one of the devotions this week, we will discuss choices. Take the opportunity to help your kids understand what you're doing as a parent.

DAY 2: HANNAH'S PRAYER

Read: 1 Samuel 1:1–18

Quick Start

Have you ever prayed to God for something every single day until He answered your request?

Quest

The Bible includes many stories of faithful people bringing their heartfelt requests to God and God granting their requests. For many years Hannah had prayed to God that she would bear a child, but the time was not right. Hannah kept faithfully praying to God believing He would answer. There was a special child God wanted to use to lead His people and He knew that Hannah would be the perfect mother for him. Hannah had promised God she would dedicate the child He gave her to His service, and God took her up on her offer. Her son Samuel would become one of the most famous of all God's prophets and guide God's people during a very troubled time. This was the prophet God would use to anoint Israel's first kings. But he himself was an answer to a mother's prayer, a mother who believed in God's ability to hear and to respond. God was kind and blessed her and her husband Elkanah with five more children! God is our heavenly Father and He understands and hears the prayers of parents for their children.

Quiet Family Prayer

Take a moment to pray a blessing over each person around your table individually. Thank God for them and ask God to encourage, guide, protect, and bless them this week.

Quiet Times

Younger Kids: Let your parent tell you a wonderful story about you. Then let them say prayers for you. Close your eyes and listen to all the great things they ask God about for you.

Older Kids: Read the first chapter of 1 Samuel. Hannah knew that the most important thing about parenting is that parents give their children to God. Thank God that you have people in your life that love you enough to take the time to teach you about God.

Day 3: Samuel in the Temple

Read: 1 Samuel 2:11–21, 26

Quick Start

Why do you think some people are nice and others seem mean and selfish?

Quest

What if you were the only person who could hear God speak? It would be a very big responsibility to tell people every word, exactly as God had told you. You could not add to what God said or forget any part of the message. You could not be influenced by powerful or rich people to say special blessings or instructions that God did not tell you. And you could not be afraid to say the hard things God said that people did not want to hear either. Although God doesn't use prophets in the same way today He still speaks to us and still expects us to love Him and to love others as He does. The old prophet Eli had sons who were only concerned about themselves; they were mean and hated by the people. Most people are not naturally either selfish or loving; it is our choices that shape the kind of person that we become. Samuel was learning this and kept making one good choice after another.

Quiet Family Prayer

Talk about how our choices can shape who we become. Pray and ask God to help each of your choices be good ones helping you to become kinder and more loving each day.

Quiet Times

Younger Kids: Have your parent read 1 Samuel 2:26 to you. Samuel knew that growing up wasn't just about getting bigger and taller—it's also about growing closer to God and learning how to get along with people. Ask God to help you grow not just taller, but deeper with Him.

Older Kids: Read 1 Samuel 2:22–30 and 3:12–13. God doesn't just want parents to teach and correct their children; it is for their own benefit to occasionally restrain or prevent them from doing wrong and help them get it right. Thank God for positive restraints as you grow up, and ask God to help you cooperate so that you no longer need any outside restraint.

DAY 4: ELI'S BOYS

Read: 1 Samuel 2:12, 17; 4:12–18

Quick Start

Do you know any bullies? Have you ever been bullied?

Quest

Eli's two sons were lazy, corrupt, selfish, evil . . . and worse, they did not respect God or even *know* Him. Eli had not trained them to love and serve God, so people were even afraid to offer sacrifices at the temple because his two sons were always intimidating and threatening everyone—they were bullies and evil people. They served at the temple only for personal gain, not to help the people or to honor God. God could not allow them to continue to harm His people and bring such a bad name upon the temple workers. They did not know that God had planned for the boy Samuel to replace their family and restore justice in the land. Soon the people would learn what a faithful priest and prophet looked like.

Quiet Family Prayer

Name your spiritual leaders. Pray for them, that they would honor God in all they do and serve and wisely lead the people in your congregation with love and care.

Quiet Times

Younger Kids: Read John 6:10–15 with your parent: Jesus knew what to do with bullies; He prayed and trusted God for protection, but He also walked away and stayed away from the bullies. If you see bullies, remember this: Pray, go the other way, and tell an adult right away. Ask God to help you remember this.

Older Kids: Read Matthew 5:38–48. "Turn the other cheek" does not mean that we should allow people to hurt us; Jesus was talking about insults, not beatings. Jesus wants us to forgive, not take revenge. We are to be kind to our enemies, but we are not to allow ourselves to be bullied. Jesus even questioned someone who hit Him unjustly (John 18:22–23). Jesus forgave bullies, but He also avoided them (Matt. 5:48). Pray for any bullies you know. Also ask God to protect you and give you wisdom for dealing with them.

DAY 5: SAMUEL HEARS FROM GOD

Read: 1 Samuel 3:1–10

Quick Start

Can you recognize your mother or father's voice calling you, even when you can't see them? Why?

Quest

Samuel must have thought he was dreaming; was someone calling his name? At first, he thought it was old Eli calling, but something very different and exciting was happening to him. He had never heard God's voice before; once he realized that God was speaking to him, he learned to recognize God's voice. This was important, because God was going to speak to Samuel often and give him important information. The Bible is not always clear about how God spoke, but it is clear that each person always knew it was God speaking, and they always knew what to do next. Today, God speaks to us through His Spirit, the Bible, other Christians, and even through some of the circumstances we face. God speaks to His people in many ways and we should always be ready to respond like Samuel did: "Speak, for your servant is listening," and be ready to obey.

Quiet Family Prayer

Ask God to help you recognize when He is speaking to you and to help you hear Him in the midst of your busy life. Ask Him to help your times spent reading his Word and praying be very special times for you so your love for Him will grow.

Quiet Times

Younger Kids: Read the story of the boy Samuel in the temple from your own Bible. Sometimes you know in your heart the right thing to do; other times, you know that you shouldn't do something. That is God helping you. Ask God to help you listen to and follow Him.

Older Kids: Read John 14:15–27 and Matthew 28:20 (Jesus speaking). Sometimes we think Jesus is far away in heaven and in one sense, that's true; He won't come back in His physical presence to reign until the end of the age. He has promised, however, to always be with us and in us through the Holy Spirit. He's still our Lord and Teacher and we can experience Him teaching us, giving us wisdom, and guiding us. Talk to God about this in prayer.

DAY 6: SAMUEL LEADS ISRAEL

Read: 1 Samuel 7:3–17

Quick Start

What place do you go to or what activity do you like to do to relax and be at peace?

Quest

Samuel was thrilled to be able to serve God and he lived a life that honored God—so God used him in mighty ways. His primary role was to call the people back to serving God; he helped them to throw away everything to do with idols and return to worshipping only God. It was a big job traveling among Bethel, Gilgal, Mizpah, and Ramah to give people counsel and wisdom and help them serve God; but the people still remembered Eli's two sons and they were pleased to have someone as their judge who was godly and just, and not corrupt and selfish. They loved and respected Samuel. He judged in Israel his entire life and there was peace in Israel. When there is peace, it means God is protecting His people and they are experiencing the blessings that come when they love and serve only Him.

Quiet Family Prayer

Read 1 Timothy 2:1–3 and pray together for the people of your country and their salvation; for your leaders; and for wisdom and salvation, so that you can live a peaceful life, loving and serving God.

Quiet Times

Younger Kids: Read Ephesians 6:3 with your parent. These verses tell kids to listen to and obey their parents as their parents teach them how God wants them to live and be. When you listen, learn about God, and follow Him, God takes care of you in everything. Ask God to help you with this.

Older Kids: Read Philippians 4:6–9 and John 14:27. God wants us to experience His peace on the inside as well. These verses give a simple recipe for that: Pray about everything. Then don't let yourself be troubled or afraid, but instead think about good and godly things; in other words, make sure your thoughts are on God and expecting Him to help you in every way, with everything, because of what Jesus did for us. If you're having trouble, just ask the Holy Spirit to help—He loves being at work inside you.

DAY 1: PARENT CONNECTION

THIS WEEK'S TOPIC: KING SAUL

Saul started out well enough as king but turned into a disaster. Although David made mistakes, he was an amazing man of God whom God used to accomplish great things. The main difference between the two was that David had a heart for loving and serving God on a personal level; Saul seemed only concerned with doing the religious things that he thought would make God happy so that he could get on with doing his own thing. It came down to heart.

Tips

Read Ezekiel 36:25–27 and 2 Corinthians 3:18; 5:16–18. The key to really living out our Christian faith is realizing that Jesus didn't just die to get us a ticket to heaven. Through His work, He gave us a new heart and put His Spirit in us to help transform us from glory to glory into that new creation—into the image of Christ. We can successfully live the Christian life because His Spirit is at work within changing us (Jude 24; 1 Thess. 5:23–24). Not because we deserve it, but because Jesus paid the price for our sanctification (making us new) as well as our salvation.

Once we're saved, we aren't just left to struggle through attempting to do our best to serve God and not sin too much. We begin in grace, and we walk in grace daily with God working in us through His Spirit. This week special emphasis is placed on directing your kids to ask for God's help in living for Him; that's because it's His help (and only His help) that can enable us to do it. Be careful that you don't *demand* that your kids do it, but instead encourage them to trust God to help them; let them know that no matter how they feel, if they trust His promise to transform them, they can be all God created them to be.

DAY 2: ISRAEL WANTS A KING

Read: 1 Samuel 8:1–10

Quick Start

How many kings or queens, princes, or princesses can you name who are alive today?

Quest

Samuel was old; unfortunately, like Eli, his sons also turned out corrupt and dishonest. The people were very concerned that when Samuel died, they would have only his sons left to rule over them. They wanted a king. God told Samuel to listen to their request, but to tell them that there would be a heavy price to pay for rejecting God as their king and turning to a man instead. The people thought a king could keep them safe from their enemies. But God protected them, so why would they need a king? God's leaders called the people to serve God and warned them that God wouldn't protect them if they didn't. They wouldn't listen—they wanted a king. This really wasn't about Samuel or his sons—they were rejecting God. When people trust in anything else other than God, they are trusting things that can and will go really wrong.

Quiet Family Prayer

Ask God to show you any area of your life where you may be trusting in someone or something other than Him.

Quiet Times

Younger Kids: Read Judges 9:8–14 with your parent. Can you imagine the bramble bush ruling over the big trees? This pretend story shows us how sometimes people follow the wrong leaders. Jesus is our King; we should follow Him and those He puts in our lives to help us follow Him. Ask God to help you be a good follower.

Older Kids: Read Matthew 23:1–12. Jesus wasn't teaching that we couldn't use respectful titles like father, teacher, or pastor. He was teaching that those people are to be beside us helping us learn to obey God our Father and follow Jesus our Master and Teacher. We should submit to their help, but when we go to them instead of God, it's just like the Israelite's asking for a king. Pray for those who help you in your relationship with God.

DAY 3: KING SAUL

Read: 1 Samuel 10:17–25

Quick Start

When have you been put in charge of an important task or responsibility?

Quest

Maybe everyone likes tall people to *rule* over them because they are already *standing* over them! Saul was bigger than everyone else, but even though he was big in stature, he was small in character. He started well as king, even giving glory to God for the victories they had in battle (11:13), but it seemed like Saul began to think he didn't need God after a while. Maybe he enjoyed being so important, or he thought his victories in battle were because he was such an imposing figure. Whatever it was, Saul slowly stopped seeking God and honoring God and soon found out that God didn't need him as much as he needed God. Even though Saul was a king, he was just a man like everyone else in God's eyes. When we want to please God and we ask for His wisdom and help—even if we make mistakes—God is patient, loves us, and keeps helping us grow. But as Saul would find out, when we forget God and purposely sin, unhappy consequences will come.

Quiet Family Prayer

Read Colossians 3:23. Pray and ask God to help you do everything well and in such a way that your work would be pleasing to Him.

Quiet Times

Younger Kids: Read the story of Saul becoming king in your own Bible. Why did Saul hide? When we're nervous about doing something for God, we should pray for courage. Pray and ask God for courage and boldness to follow and obey Him.

Older Kids: Read the whole story of Saul becoming king (1 Sam. 10:1–11). When Samuel told Saul what would happen on the way home and it all happened, God clearly showed Saul that He was in control and that He would put His Spirit on Saul when he needed it. God did all this to show Saul how to rule by trusting and obeying Him; eventually, Saul forgot. Ask God to help you remember all He teaches you and shows you.

DAY 4: SAUL DISOBEYS GOD

Read: 1 Samuel 13:5–15

Quick Start

What kinds of things do you do when you are impatient? Have you ever gotten into trouble because you were in a hurry and weren't paying attention?

Quest

Saul was impatient and scared. He was desperate to give his frightened soldiers some courage; but his impatience only made matters much worse. He must have forgotten about Gideon routing 135,000 soldiers with only three hundred men! Saul's enemy only had thirty thousand chariots and six thousand horsemen, and a large army. Saul had forgotten how big and mighty God is, and that He already had defeated the Egyptians, the Amalekites, the Philistines, and everyone else that came against His people as long as they were faithful to Him. Saul forgot that God is always in control, that He cares and that He is never late. In his hurry, Saul decided God and Samuel needed his help; but his actions were disobedient. Sometimes trusting and waiting upon God can be difficult to do; but our patient obedience shows God that we trust Him. Saul's impatience showed he was unworthy to lead the people, and God began to prepare someone to replace him: a shepherd named David.

Quiet Family Prayer

The Bible says we receive God's promises through faith and patience (Heb. 6:12). Patience and faith work together; ask God to help you grow in faith and in patience as you trust Him with the challenges you face in life.

Quiet Times

Younger Kids: Read the first phrase in 1 Corinthians 13:4 with your parent. Talk about it. God is patient with us; this is why He's always kind to us. Pray and ask God to help you be patient and kind to everyone like He is to you.

Older Kids: Read Samuel's farewell address in 1 Samuel 12. Pray before you start asking God to help you learn and grow. Read it slowly and think about each part. Put yourself in Samuel's shoes and then in the place of his hearers. Talk to God about whatever lesson or thought stands out to you.

DAY 5: JONATHAN AND THE PHILISTINES 117

Read: 1 Samuel 14:1–15

Quick Start

Are there any crazy extreme sports you would do that other members in your family would never do?

Quest

Some people would call what Jonathan did foolish; others see it as very brave. There were twenty Philistine soldiers against only him and his armor-bearer. But one plus God is always a majority. Not only did God give Jonathan strength to defeat the enemy soldiers, but He caused an earthquake that confused the Philistine camp. God's actions gave courage to the Israelite soldiers and brought them back. It is exciting to be around people who see God as mighty. When people step out in faith and trust God, they see God do so many more things. People who do not believe in Him rarely see His power displayed. In 1792, pioneer missionary William Carey said, "Expect great things from God, attempt great things for God." God does not ask us to be reckless and foolish, but He wants us to be listening and obedient when He calls us to step out in courage and in faith.

Quiet Family Prayer

Jonathan was being nudged by God; but he wasn't sure, so he prayed for guidance and then went. Ask God to help you recognize when He's "nudging" you so you can go in courage with His strength.

Quiet Times

Younger Kids: Read the story of Jonathan's courage in your own Bible. It's very exciting to be part of what God is doing in people's lives and to see God make a difference. Pray that God would use you in His plan.

Older Kids: Read 1 Samuel 14:1–15 again. So many people are into extreme sports today because of the thrill. There is no thrill like the thrill you get when God's Spirit works through you, showing you what to do and to say, using you to help others and seeing their lives changed forever by God's power. Ask God to help you be a modern-day Jonathan defeating the power of darkness in people's lives.

Read: 1 Samuel 16:1–13

Quick Start

Do you know anyone who has undergone an organ transplant? How do you think you would feel having a part of another person in you?

Quest

Sometimes the youngest member of the family is overlooked because they have not yet grown up like their older siblings. Their older brothers or sisters do not give them very much respect because they're smaller, and haven't done as much to earn respect. But God does not look at the visible things that we see (our accomplishments, appearance, our voice, skin color, etc.). He looks at the heart—the inside of a person. In young David, God saw a heart that loved God and wanted to serve Him (13:14). No one could have guessed that this boy would write songs (Psalms) that God's people would sing for thousands of years; fight a giant and win; become a great warrior, a great king, a prophet; and serve as a great example of someone who loved God. No one but God sees the heart; when we become Christians, God makes us new on the inside (2 Cor. 5:17) and gives us a new heart to love Him. What an amazing gift! No matter what we feel inside, we can trust God to teach our hearts to love and obey Him.

Quiet Family Prayer

Read Ezekiel 36:25–27. Thank God for your new heart and for His Spirit who works in you helping you to love and follow Him.

Quiet Times

Younger Kids: Read the story about Samuel anointing David as the next king. David was great because of his heart for God; believe it or not, God has given you an even better heart with Christ living in us. Thank God for the awesome present He's given you!

Older Kids: Read 2 Corinthians 5:12–17. Ask God to help you trust Him to work in your heart, changing you. Ask Him to help you not judge other Christians by what you see and hear, but to give them the same grace and understanding God gives you, as God works in them.

THIS WEEK'S TOPIC: DAVID BECOMES KING

This week we follow David on his journey from shepherd to king. We see how God took all that David had learned as a shepherd and applied it to his role as a king. Your family will learn how David believed in God's power and that He can do anything through anyone who'll trust Him. You will also learn David's secret for how to make the best of waiting-on-God times. You'll also read the Bible's best story about true friendship and learn how God will care for and use us in His plan when we put Him first. It's going to be a great week of lessons and conversations!

Tips

Read Matthew 6:33 and 1 Timothy 6:17. Throughout this devotional and in this week, we talk much about the proper life-focus of a Christian. God wants us to put seeking Him and His kingdom first, knowing that effecting lives for eternity is more important than the race to accumulate stuff. God will take care of us during our journey here as we put Him first. Of course that doesn't mean that we shouldn't get an education and employ God's principles for working hard; but it does mean that our decisions (including those about education and career) should be directed by God and a motivation to serve Him—not by a desire to get an address on Easy Street.

As you just read in Timothy, God wants to bless us with good things to enjoy; it's just not to be our focus. As parents, we want to see our children well-provided for, but we need to be careful not to point them toward the best money-making careers instead of God's path. Point them toward God; know and trust that God will provide them with what they need to richly enjoy as they serve and follow. We, of course, need to not just point, but also lead the way.

120 DAY 2: DAVID PLAYS FOR THE KING

Read: 1 Samuel 16:14–23

Quick Start

What is one skill or ability that you are trying to improve in your life?

Quest

David could sing and play music for hours out in the fields while he watched the sheep. Those fields were the same ones where the angel chorus would one day appear announcing the birth of Jesus to other shepherds. God loves music, and He gave David the ability to play it beautifully. David practiced his instrument a lot and became so skilled that he was good enough to play for royalty! This opportunity put him in the place where he would meet his new best friend Jonathan, his future wife Dinah, and eventually, where he would live as king. David could have just complained about being bored out there in the fields, or he could have wasted his time teasing the sheep or doing other pointless activities. Instead he used his time wisely by praying, worshipping, and getting closer to God. He practiced his music and honed his skill with the slingshot. Protecting the sheep against lions or bears gave him confidence to trust God against much larger odds. God took all of these talents and skills and used them for His glory.

Quiet Family Prayer

Ask God to help you use each moment wisely so you can develop the skills and the talents God may want to use for His glory in the days to come.

Quiet Times

Younger Kids: Read and talk about Proverbs 22:29 with your parent. We learn what our gifts are by trying different things to see what we enjoy and are good at. Ask God to help you discover and practice your gifts.

Older Kids: Read 1 Timothy 4:14–15 and Proverbs 22:29. As with David, the gifts God gives you match your purpose and calling in life and it's important for you to spend time doing your part; talk to God about this.

DAY 3: DAVID AND GOLIATH

Read: 1 Samuel 17:1–51

Quick Start

In what situations is bigger not always better? (Needles, trouble, debt, etc.)

Quest

The Israelites shook with fear at all ten-and-a-half feet of Goliath; no one dared to think they could beat him in battle. Obviously, none of them believed God would help them conquer this giant. They all forgot how God used small numbers and ordinary people to defeat large numbers in the past. Now only one man (albeit a very large man) taunted and mocked God's people, and they were terrified. Only David believed God could use anybody to do great things—including him. He had battled a bear and a lion with God's help and killed them both; Goliath would be no different. The odds could not have been stacked higher against David—a teenager against a human war machine. David was armed with only a slingshot; Goliath a sword, a shield, and a spear. David ran out wearing his normal clothes, and Goliath wore blood-stained battle armor. Goliath never stood a chance, because one person trusting and following God can do anything God can do. David may have slung the stone, but God guided the rock and sunk it into the giant's forehead. No more jeering and mocking; and only a young boy serving a mighty God was left standing on the battlefield. Like David, we need to know that God can use us against all odds if we're willing.

Quiet Family Prayer

Ask God to help you have David's kind of faith and believe that God can use you too—despite any odds that are stacked against you.

Quiet Times

Younger Kids: Read the story of David and Goliath in your own Bible. David knew that God can use anyone to do great things. Pray and ask God to use you.

Older Kids: Read Isaiah 6:1–8. Isaiah knew that he wasn't perfect, but he volunteered quickly to be used by God. Make Isaiah's prayer in verse 8 your prayer.

Read: 1 Samuel 18:5–16, 28–19:1

Quick Start

When have you had to wait a long time for something?

Quest

It was very confusing for David; Samuel had anointed him to be king, while Saul, the current king, was trying to kill him. Many times David barely escaped with his life. Spears were thrown at him, a royal decree demanding his murder was declared, and he had to flee, hiding in caves and in faraway places. But God's hand of protection was upon him; no one would be allowed to harm him. David knew he could not take the throne by force, because that was not God's plan; he had to wait patiently for God to work things out in His way. During those difficult days, David learned about the people he would govern; how to be a better leader; and how to depend upon God for everything.

Many of God's servants waited patiently to see the fulfillment of God's promises for their lives. They realized that the in-between waiting times are when God can teach us many important lessons. David waited patiently when he was a young shepherd, now he waited patiently again for God's perfect timing. When we trust that God knows best and that His timing is always perfect, use the waiting time to learn and grow.

Quiet Family Prayer

Talk about waiting for God's perfect timing. Ask that God would help you to always use the in-between times wisely.

Quiet Times

Younger Kids: Read the story about David and Goliath again. What parts of the story do you like the best? What do you like about David? What can you learn from David's example? Talk to your parent and pray about this.

Older Kids: Read 1 Samuel 23:1–14. One of the things David learned while waiting for God and running from Saul was to get instructions from the Lord before making decisions. Ask God to help you learn to get into the habit of seeking Him for His wisdom and direction.

Day 5: David and Jonathan

Read: 1 Samuel 18:1–5; 19:1–7; 20:31–42; 23:15–18

Quick Start

How would you describe what a true friend is like? Would you say you are like this?

Quest

Jonathan was not only a better soldier than his father, he was wiser, godly, and more courageous, because he was willing to trust and obey God. As the next in line for the throne, he did not feel threatened by David, or his success and popularity. He trusted that God loves us and has different purposes for us all. He wanted God's will; if God wanted David to be king, then Jonathan wanted that too. Jonathan saved David twice from being killed by his jealous father. He was a loyal friend and had made a commitment before God to be David's friend; he kept his promise. When Jonathan was killed in battle with his father and brothers, David was broken-hearted. Jonathan didn't become a king, but God used him for something even greater—as the Bible's example of what a true friend is to be. A true friend wants God's very best for your life and will help, support, and encourage you in that, no matter what. When David finally became king, he took care of Jonathan's disabled son Mephibosheth for the rest of his days. Follow Jonathan's example; true friends make your life richer and more meaningful, and the best way to have true friends is to be one.

Quiet Family Prayer

Talk about true friendship. Ask God to help you choose good friends and also to help you be a true friend.

Quiet Times

Younger Kids: Read the story about Jonathan's friendship with David. Jonathan was a great friend! Pray for your friends and ask God to help you be a true friend.

Older Kids: Read Proverbs 18:24. Sometimes we think that friends are just people we can have fun with. Unfortunately those kinds of friends disappear when the fun stops. Find true friends and be a true friend; those friendships will be a blessing in fun times and in hard times. Pray about each of your friendships and ask God for His wisdom.

DAY 6: DAVID BECOMES KING

Read: 2 Samuel 2:1–7; 5:1–5

Quick Start

What do you think is the most important thing in life? Would you say this is your top priority, or not?

Quest

By the time David ascended the throne, he was a well-respected warrior and leader. He had fought the Philistines more times than he could count and still had Goliath's sword as a souvenir. People understood that to fight against David meant fighting against God.

He established Jerusalem as the capital of Israel, and it would forever be known as the City of David. He ruled well and took time to gather all the supplies and material for his son Solomon to build a majestic temple for God. Although David was far from perfect, he is most remembered for his heart for God. He loved Him and desired to know Him and do His will, which was the foundation for his every success. David knew that he hadn't made himself successful nor did he deserve to be made king—his beloved God gave him this great honor. When we focus on loving and serving God, He takes care of us and places us in the center of His plans.

Quiet Family Prayer

Talk about how God took David and lifted him up to a position of great responsibility. Pray that God would use you in His plan as you seek and serve Him.

Quiet Times

Younger Kids: Read the story of David becoming king. God wanted David to be a king of His people; He has a part for you to play in His plan as well. Pray that God would help you love and follow Him as David did.

Older Kids: Read Matthew 6:33 and 1 Timothy 6:17. We live in a world where the race to get more and to get ahead is prominent. Just like David, Jesus and Paul knew that the way to abundant life isn't to chase after money and things, but to chase after God. When we do, we get to know Him; we experience His peace; He uses us to make a difference; and He takes care of us. Pray about this for your life.

DAY 1: PARENT CONNECTION

THIS WEEK'S TOPIC: DAVID'S PSALMS

This is a great week! David dances before the Lord, and we learn how a king can love and serve God without shame. He worships God with passion, and we learn what it means to worship God in Spirit and in truth. David uses Psalm 1 to show us the difference between the godly and the ungodly; we see the need to love, learn, and live God's Word and shun the counsel of the world. He reflects on how the Lord is His Shepherd; we learn about love and care of the Good Shepherd. And finally, David sins and repents; we learn how to go to God for forgiveness, how to be set free, restored, and filled with the joy that we need for moving forward on our journey. Enjoy!

Tips

Two tips this week. First, when it comes to dealing with our children's sins and mistakes, we need to follow God's example. Because of Jesus' death, God sees us and treats us as His righteous children. He knows we are learning and growing, but He views us from the standpoint that we are "good kids." We need to believe that God is at work in our children, and always see them as a work in progress.

When they do sin, imitate God's actions towards us: Forgive right away without berating them; forgive the transgression; and move on to teaching. Hear them out and lovingly teach them how they should have done it correctly. Move quickly to loving hugs of restoration, confirmation of your faith in them, and complete forgetfulness (not holding it against them or bringing it up again). We help build our child's identity; they will emulate the kind of child you believe and affirm them to be.

Second, Sunday at church is not the time to try and make your children understand worship. They need to be taught at home how to concentrate on God, enter His presence, and worship Him. When it comes up this week, take the opportunity to worship together and start teaching them.

DAY 2: DAVID DANCES

Read: 2 Samuel 6:11–23

Quick Start

What are your favorite dances to do? Which ones are the hardest to do, or the funniest to watch?

Quest

People cheer at games, shout when they win, and dance to celebrate—so why not celebrate God too? David had happy feet knowing that God's Ark of the Covenant was coming home! He couldn't help but sing and dance in celebration of God's goodness. Many kings would have reconsidered or taken dance lessons so they didn't look silly in front of everyone; David didn't care, because he did everything to please God. He was loved by the people, respected by his army, and feared by his enemies—but he knew that God had given him all of that. Putting God first again, David showed God just how happy he was whether people approved of it or not. In his Psalms, David says to clap your hands, shout for joy, dance, celebrate, rejoice, and sing before the Lord. His wife felt it was undignified for a king to dance around in public and to be without his important-looking royal robes. There are many things we do as Christians because we love and serve God that others may not understand or approve of. David showed us that we should not stop doing them because of that.

Quiet Family Prayer

Ask God to help you to never be ashamed of believing in and serving God but to be bold in your faith.

Quiet Times

Younger Kids: Read the story of David dancing. Have you ever been really excited to see someone? God loves us and rejoices over us like that, and He loves it when we celebrate Him too. Thank God for His love for you.

Older Kids: Read 2 Samuel 6. The first time David tried to move the Ark, he did not follow God's instructions for moving it and someone died. David was upset, but he learned and did it right the second time. When his wife criticized him for not doing things in a kingly way, this time David refused to budge. He was all about pleasing God, not people. Ask God to give you this same attitude.

Day 3: David Worships

Read: 2 Samuel 6:17–19

Quick Start

People sacrifice a lot to get what's important to them. Is there anything you would not be willing to give up for God?

Quest

When David worshipped God, he stopped everything else to focus on God; he was willing to sacrifice all he had. When Ornan offered to give David a suitable place to offer a sacrifice to God, David insisted on paying the full price. He would not offer something to the Lord that didn't cost him anything (1 Chron. 21:24). Worship is something we bring to God from our hearts, not something we get at church. David knew that everything he had was given to him by God: the palace; peace in the land; his family; his victories in battle; and the love and respect of his people. Nothing was too good to give to God, and only the best was worthy of such a great God. David gave us a great example of what true worship looks like—it is from a sincere heart of love and an attitude of gratitude. We don't sacrifice animals anymore, but we should sincerely and passionately give all our hearts and all we have to show God our love and thankfulness.

Quiet Family Prayer

Read John 4:23–24. Spend some time worshipping God together. Sing and talk out loud and in your heart, but most importantly concentrate on God. Direct all your words and actions at Him.

Quiet Times

Younger Kids: Read Psalm 150 with your parent. Spend some time telling God how much you love Him and telling Him what you're thankful for.

Older Kids: Read John 4:19–25. Don't get caught up in details such as what songs to sing, what kind of music, what instruments, hands up or hands down, where, and when. Christians are the temple of the Holy Spirit and God cares whether we come to Him with sincere, loving hearts. Concentrate on Him and worship Him. If you have trouble or you've never truly worshipped before, God's Spirit in you will help—just ask Him.

DAY 4: PSALM 1

Read: Psalm 1

Quick Start

When have you seen a big, healthy tree with lots of fruit hanging from the branches?

Quest

The very first Psalm sets the tone for the whole book. It tells us the difference between those who follow God and those who don't. Will we live in a way that pleases Him? God tells us that He watches how we live our lives, and that He is ready to bless us when we live His way. He says we'll be like a healthy tree planted by water that yields wonderful fruit. But the way of the ungodly will perish. *Perish* means to be destroyed or to waste away to nothing. The key difference between the two types of people is that the godly learn God's Word and live it; the ungodly listen to other ungodly people and make the same mistakes. Learning God's Word and honoring God will be an example to others and leave a legacy of faith and blessing that lasts. As Christians, God has called us to live His way and He's even given us His Spirit to help us do that.

Quiet Family Prayer

Read John 15:5 together. Sometimes we feel like we can't do the right thing. Jesus understands. He told us that apart from Him we can't; but we're not apart from Him. Ask God to help you rely more on God's Spirit to help you live His way with each decision—He is in you to help.

Quiet Times

Younger Kids: Read and talk about Psalm 1:3 with your parent. Ask God to make you and your life like a big healthy tree that gives lots of good fruit.

Older Kids: Read John 14:26 and Psalm 1 again. Notice that the godly person does *not* get his advice from the ungodly, or do things the way they do. Be careful when you're listening to others that you don't just take in what they say. Learn the truth from God's Word and use it as a filter. His Spirit will help by reminding you of the truth you've learned. Ask for God's help with this.

DAY 5: PSALM 23

Read: Psalm 23

Quick Start

Have you seen someone very gently and lovingly taking care of an animal that they love?

Quest

Psalm 23 is probably the most loved of all the Psalms. It talks about the Lord as a shepherd who guides and protects His sheep with great care and compassion. David was a shepherd as a boy; he protected the sheep and managed their welfare. He knew how dependent the sheep were on the shepherd, so when he calls the Lord his own shepherd, he was saying how much he needed God in his life. He needed the comforting guidance and safety only God could provide; he wanted to stay near the shepherd's house all the time. Jesus is God the Son, and He called Himself the Good Shepherd. Through His ministry and teaching, he showed us that we could rely on Him to care for us, lead us, give us peace and rest. He can also restore us, comfort us, bless and provide for us. His goodness and mercy ensures hope of eternal life with Him forever. The Good Shepherd is in us through His Spirit and we can trust Him daily for all of this. No wonder this Psalm is so loved!

Quiet Family Prayer

Pray through the Psalm aloud together, thanking Jesus for being your Good Shepherd and caring for you in each of these ways.

Quiet Times

Younger Kids: Talk about Psalm 23 with your parent. Which actions of the Good Shepherd do you like best? Talk to God about them in your life.

Older Kids: Read John 10:1–31. Jesus was telling them that He was the Good Shepherd that the Old Testament talked about—but they didn't understand, because that would make Him God. Jesus finally made it crystal clear by saying that He and the Father are one. Knowing Jesus cares for us in all these ways is very comforting. Ask God to help you understand and receive all of the Good Shepherd's help daily.

DAY 6: PSALM 51

Read: Psalm 51:1–13

Quick Start

Can you recall a time you were very sorry for something you did? What did you do about it?

Quest

David had a deep love for God, but he also sinned and caused others a lot of pain. When the prophet Nathan confronted King David with his sin, David did not get angry or make excuses; he was saddened, for he knew he had disappointed God. This Psalm became a great example to others of how to repent from sin and live a life that honors and serves God. David didn't just ask for forgiveness, but for God to completely remove the sin. David asked God to forgive him; remove the sin and the desire to sin; help him never do it again; and even to free him from the guilt by providing a clean heart so he could be joyful again. When we sin, we should quickly ask God to forgive us and to cleanse us in the same way David asked. If others are involved, we can ask God to help us make amends. God will answer all this, help us get through the consequences with His love, and even restore our joy.

Quiet Family Prayer

John wrote the same thing in 1 John 1:9. If we ask, God will forgive us *and* cleanse us from the sin. Have everyone pray silently and ask God to cleanse and free themselves from any sins that have been hampering them.

Quiet Times

Younger Kids: Read the story about Jesus rising from the dead. We can be forgiven for our sins because Jesus died for us. Thank Jesus for His amazing gift.

Older Kids: Read 1 John 1. John knew that freedom from sin is a growth issue; he also knew we could have joy knowing that if we sin, we are instantly forgiven and set free from the sin so we can continue to walk in the light and in fellowship with God. Jesus took your sin and guilt on Himself. Pray for forgiveness, freedom, and joy.

DAY 1: PARENT CONNECTION

THIS WEEK'S TOPIC: SOLOMON

This week is all about wisdom and success. With Solomon becoming king, we see that when we follow God's will—even when that means repenting and getting back on track—He works everything out and keeps us heading in the right direction. Solomon's famous prayer for wisdom shows us that wisdom is a prayer priority; because of Jesus, we too can make it a priority in each and every circumstance. We will, of course, discuss the difference between God's wisdom and the world's wisdom; being wise in our own eyes; and being wise in God's eyes. We'll also talk about the wisdom (or lack thereof) of seeking wealth and riches instead of God, His will, and His blessings. And we'll end the week up by discussing the wisdom needed for true success, and the difference between praise and flattery.

Tips

When Jesus talked about how difficult it was for a rich person to enter the kingdom, His disciples were shocked (Matt. 19:23–26). They had been taught by their culture that being rich was the equivalent to being blessed by God. Our culture equates success and being rich with wisdom, skill, talent, and/or intelligence. Some people believe if you've "made it," you're one of the smart ones and you deserve rewards and respect. So pop stars, movie stars, professional athletes, and even some poker players are all admired. Unfortunately they're famous in spite of how they behave and what they did to become successful. Our kids need to know that just because someone is rich or famous, it doesn't mean that person should be a role model for others. This week as you read and talk about Solomon, wisdom, and wealth, we'll be providing you a few opportunities to bring God's thoughts to these topics. Take the opportunity to talk about true riches, what God values, and the difference between chasing riches and being blessed by God.

DAY 2: THE NEW KING

Read: 1 Kings 1:28–40

Quick Start

What would be your first decree if you became king or queen over a country?

Quest

When God chose Solomon to be the king after David, it was a very interesting choice; it showed how God can make good things come from trouble and disappointment. Even though David had several wives and many sons, he took Bathsheba (Solomon's mother) as his wife although she was already married to one of his soldiers, whom David ordered to be killed. David faced God's punishment because of it; when David repented, however, God forgave him because God always looks to the future and what He has planned for His people. God doesn't hold grudges; He forgives us when we repent and helps us move on from there. He wanted a wise leader for His people and He found such a man in Solomon. There was much to do to take the people from being a small nation always at war to a prosperous nation living in peace. God is wise and sovereign and nothing we do can throw His plans off track. Our sins cause pain and grief; when we run back to God, He forgives us and puts us back on track.

Quiet Family Prayer

Thank God for how He forgives and forgets our sins; ask Him to help you do the same thing with your sins and the sins others do against you.

Quiet Times

Younger Kids: Read the story of Solomon becoming king in your own Bible. God loves everything about you and He will use you in His plan if you love and follow Him.

Older Kids: Read Romans 8:28–29. God has predestined all Christians to be transformed into the image of Jesus. His Spirit is at work in you, teaching and changing you, as you trust Him. So whatever happens in your life God will use it and turn it around for your good—to help you become more Christ-like. Thank God that nothing can hold you back from His will for you and for Him to help you cooperate with your transformation.

DAY 3: SOLOMON'S DREAM

Read: 1 Kings 3:4–14

Quick Start

What would you ask for if God asked you the same question He asked Solomon?

Quest

Can you imagine God offering to give you anything you asked for? Maybe a fancy sports car, a billion dollars, or your own professional sports team? Many people would have made a poor choice if given this opportunity—but Solomon didn't. He realized that he was now king and that he didn't really have a clue how to govern this nation of God's people. Solomon chose wisely and asked for the one thing that could help solve a whole lot of problems. Wisdom. At the beginning of his book, Proverbs 1:7, he says, "The fear of the LORD is the beginning of knowledge; fools despise wisdom and discipline." Solomon was no fool; he chose wisely, and God blessed him because of it. God always wants to give us the best things and the important things in life such as wisdom, God's kingdom, godliness, love, great relationships, salvation for others, and peace. These should be our prayer priorities.

Quiet Family Prayer

Talk about your prayer priorities and pray together for the things that really matter for your life and then pray for others.

Quiet Times

Younger Kids: Read the story about Solomon asking for wisdom. James said that we should ask God for wisdom whenever we need it (James 1:5). Ask God for wisdom for the things that you are doing in your life now.

Older Kids: Read James 1:1–8. When James wrote about trials, he said we could ask God for wisdom anytime and get it. So God will help us with His wisdom no matter how tough and impossible the situation is. But He says that we must trust that He'll answer. Ask God to help you get into the habit of asking and trusting Him for wisdom in everything. You can ask once like Solomon did, but God wants you to come to Him in each situation as well. He gave Solomon a measure of wisdom; through Jesus, however, He's given you access to all of His wisdom (1 Cor. 1:30).

Day 4: The Wisdom of Solomon

Read: 1 Kings 4:29–34

Quick Start

Have you ever heard a riddle or a mystery that you were not able to solve?

Quest

Solomon was so smart that there was no riddle he could not explain, no puzzle he could not complete, no question he could not answer, and no mystery he could not solve. People tried to stump him with questions and riddles, but they were amazed at how easily he figured them out. It seemed everything he did was successful. There was no one who compared to him in wealth and wisdom and his reputation was known throughout many lands. The Bible tells us he spoke three thousand proverbs and wrote over a thousand songs. He knew about animals, plants, fish, and birds; about military strategy, architecture, and engineering; and about international diplomacy, business, and trade. You name it, he knew about it. When God is with you, you have access to all that God knows. If you have the wisdom of God, you are able to face any challenge with strength and knowledge. When we try to be wise in our own eyes, we will fail. When we are wise in God's eyes, we cannot fail.

Quiet Family Prayer

The Bible is full of stories of God making those who loved Him and served Him wise in many different ways. Ask God to give you wisdom and understanding in all your areas of your life.

Quiet Times

Younger Kids: Talk to your parent about what your strengths are. Pray and ask God to help you be wise and smart in all you do and in everything you're learning.

Older Kids: Read Proverbs 3:5–8 and Matthew 11:29. Before sin, in the Garden of Eden, God walked with Adam and Eve and taught them. Instead of becoming wise when Eve ate of the wrong tree, what actually happened? Today we live in Eve's world—a world filled with people who try to figure things out without God. Through Jesus, God calls us to abandon Eve's ways and learn from Him. Ask God to teach you and help you learn all He wants to teach you.

Day 5: Solomon's Riches

Read: 1 Kings 10:14–29

Quick Start

What would you say was one of the happiest times in your life?

Quest

There was no one in the Bible who amassed more wealth than Solomon. He would have been the right person to build God's temple because he had all the money and resources to do it. When the temple was completed, it would have been an incredible sight that could be seen for miles. The gold on it would have glistened in the sun and reflected the light of the moon at night. Solomon wrote the Bible book of Ecclesiastes, which tells us that riches don't make you happy. He learned that it's best to serve God, to do what He asks you to do, and to enjoy what He provides for you. God provided Solomon the wealth he needed to do the work He wanted him to do; but the riches Solomon *continued* to gather made him unhappy and too busy taking care of all his things. When we put God first instead of wealth, fame, or power, He will make you truly happy in your work and your life.

Quiet Family Prayer

Read Matthew 6:33. Ask God to help you put Him and His plans first in your lives and thank Him for providing for you and blessing you in the process.

Quiet Times

Younger Kids: Read the story about Solomon's great riches and accomplishments. When we do what God wants us to do, whether it's big or small, it'll make a difference in His kingdom. Ask God to help you understand what your job is in His kingdom.

Older Kids: Read Ecclesiastes 5. Solomon rightly concluded that striving after riches is a waste of time that steals your life and joy. When we follow God's purposes for our lives, He provides His resources, His joy, and His blessing for our lives. It will also help us keep our priorities on the things that matter: building a wonderful relationship with God and the people in our lives; growing in Christ; increasing God's eternal kingdom; and making a difference. Ask God to help you walk on the pathways He has prepared for you to walk on.

DAY 6: THE QUEEN OF SHEBA

Read: 1 Kings 10:1–13

Quick Start

When people say nice things about you, do you think they mean what they say, or that they are trying to get something from you?

Quest

There was never a king over God's people before or after like Solomon; no one was wiser, no one was wealthier, and no one amassed more land, or had greater influence than Solomon. The visit by the Queen of Sheba helps us understand just how impressive Solomon's great wisdom and amazing accomplishments were. But sometimes, what we own begins to own us. That can happen when other people praise or flatter us, and we begin to enjoy the praise. Then we start to think that the influence we have over others and all God has given us are things we got on our own and that we even *deserve* them. Though Solomon was wise in the eyes of the people around him, in the end, he became foolish in what he gave his heart to in the eyes of God. We often judge others by what they have or what they have accomplished; but God knows our hearts, and He honors the person who is rich in character and who accomplishes His will with humility.

Quiet Family Prayer

Talk about how we tend to see successful people as admirable. Ask God to help you always give Him the credit for what you have accomplished and for who you have become.

Quiet Times

Younger Kids: Talk about the Queen of Sheba's visit with your parent. Ask God to help you be a humble person who does not let the flattery of others influence you.

Older Kids: Read Proverbs 27:19–21. Compliments feel good, but if you start doing things in order to earn people's praise, you will begin to follow people instead of God. In fact, flattery is what people use to control you. Do what's right and what pleases God; if you get compliments along the way, don't be distracted—say thank you and keep moving.

DAY 1: PARENT CONNECTION

THIS WEEK'S TOPIC—PROVERBS

The book of Proverbs was written to young people who need to learn wisdom to navigate life; this week we'll be covering some highlights. First, we'll talk about the three Bible books Solomon wrote and their missing ingredient. Then, we'll learn about trusting in the Lord with all our hearts and receiving His direction. Next, we'll talk about loving what God loves and hating what God hates. We'll see how Proverbs compares the wise person to the fool and clearly shows what both of them will end up looking like. The week wraps up by discussing Solomon's instructions to parents and to children. Since there are thirty-one chapters in Proverbs—one to correspond with each day of the month—consider tackling a chapter a day, thinking and praying about (and sometimes memorizing) what they read.

Tips

Proverbs encourages us to do what it takes to get wisdom and to continually learn and apply what we learn. A child who enjoys learning is a child who will take initiative instead of reminding; encouragement and training is the key to getting them there. Every time your child wants to learn something, praise their desire to learn, happily explain how to do it, demonstrate doing it, and then help them try it. Stay with them and encourage each attempt until they have it; lavish praise on them not just for learning something, but also for doing such a great job of learning. Use every teaching opportunity—baking cookies, riding a bike, throwing a ball, worshipping God, etc.—as an opportunity to teach your child. The true difference between a wise person and a fool is that the fool thinks they know everything, and the wise person wants to learn from God and others. Take this week to watch for opportunities to teach your child how to be wise.

DAY 2: SOLOMON WRITES

Read: Proverbs 1:1–4; Ecclesiastes 1:1; Song of Solomon 1:1

Quick Start
If you wrote a book, what would your book be about?

Quest
Three thousand proverbs, a thousand songs, and three books of the Bible—that's a *lot* of writing. Solomon wrote down what he wanted to pass on to his children and others who desired wisdom. People all over the world quote Solomon's wise sayings about life from his book of Proverbs. His book of Ecclesiastes compares two ways of living. He had tried both ways; he wrote that he had done it all and owned it all, but in the end it was meaningless without God at the center. Finally, the Song of Solomon is the Bible's wisdom for romance in poetic form. You could sum up all that Solomon taught this way:

- First, honor, love, serve, and trust God, then He will guide you, provide for you, and give you joy.
- Next, learn God's wisdom for every area of your life and practice it so you can find what God has for you to do and do it well with joy.
- Last, focus on what's important: loving God, loving your family, loving and helping others, and enjoying your life and all of God's blessings—all in proper balance.

Quiet Family Prayer
Solomon was wise in many ways because God gave him his wisdom. Ask God to help you live with the help of your Lord and Teacher, Jesus, who gives us wisdom today, each minute in every day.

Quiet Times
Younger Kids: Have your parent tell you about one of their favorite writings of Solomon. Pray about what you learned.

Older Kids: Read 1 Corinthians 1:24; 2 Timothy 1:9; and Revelation 19:6–9. Although Solomon lived before Jesus' birth, many Bible teachers feel that God put Him in Solomon's teachings. He is our Wisdom, He is the One who makes life purposeful, and He is the Groom waiting for His bride, the body of Christ. Thank God for Jesus your Savior who died to give you everything you need to be happy and fulfilled.

DAY 3: PROVERBS

Read: Proverbs 3:1–12

Quick Start

What do you think it takes to be a successful person?

Quest

One of the most quoted verses in Proverbs is 3:5–6. Here, Solomon gives wise words to young people who are trying to figure out what their place in the world is going to be. God gave us brains to use, and we can spend a lot of time learning knowledge from books and other people, but Solomon reminds us that it is not how smart we are that determines our success in life; it is humbly submitting to God that will ensure success. When we seek to please God in everything we do, He will guide our steps, open doors for us, protect us from harm, and help us know what to do when the way is not clear to us. Success takes much more than intelligence, much more than university degrees, much more than having good business sense; it takes trusting the Lord to direct or change what you know. He doesn't want us to rely on our own understanding, but to ask for His direction and wisdom in everything. Why? Simply put, He knows everything—our future, what's best, and what He created us for—and He wants to show us His love by teaching, helping, and guiding us.

Quiet Family Prayer

Pray together and thank God that He wants to help and direct you. Ask Him to help you learn how to ask for and receive His direction in everything.

Quiet Times

Younger Kids: Read Proverbs 3:13–15 with your parent. Wisdom is better than loads of treasure. Ask God to give you lots of wisdom.

Older Kids: Read 1 Thessalonians 5:15–18. Think about what each verse teaches. Whatever God asks you to do, He'll help you do. Read verse 17 again. God wants to help us develop the habit of sensing His presence, talking to Him, and receiving His wisdom as we walk through life. That's the way to acknowledge Him in all your ways (Prov. 3:6). Ask God to help you develop this amazing habit of walking and talking with Him.

DAY 4: PROVERBS

Read: Proverbs 6:16–19

Quick Start

If there was one thing that you really hate, what would it be?

Quest

Did you know that God hates some things? It's true (see also Deut. 12:31; Ps 5:5; Zech. 8:17). When God "hates" something, He sets Himself up against it. God hates the destruction that sin has caused in the world, and the harm it has caused people. God does not hate people, but He hates the wrong they do. In plain English, Solomon said that God hates it when we think we're better than others, lie, do bad things to good people, think about doing bad things, or when we are eager to do something we know is wrong. It also displeases Him when we gossip or tell untruths about others, and when we cause arguments and strife. Of course, we know now that He sent His One and only Son to die for the sins of the world. He did this out of His great love for us; as God's people, we should love good and hate what God hates—even when we see it on television (we shouldn't call what God hates "entertainment"). We should trust God to help us not do these things and to walk away from those who do.

Quiet Family Prayer

Ask God to help you hate the seven items from today's Scripture and to help you remove any trace of them from your lives.

Quiet Times

Younger Kids: Read and talk about Proverbs 4:23 with your parent. It's important that we guard our hearts like we would guard treasure. If we put yucky stuff in our hearts, our hearts get yucky. Ask God to help you keep a clean heart.

Older Kids: Read Proverbs 4:8–27. Verse 23 tells you to diligently guard your heart. The following verses tell you how: Watch what you say and what you look at; think about the path of your feet. Watch where you go, what you do, and who you spend time with. Your choices either pollute your heart and life, or protect it. Ask God to help you get into the habit of passionately guarding your own heart with His help.

Day 5: Proverbs

Read: Proverbs 10:1–32

Quick Start

Have you ever gotten lost? What did you do?

Quest

Many of Solomon's proverbs compare a wise person to a foolish person. The wise person seeks justice, welcomes advice from others, works hard, speaks truthfully, is helped by God, and is respected by all. The foolish man perverts justice, despises wise counsel, is lazy, tells lies, will be destroyed by his evil ways, and has a bad reputation. Each of Solomon's proverbs offers the reader a choice; we can follow God's narrow road that leads to life and happiness, or we can follow the broad way that many others take that looks good at the start, but leads to destruction. Much like Joshua's challenge to his people (Josh. 24:15) to choose whom they were going to serve, Proverbs offers us a challenge. You can drive by prisons and jails and see the consequences of people's choices. You can read in the paper about people's choices and see that many times, they chose poorly. Choose wisely; following Solomon's advice has proven rewards that will lead to where you ultimately want to be. We cannot act like fools and receive the rewards of the wise.

Quiet Family Prayer

Talk about how God's Word is our map for life. Ask God to help you listen to wisdom and follow the way of the wise and not the way of the fool.

Quiet Times

Younger Kids: Read and talk about Proverbs 10:17 with your parent. Ask God to help you always listen to wise instruction and correction.

Older Kids: Read Proverbs 10 again but slowly, thinking about each verse. In Joshua 1:8, the Lord told Joshua to meditate on His Word. God's Word is alive and is meant to change us—that doesn't happen when we skim it or speed-read it. Pray as you read and think about how to apply it. Choose one of the verses that made sense to you for your life and memorize it.

DAY 6: PROVERBS

Read: Proverbs 22:6; 23:13–26

Quick Start

What is the best advice your mother or father ever gave you?

Quest

Solomon truly wanted his children to be wise. He wanted them to make good choices in their lives so they could enjoy the blessings of God. He tells parents to provide the best training possible to their children, to help them love God, and to be good examples for them. Solomon also offers advice to children: Show respect for your parents and listen to them, learn from them, and obey. Sometimes children are tempted to disregard their parents' advice or be disrespectful to them; God gave parents the responsibility to correct their children's poor behavior and to set consequences. He knows that children who get into the habit of not listening become fools. God loves us enough to teach, guide, and correct us. Parents also love their children and are to follow God's example. Discipline and correction are not always fun to endure, but if we learn from them, they will prevent us from having to face far harsher consequences in our lives down the road.

Quiet Family Prayer

Talk about a parent's job (loving, teaching, training, and correcting) and a child's job (respecting, listening, learning, and obeying). Take turns asking God to help you do your job well.

Quiet Times

Younger Kids: Read Proverbs 23:24–25 with your parent and let them tell you how happy you make them. Pray and ask God to help you always be a joy to Him and your parents.

Older Kids: There are 31 chapters in Proverbs; some people make a habit of meditating on one a day each month. Whatever date it is today, turn to the chapter that has the same number and read, think about and pray your way through it. Pick one to memorize.

Day 1: Parent Connection

This Week's Topic: Two Kingdoms

This week's discussions can be summed up in five points:

- Blindness says that God's truth doesn't matter; and sin and compromises pave the road that leads us there.
- He who seeks God finds wisdom; He who seeks wisdom without God becomes a fool.
- God will always find and use the faithful to bring about His plans; demonstrate your availability with your faithfulness.
- Compromising God's truth is a hereditary disease that grows worse with each generation.
- There's no question that God's plan will happen—yet the question remains, however, will you take part and share in the joy, glory, and rewards?

Tips

Faith is in decline in some countries around the world, and church buildings are being sold off for lack of attendance. Israel and Judah experienced the same thing more than 2,500 years ago. We read about them 'forgetting God' and we think, "How could they?" What we don't realize is that usually several—if not many—generations had passed between a godly generation and a wicked one. God's Word is clear (for the Israelites and for us now) that parents are to diligently pass their faith on to their children. When parents don't, the next generation grows up a little further away from God than their parents were, and the cycle continues with each subsequent generation straying a little further away from God. The same thing happens when parents live their Christian lives compromising with the world—each successive generation will compromise further until a generation arrives that has forgotten God. The solution isn't to scream at the world, but to teach and encourage parents to live for God and to raise their children to walk with Jesus without compromise. Keep up the work you have begun with your own family, and perhaps encourage other families to do the same. It's never too late.

DAY 2: SOLOMON'S MISTAKE

Read: 1 Kings 11:1–13

Quick Start

If you were to set a trap to capture a wild animal, what sort of trap would you make that would not harm the animal?

Quest

Solomon knew that God was against him having many wives and marrying women who didn't love God. But this was "business"; Solomon compromised in order to make strategic alliances with other nations . . . at least, that's how it started. In all, he collected over a thousand women for his palace! Solomon should have known better. No matter how wise we are, compromise (even small ones) leads to blindness, which leads to more sin. Solomon must have thought that he was wise enough to get away with his compromises; little by little, however, his sins grew, blinding his judgment. By the time Solomon was old, he had set up places where God's people could worship foreign gods and idols. Solomon started out as a great blessing to God's people, but ended up turning their hearts away from God. Greed, foolishness, jealousy, and hatred took root in people's hearts, and the nation of Israel slipped into a very dark time from which they would never fully recover. Compromise is a trap that potentially ensnares us and others.

Quiet Family Prayer

God would have shown Solomon how to make strategic alliances without compromise if he had refused to sin. Ask God to help you trust Him when compromise tries to lure you away.

Quiet Times

Younger Kids: Read the story of Solomon's rule. Everything God tells us is for our own good. Solomon needed to listen and *remember* what God told Him. Ask God to help you listen *and* remember.

Older Kids: Read Proverbs 3:1–2; 4:5–13, 20–21. Solomon strongly advised that we *not forget* what we've learned. Unfortunately he underestimated the power of slow, progressive blindness that makes us unaware when we start down the road of compromise. Remembering God's truth and asking Him to help us refuse the small sins keeps us on track. Ask God to help you be resolute against little compromises.

DAY 3: REHOBOAM

Read: 1 Kings 11:43; 12:1–15; 14:21–22, 25–30

Quick Start

Have you ever broken a promise to someone that hurt your friendship?

Quest

Only Saul, David, and Solomon ruled over all of God's people. The kingdom was divided in two because of Solomon's great sin; his son Rehoboam only ruled over the tribes of Judah and Benjamin. And thanks to his father's idolatry, Rehoboam also proved to be unwise and ungodly. You would think that the son of Solomon would have at least tried to start his rule wisely. But with bad counselors comes bad decisions. Rehoboam tried to be wise, but he didn't seek God; so God's wisdom was hidden from him. And having the kingdom divided under him was just the start! The king of Egypt attacked Jerusalem and took away the riches his father had gathered. Just as Israel had plundered Egypt when they left as slaves, now God permitted Egypt to plunder His people because of their sins.

God never takes pleasure in seeing His people hurt, but He cannot bless us when we disobey Him. He who seeks God finds wisdom; He who seeks wisdom without God becomes a fool.

Quiet Family Prayer

Pray together and ask God to help you always seek Him and receive all of His benefits as a result of your love relationship with Him.

Quiet Times

Younger Kids: Read the story of Rehoboam. Rehoboam listened to his young friends instead of older, wiser people—that wasn't wise. Ask God to help you always listen to wise and godly people.

Older Kids: Read 1 Kings 12:8–10, 15. Fools listen to fools and help each other destroy their lives. When you find yourself thinking that your young friends (who don't have God's wisdom and have very little life experience) are wiser than your parents and the godly people you know—*stop*!! You're falling into Rehoboam's trap. Ask God to help you choose your counselors wisely and to keep you from taking the path of fools.

DAY 4: DIVIDED KINGDOM

Read: 1 Kings 12:16–24; 14:30

Quick Start

Can you think of something that has happened to you that helps you know your life is a part of God's plans?

Quest

If it were not for God's intervention, His people would have been wiped out by each other or by other more powerful nations. But God had a plan and had made promises to certain people, such as Abraham and David. God had promised them that one of their descendants would bless all the nations on Earth and sit on David's throne forever.

You see, even though His people kept rejecting Him and trusting in other gods, He always had those who sought after Him and wanted to honor Him, even when most didn't. God used those people to keep His plan moving and they were blessed. Many, many years later a boy would be born to Mary and Joseph who came from the line of Abraham and David—the King of kings. His death and resurrection are bringing God's blessing of eternal life to all nations, just as God had promised. God is still looking for those who will be faithful and help with His plan to share the gospel. Whatever God promises to you He will be faithful to do, as you are faithful to help. Don't take yourself out of God's plan and miss the blessings He has for you.

Quiet Family Prayer

Talk about how God's plan included Jesus from the start. Pray that God would use your family to help others know Jesus.

Quiet Times

Younger Kids: Read the story of the Holy Spirit's arrival at Pentecost. Talk to your parent about how you can help others know Jesus and ask God to use you.

Older Kids: Read 1 Peter 3:14–16. Always be loving and respectful; sharing your own faith experience can be powerful, so pray silently for help; trust God to give you the words; and know some basic Scriptures (John 3:16, Rom. 10:9–10, etc.). Ask someone to help you be prepared. Pray about this; there's nothing greater than helping someone receive eternal life.

Day 5: Israel

Read: 2 Kings 13:1–3

Quick Start

Do you know someone who is always getting into trouble?

Quest

The ten tribes of Israel (northern kingdom) began under Jeroboam in 975 BC and ended with King Hoshea in 721 BC. None of their kings truly served God. It was 254 years of seeking other gods and making alliances with pagan nations, trusting everyone else *but* God. They didn't tell stories of God's great miracles and help, or commemorate God's goodness and protection with important events like the Passover; instead, they lived like all the other nations. God sent prophets to call them back, but they didn't listen. Israel could have lived a life of blessing and peace, allowing God to use them to display His might and His glory, but they forgot God gradually by compromising and thinking little sins don't matter. God was no longer a priority; they were too busy to learn how to follow Him, or to teach their children to follow Him. As each generation made more compromises, they strayed further away from God; and eventually, He was forgotten.

Quiet Family Prayer

Talk about how this is happening today, as some countries step further away from God with each generation. Pray together for your country.

Quiet Times

Younger Kids: Read the Parable of the Sower in your own Bible (Matt. 13:1–9, 18–23). Jesus taught that when we love God, things in this life try to distract us like weeds trying to take over a garden. Ask God to help you keep your love for Him free from weeds and thorns.

Older Kids: Read Matthew 13:1–23. Think and pray about it. What is fighting against the seed? What types of distractions try to make you slowly forget what you know about God? Read verse 15 again. Ask God to help you want Him, His plan, and His blessing so you won't be distracted and forget.

DAY 6: JUDAH

Read: Kings 18:1–7

Quick Start

Have you ever cheated in order to win in a game? How is that like compromising God's Word in our lives?

Quest

The kingdom of Judah was small. Its capital was Jerusalem, where Solomon's temple and the king's palace were located. Out of their twenty kings, two-thirds of them followed God. So 263 of their 393 years as a kingdom were under God-seeking kings. Their kingdom lasted nearly twice as long as Israel's, who had no God-seeking kings.

God is famous for using small things to accomplish great feats. Remember Gideon's little army? Many times the people in Judah asked God for help and He protected them from huge enemy threats. But eventually, even Judah slowly forgot God and they were taken captive by foreign nations. By 586 BC, there was little left. Their city walls lay in ruins, their temple was smashed, and their royal palaces had been burned. There was nothing left to indicate they were chosen by Almighty God to be His people. It would be many years before they would seek after God and serve Him once again. But God was still at work and His salvation plan was still on track. What we need to ask ourselves is, do we want to serve Him and to be part of His plan and glory—or follow in Judah's footsteps?

Quiet Family Prayer

Talk about how Jesus helps us to stay faithful by His Holy Spirit, who is in us. Ask God to use you in His mighty salvation plan for the world.

Quiet Times

Younger Kids: Read Jesus' parable about the pearl in your own Bible (Matt. 13:45–46). With this story, Jesus is telling us that the greatest treasure in this life and in heaven is to know Jesus, follow Jesus, and be part of God's plan. Ask God to help seek this awesome treasure.

Older Kids: Read Matthew 13:44–46. Four simple verses with profound, life-changing meaning. Pray about these verses and write down what you think Jesus means. Ask God for the help and courage to live your life this way.

DAY 1: PARENT CONNECTION

THIS WEEK'S TOPIC: KINGS

This week, we're going to look at some of the kings, good and bad, who ruled the kingdom of Judah. Jehoshaphat and Hezekiah were godly kings; we can learn a lot from their prayers that moved God to save Judah from certain destruction. We'll also learn that when we desire to please God, we'll end up loving and serving others—because that's what pleases Him. We're going to talk about how good leaders make a difference, and about the importance of praying for our leaders.

We have plenty to learn from ungodly kings, too—like how doing the wrong thing is sometimes easier in the moment, but never beyond that. Finally, we'll talk about the two children who became kings, and what happened when one stopped serving God. History is a great teacher.

Tips

"The oldest trick in the book" can only truly refer to the one Satan used on Eve, resulting in her questioning God and His motives. It's a trick he's still using.

Each time we teach our children about one of God's instructions, the enemy will try and convince them that God's way doesn't work, or that it isn't fun, or is out of date, or it is way too difficult and/or doesn't work in the real world. We need to arm our children against this trick; when teaching about one of God's principles, make sure you let them know why it works and why the wrong way doesn't. For example, if you're teaching your children not to lie, explain how lies are revealed and cause distrust. When people trust you, they are willing to let you in and give you opportunities. When people don't, they'll keep you at a distance, which means your opportunities for most things in life—friendship, adventure, advancement—dry up. Help them understand the reason for the rule. "Because I (or God) said so!" isn't enough.

DAY 2: JEHOSHAPHAT

Read: 2 Chronicles 20:1–25

Quick Start

When was the last time you praised God and celebrated His answers to your prayers?

Quest

Judah had some kings who pleased God; as a prince Jehoshaphat watched his father King Asa rule wisely with God's help. Jehoshaphat had a keen desire to please God and—like his father—when he became king, he was fairly ruthless with those who refused to abandon their idols and worship God only. In return, God richly blessed the king and his people. Even in battle, God was with them and protected them. When Moab, Ammon, and Mount Seir came to destroy them, God caused them to destroy each other instead. Jehoshaphat and his men went to battle with the worshippers leading the way. When they arrived, all they found were dead soldiers and more plunder than they could even carry home. Many say that Judah enjoyed more prosperity and peace under the rule of Jehoshaphat than under any other king since Solomon. It is a wonderful feeling to know that the person governing you is seeking God's wisdom and guidance. We can always trust a leader who is trusting God.

Quiet Family Prayer

Talk about verses 13 and 22. Pray together for whatever you need and when you're finished, praise God together for His love, His care for you, and for hearing your prayer.

Quiet Times

Younger Kids: Read the story of the children praising Jesus (Matthew 21:14–17). *Hosanna* means, "Please save!" It was a prayer for help, a praise to the Lord, and a celebration of God's answer. Pray for what you need, then praise God and celebrate like Jehoshaphat did.

Older Kids: Read Matthew 21:14–17. *Hosanna* means "Please save!" It was a prayer for help, a praise to the Lord, and a celebration for God's answer, all wrapped up in one word. Jehoshaphat's prayer was like that; it involved a request for help; praise to God for His promise and faithfulness; and a celebration for God's answer before they even saw it. Pray following the Hosanna pattern.

DAY 3: HEZEKIAH

Read: 2 Chronicles 29:1–11; 2 Kings 19:8–12, 14–19, 25

Quick Start

What interesting thing would you want to have in your palace if you were a king or queen?

Quest

Hezekiah means, "The Lord is my strength." He was the thirteenth king over Judah and fortunately he was *not* like his father; he re-opened the temple and re-established the worship of God. He encouraged both the tribes of Israel in the north and Judah in the south to worship God once again. When a huge army camped outside the city's walls, mocking God and planning to destroy Judah, Hezekiah prayed and an angel wiped out 180,000 soldiers in one night. When the enemy leader who had mocked God saw what had happened, he quickly went home. Hezekiah was not a perfect king, but he sought to live righteously and to influence those around him to return to God as well. Often people use positions of power for personal gain and personal recognition, but those leaders are not remembered or respected; only leaders who leave a legacy of helping those they governed and bettering society are remembered with fondness and respect. When you desire to please God and ask for His help, you'll end up loving and serving others well because that's what pleases Him and what He helps us do.

Quiet Family Prayer

Ask God to give you a caring and serving heart that always wants to see, and to work for, God's best for everyone.

Quiet Times

Younger Kids: Talk to your parent about Jesus. Even though He was God's only Son, He spent His time loving and caring for people who were sick and lonely and hurting. Ask God to give you a heart like that.

Older Kids: Read Matthew 20:20–28. God showed us His idea of greatness in Jesus. Jesus came to love, serve, and give Himself for the benefit of others. Ask God to help you always use any influence you may gain or leadership position you may hold to help others instead of just yourself.

DAY 4: GOOD KINGS

Read: 2 Chronicles 31:20–21; 1 Timothy 2:1–6

Quick Start

Would you say it is easier to be good, or to be bad?

Quest

Of the forty-two kings who ruled over Israel and Judah, only ten of them sought to honor God. While the king and the people worshipped God, they were blessed and protected; as soon as they turned away from God, He withdrew His blessings and His protection over them. Often the kind of political leaders we have over us in this world can still seriously impact us. With bad leaders, life can be more difficult. With good leaders, life can be better. Paul instructed us to pray that our rulers would listen to and follow God. Some governments and rulers try and put laws in place that prevent the gospel from being preached or that persecute Christians that makes our job of sharing the gospel and growing His kingdom difficult. We need to always pray for our leaders, that they would be good and fair rulers who govern with compassion and grace, and who will not oppose God's agenda in any way. As you pray, remember you are part of His kingdom and God will faithfully bless and protect you no matter what your rulers are doing.

Quiet Family Prayer

Discuss the names of your political leaders and pray for each one of them that they would seek and follow God.

Quiet Times

Younger Kids: Talk with your parent about other countries that your family is connected with or knows about. Pray together for the leaders of those countries.

Older Kids: Read Psalm 2. God has sent His Son Jesus and has now given Him all authority in heaven and earth. Jesus is the King of kings. He's called us to build His kingdom by spreading the gospel. This psalm prophetically looks forward to our time and warns the leaders of this world not to oppose the gospel. Pray for leaders around the world that God would help them not oppose His plan.

DAY 5: BAD KINGS

Read: 2 Chronicles 28:22–27

Quick Start

How do you feel when you do something bad? Do you feel guilty?

Quest

Sometimes it seems easier to be bad than to be good. You just have to do whatever you like; take things that belong to others, call people names, or beat them up when they don't give you what you want. You don't have to keep your promises if you don't want to; tell people whatever they want to hear, but don't mean what you are saying; and only think of yourself all the time. See—easy. Of course, you won't have any good friends, just bad ones whom you cannot trust. You won't truly enjoy your stuff because you will be afraid other bad people will take it from you. You will be a disappointment to your family, and at some point you will have to face God's judgment. The thirty-two bad kings that ruled God's people had nothing left to show after their reigns were over; no nation, no people, no riches, no fame, and no one who was sad to see them go. Doing whatever you want is only easier in the moment; every time you do something the wrong way, it makes your life more difficult and more miserable.

Quiet Family Prayer

In God's kingdom, obedience always brings blessings. Talk together about the consequences of obeying God versus disobeying God. Ask Him to guide your heart and mind to *want* to obey Him at all times regardless of what others around may be doing.

Quiet Times

Younger Kids: Talk to your parent about how God knows that we're all growing and we make mistakes. Thank God for being such a nice and patient teacher who corrects us, forgives, and loves us.

Older Kids: Read Galatians 6:6–10. Paul makes it clear that thinking that we can sin and get away with it (even as Christians) is in essence mocking God. Jesus died to forgive our sins and to set us free from sin all together. If we choose to sin, we have chosen the trouble it brings with it—and no sin is worth the price the devil charges. Don't be deceived; pray instead that God helps you make right choices.

DAY 6: KID KINGS, JOASH AND JOSIAH

Read: 2 Chronicles 24:1–4, 14–19; 34:1–3

Quick Start

Have you ever quickly stopped doing something that was wrong when you heard your parents walking into the room?

Quest

Joash was seven years old and Josiah was eight when they were crowned as kings. Joash's rule started well, but ended poorly. Joash had a wise and godly advisor named Jehoiada; as long as Jehoiada was alive, Joash ruled well. But after his godly advisor died, Joash listened to evil men and followed their advice. God sent the king of Syria to come and destroy all the leaders in Jerusalem and send all the treasures off to Damascus; Joash was killed by his own servants. Josiah was an extraordinary boy king who sought the Lord as a child; he was a powerful and noble king all of his days. He never stopped pleasing the Lord, and God blessed him. When he finally died, all of Judah mourned for him and the prophet Jeremiah wrote a song for the people to sing commemorating him. Josiah's rule started well and ended well. It is important to be careful from whom we take advice, but more importantly we need to make a personal decision to love and follow God ourselves. Joash was a follower, and just did what others told him to do. Josiah was a leader, and decided in his own heart to seek and obey God—no one could tell him to do otherwise.

Quiet Family Prayer

Talk about the two kid-kings. Ask God to help you make your own unshakable decision to love and serve Him.

Quiet Times

Younger Kids: Read and/or talk about Josiah with your parent. You're never too young to make the most important decision of your life—to serve God and follow Jesus with all your heart. Once you've made that decision, you're also not too young for God to use you in His plan; pray about these two things.

Older Kids: Read about Josiah in 2 Chronicles 34. Think and pray about how he responded to God and to God's Word. Ask God to help you always respond to Him and His Word with urgency, faith, and passion.

Day 1: Parent Connection

This Week's Topic—The Prophets

This week we'll learn some powerful lessons from some powerful prophets who ministered during the decline and fall of the two kingdoms. From Elijah's story, we'll see how our prayers can be powerful and effective. Through Elisha's life, we'll see that it's God's job to decide who gets used for what task in His work—and it's our job to let His Spirit prepare us and to obey as He leads us. By talking about Isaiah, we can gain comfort from the fact that God knows the future and that He can prepare us for ours as we stay close to Him. By looking at the prophesies of Jeremiah and Ezekiel, we'll see what God had planned for us through Jesus' work on the cross, and how it's meant to transform us and our lives—and bring God glory. So this week takes us from their amazing stories to our own amazing stories.

Tips

Emphasizing the power and effectiveness of prayer, James encourages us to pray for one another (James 5:16–18) and cites the example of Elijah the prophet, whose prayers caused and ended droughts and brought fire down from heaven.

Sometimes, however, we're afraid to pray in front of others and allow ourselves to think our prayers won't make a difference; then, we can be absolutely sure that nothing will happen. Unfortunately our children won't see and learn how powerful prayer can be either.

With God's help, set an example for your children; when you feel afraid to pray, pray boldly—and ask Jesus to help your unbelief. Pray silently before you pray out loud, ask God to guide you in prayer, to show you what to pray, and to give you confidence (Luke 11:1; 1 John 5:14–15). Our job is to pray boldly about everything and believe God will answer (Heb. 4:16; Phil. 4:6). God's job is to teach us to pray, reveal His will, help us believe, and to answer our prayers. God's doing all the heavy-lifting, but it starts with us.

DAY 2: ELIJAH

Read: 1 Kings 18:17–39, 42–46

Quick Start

Can you imagine fire coming down from heaven when someone prayed? Would you be amazed or terrified?

Quest

Elijah is one of the most respected and admired prophets in the Old Testament. His name means, "Whose God is Jehovah," and he was anointed as God's prophet and sent to warn Israel's King Ahab. Ahab's wife Jezebel is known as one of the most evil women in the Bible; she hated Elijah because she refused to worship Elijah's God. Elijah did many amazing miracles but is most famous for beating Jezebel's 450 pagan prophets of Baal and four hundred pagan prophets of Asherah in a contest on Mount Carmel that determined whose god was real. Elijah had prayed that it not rain for three years, and it didn't; now that the Israelites had seen Elijah defeat the false prophets and they decided to serve God again, it was time for rain. Notice how Elijah believed that God would answer and therefore continued to pray until he saw the answer coming. No other person had such an exciting exit from the earth—God took Elijah up to heaven in a blazing chariot of fire (2 Kings 2:11)!

Quiet Family Prayer

Read and talk about James 5:16–18. Ask God to help you understand and believe that your prayers can really make a difference.

Quiet Times

Younger Kids: Read the story of Elijah in your own Bible. Ask God to help you stand strong against your enemies and to have faith like Elijah's.

Older Kids: Read 1 Kings 18 again and go back and think about verse 21; read Luke 6:46 as well. Elijah and Jesus make the same common sense point: If we believe in God, Jesus, and the Bible as God's Word, then we need to respond and live our lives accordingly. The Israelites said nothing to Elijah's question because they realized that stating a belief in God without living His way makes no sense. Ask God to help you always live what you say you believe.

DAY 3: ELISHA

Read: 2 Kings 2:1–14

Quick Start

Elisha's name means "God is salvation." What does your name mean?

Quest

Have you noticed that none of the prophets *volunteered* for their jobs? God chose them. Elisha was plowing with oxen in a field when God called him into service. He had a tough job to do—he was appointed to replace Elijah, a well-known and powerful prophet. But he made a request to God: to be given a double portion of power that Elijah had (v. 9). When we look over his ministry, we see that he actually did perform about twice as many miracles as his predecessor; he anointed kings, healed the sick, raised the dead, performed miracles, and led schools of prophets. None of these are things that Elisha could have done without God; that's why God decides whom He uses—it's *His* work. He was called to serve during the rules of Israel's most notorious kings—Ahab, Ahaziah, Jehoram, Jehuy, Jehoahaz, and Jehoash; his obedience, therefore, was crucial. God always looks for those to whom He can trust important tasks and give important messages to share on his behalf. Would you be ready if God called you to serve Him?

Quiet Family Prayer

Talk about how we can cooperate with God's Spirit preparing us. Let God know that you're willing to be used for His work and ask Him to help you be prepared.

Quiet Times

Younger Kids: Read about Elisha in your own Bible. Elisha did amazing works because God chose him for those tasks. God always helps you do what He chooses you to do—even in learning, growing, and obeying your parents. Ask God for His help.

Older Kids: Read more about Elisha in 2 Kings chapters 2–7; read as much as you can. Before you start to read, ask the Lord to teach you while you are reading these stories. When you're finished, pray about what you've learned.

DAY 4: ISAIAH

Read: Isaiah 6:1–8; 9:6–7

Quick Start

How far ahead do you like to plan: one day, one week, one year, or more?

Quest

Isaiah served during the reign of four kings in Judah, and his ministry may have lasted more than fifty years. One of the most famous passages in Isaiah's writings is Isaiah 6:1–8; he had a vision of God in his temple, surrounded by angels, proclaiming God's holiness. In this vision, God calls Isaiah into service as His prophet; he was to warn the people about God's coming judgment. Isaiah also wrote prophecies about Jesus seven hundred years before Jesus was born (7:14; 9:1–2; 11:1–10; 50:6; 53:1–9); they all happened exactly as he had said. Sometimes, God opens a window into the future and tells His people what He is going to do to give them hope and encouragement. King David, Daniel, Isaiah, and others wrote many details about what God would do with and through Jesus. These prophecies were so precise that the Wise Men from the East used them to predict when Christ would be born in Bethlehem. God knows the future and already has plans for us; it's important to stay close to Him so He can prepare us for what He has in store.

Quiet Family Prayer

Talk about how God has a good future for us, but we need to respond by trusting, following, and obeying Him. God knows that you need His help getting there—go ahead and ask Him.

Quiet Times

Younger Kids: Read and talk about Isaiah 9:6–7 with your parent. Isn't it amazing that Isaiah wrote this many years *before* Jesus was born? Thank God that you can obey Him and trust Him with your future.

Older Kids: Look up and re-read some of the prophecies Isaiah wrote about Jesus. If possible, use a Bible with cross-references and look up the New Testament verses that record the fulfillment of each prophecy. Thank God that He knows the future, and that He has a good plan for you that He can easily fulfill; ask for help to trust and follow Him.

Day 5: Jeremiah

Read: Jeremiah 1:1–9; Hebrews 8:8–12
(quoted from Jeremiah 31:31–34)

Quick Start

Have you ever had to share bad news with someone? How did it make you feel?

Quest

Jeremiah's name means "the Lord exalts." If you ever wonder if God has a plan for you, remember Jeremiah 1:5—God had plans for Jeremiah even before he was born. Jeremiah was to be a special messenger, even though the people would not listen. Jeremiah suffered at the hands of ungodly rulers, but he remained faithful to God and spoke exactly what God told him to say. Jeremiah pointed out the sin of the people, and spoke of a New Covenant with God. God showed Jeremiah that He would give His people a new heart and cause them to know Him and follow Him; thanks to Jesus, we have that promise, too. Jeremiah was a bad news/good news kind of prophet. God knew that the hard-hearted Israelites would not listen, but we have a different choice. When Christ lives in us, we have the Way, the Truth, and the Life in us to help us live God's way—and it is our privilege to share that good news with others.

Quiet Family Prayer

Thank God for Jesus and how you can have a changed heart, you can know and do God's will, and you can know God because of what He did for us.

Quiet Times

Younger Kids: Read and talk about Jeremiah 32:39–40 with your parent. Jeremiah was actually talking about what Jesus would one day do for us. Thank God that He's given you a heart that wants to obey Him and that He is doing good things for you.

Older Kids: Read Jeremiah 1; God showed Jeremiah that it was God's calling and equipping that was important, not his age. Remember, it is God who will teach you and prepare you for what He wants you to do in the days to come, no matter your age. Don't put off obeying and learning from God now just because you're still young.

Day 6: Ezekiel

Read: Ezekiel 36:22–36

Quick Start

Have you ever seen something that had been old and ugly restored to look new and beautiful again?

Quest

Ezekiel's name means "God will strengthen"—and he needed strengthening. Can you imagine lying on one side for 390 days then turning over onto the other side for forty more? Ezekiel acted out some of the prophecies God gave him so it would have a greater impact; he was willing to be embarrassed for God. Like Jeremiah, Ezekiel also had to endure the punishment of his people, and was taken captive to Babylon where he lived out the rest of his life. But through Ezekiel, God promised hope for the future. Keep in mind that God always planned to send His Son Jesus, and His chosen people would one day be called Christians. The Promised Land was to the people of Israel what heaven is for Christians today. Ezekiel was describing what God would one day do through His Son Jesus: forgive and cleanse us from sin; give us new hearts and place His Holy Spirit within us; and restore us as we trust and follow Jesus. People around us who see what God has done in us and in our lives should be amazed.

Quiet Family Prayer

Ask God to continue restoring you, your family, and your lives to make you a testimony to what God can do.

Quiet Times

Younger Kids: Read the story of Nicodemus (John 31:1–16) and Jesus. Jesus and Ezekiel spoke of the same condition: being forgiven, reborn, and having God's Spirit live in us. Thank God for making you new because of what Jesus did.

Older Kids: Read Ezekiel 37:1–14 and John 3:1–10. Jesus was probably reminding Nicodemus of this story when He talked to him about being born again (John 3:8). Before rebirth we are just like dead, dry bones. But because of Jesus, we've been raised to new life, filled with His Spirit, and made to be part of His army. Thank God for His Spirit in you, giving you real life.

DAY 1: PARENT CONNECTION

THIS WEEK'S TOPIC: TAKEN AWAY

This week is the last week we'll talk about God's disobedient people being destroyed and taken away. Next week we will follow them to their captivity in Babylon, but first we have a few more important lessons to learn. First one from Jonah the runaway prophet: when we are following God and enjoying His grace, we have an obligation to lovingly reach out to those who are not. We also have a responsibility to be an example to others of what it means to serve God and be blessed and cared for by Him. Next we all need to know and remember that consequences for our actions don't just show up if we're caught—they always come. From the book of Lamentations we'll see that sin is a yoke that traps us but that Jesus took on that yoke and gave us His. And finally before moving on to Babylon we'll see that although God gives us wisdom and often helps us understand what He's doing, we need to know that He sees the bigger picture and trust Him whether we understand or not.

Tips

The gospel message has two key elements that our children need to understand how to live out in balance. First, as Christians we have become God's children and He wants to teach us, care for us, grow us, and bless us. Second, we are part of God's army called to fight in the current war to set the captives free and see the lost transferred from the kingdom of darkness into God's kingdom. We are to enjoy our relationship with God and show the world what it means to be loved and blessed by Him, but we are also called to sacrifice in order to see the kingdom advanced and more people saved. For kids it starts with God's blessing (Eph. 6:3) but the focus is to change as they mature (Matt. 6:33). Let your kids know that it's like being born as a prince or princess—you have many blessings and privileges but you also have an obligation to commit your life to being a noble example and a servant to others. When we don't understand this balance, Christianity can seem like it's either all about us being blessed or all about sacrifice.

DAY 2: JONAH

Read: Jonah 1; 2:10; 3; 4:5–11

Quick Start

Can you each name five people who you know are not Christians yet?

Quest

Jonah is a whale of a story! Some have a very difficult time believing that this story could be true. Well, Jesus told us it was true (Matt. 12:40). Jonah's story was a picture of what would happen to Him—He spent three days and three nights in the grave and rose again to bring salvation to the Gentiles. Jonah was an unwilling prophet. He seems happy to bring a message of hope to Israel (2 Kings 14:25) but reluctant to bring a warning to Nineveh. His four-chapter book starts with running away from God and ends with him complaining to God. Sadly we can be like Jonah today—enjoying our salvation and God's blessings but not wanting to make much of an effort to bring the gospel's message of hope to others; instead we judge them. We are not to judge others; we are to love them just as Christ has loved us, knowing that we are no better than even the worst of sinners—the only difference is that we have already received God's grace in salvation and they haven't yet. God is loving and merciful and wants to see all people saved and we should be the same.

Quiet Family Prayer

Talk about Jonah's attitude and pray that God gives you a heart to see God's salvation and blessing come to everyone. Pray for people you know, who don't know Jesus.

Quiet Times

Younger Kids: Read the story of Jonah in your own Bible. Jonah forgot that the whole reason God chose the Jews was to bring salvation to the whole world. Ask God to use you to tell others about Jesus.

Older Kids: Read the book of Jonah. The plant that God provided for Jonah is like the salvation, protection, and blessings God gives us because we're Christians. We can't sit under our plant wanting to see God judge others. God challenges Jonah (and us) to have compassion on sinners because they don't yet know and understand the truth (4:11). Ask God to give you a compassionate heart for the lost and to use you to help reach them.

DAY 3: THE FALL OF ISRAEL

Read: 2 Kings 17:1–18

Quick Start

On a scale of 1 to 10, how good of an example are you to others?

Quest

None of Israel's kings had followed after God since they broke away from Judah. God had sent them many prophets, but they refused to listen. People in every town performed pagan rituals to foreign idols, and no one sought after the One True God, the One who had delivered them from Egypt, the One who had performed miracle after miracle to feed them, protect them, and fight for them against their enemies. Things could have been so different, but the people in Israel chose to reject God. So God used the King of Assyria to invade Israel, defeat their armies, and take the entire people captive. Israel was to be an example to the nations. They were to show what God is like, how we should serve Him and how He would reward those who serve Him. Instead they became like everyone else. Today, as Christians we are to be an example to unsaved people—they should see from our lives what it means to follow and be blessed by God. Just like with Israel, God can't bless us if we don't obey Him—if He did, others would see the wrong example.

Quiet Family Prayer

Ask God to help you be an example of both what it means to serve Him and be blessed by Him.

Quiet Times

Younger Kids: Talk about what Jesus said about salt and light (Matt. 5:13–16). Jesus died to take away our sins so that we can be like Him. When we live His way, others see how great it is to love, serve, and be blessed by God. Ask God to help you be an example.

Older Kids: Read what Jesus taught in Matthew 5; read verses 16 and 48 twice. Christianity isn't just about what you believe; it's about how you live because of what you believe. God used the Israelites to show us that living God's way leads to real life and blessing and that living the world's way leads to destroyed lives. Jesus came to teach us how to live, and He died and rose again so that we'd have the freedom and ability to live that way—as we do, our lives become a desirable example. Ask God to make you and your life an example that others will desire.

DAY 4: TAKEN CAPTIVE

Read: 2 Kings 17:18–23

Quick Start

Have you ever been really sorry for something *after* you found out what the punishment was?

Quest

Children can plead with their parents to relent, but sometimes punishment must come as a reminder of consequences. Some think consequences only come when you're caught—not true. Every time we do something wrong we sow bad seeds in our lives that will grow and help make our lives miserable. A parent's loving punishment helps remind us that bad behavior wrecks our lives. Saying you're sorry is nice but the important thing is changing your behavior so you stop wrecking your own life. Israel didn't understand that they were destroying themselves and so they never changed. God needed to be drastic so that they'd finally understand. Israel was sorry for rejecting God as they saw their homes and cities grow smaller and smaller in the distance as they were carried off to Assyria, but it was too late. When we really understand that doing things God's way makes our life great and doing wrong messes it up—we won't need punishment—instead we will just learn God's way and happily do it.

Quiet Family Prayer

Talk about how God knows how life works best. Ask God to help you have a heart that wants to simply learn and do things His way so that you're always planting good seeds in your life.

Quiet Times

Younger Kids: Talk about Hebrews 12:5–6 with your parent: God wants you to be the best you, living the best life, possible. So just like parents He lovingly teaches and sometimes corrects you to help you learn. Thank God for loving you so much that He helps you get it right.

Older Kids: Read Hebrews 12:1–17. You are God's child and He's committed to transforming you (2 Cor. 3:18) so you can live the best possible life with Him. It works the same with God as it does your parents; if you simply learn and do, you receive praise and further instruction, but the more you dig your heals in, the tougher the discipline gets. Ask God to help you respond to Him and your parents, so the discipline never needs to go to another level.

Day 5: Lamentations

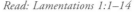

Read: Lamentations 1:1–14

Quick Start
Have you ever tried to carry something that was just too heavy?

Quest
Jerusalem was once a beautiful, prosperous, vibrant city. People would come from far off lands just to see how amazing it was. Solomon's temple radiated the sun for miles around. Time and time again God had come to their rescue against attacking armies, but this time as the enemy approached God was silent. The walls were breached, the gates were broken down, the temple and palace were ransacked and everything was burning to the ground. The people were overrun and treated mercilessly. God's heart was broken. The book of Lamentations poetically describes what the lives of people who live in sin without God look like—devastated, lonely, broken, empty, and full of pain and despair. Verse 14 of chapter 1 explains the problem. Our sin becomes a heavy burden tied on our necks that we cannot hold up under or get free from. But God knew that Good News was coming. Read Matthew 11:28–30. Jesus bore the burden of our sins on the cross. He comes to each of us, removes our burden, lifts us up, and gently yokes/ties us with Himself. He then carries us and begins to teach us, strengthen us, and help us know God and live life His way. He restores us and makes us like Jerusalem at its best.

Quiet Family Prayer
Thank God for sending Jesus. Ask Him to help you walk with Jesus daily, learning from Him and being changed.

Quiet Times
Younger Kids: Read the story of Jesus and the children. You can go to Jesus and be rescued too. Thank Jesus that He's always with you helping you know God and helping you live His way and be blessed.

Older Kids: Read Matthew 11:20–30. Jesus speaks woes on cities of His time similar to the book of Lamentations. But He goes on to talk about the solution; when we come to Him as individuals, families, or cities, He forgives us, begins to reveal the Father to us and helps us walk with Him and be restored. Pray this for yourself, your family and your city.

DAY 6: BABYLON

Read: 2 Kings 20:12–18

Quick Start

Have you ever had to go somewhere you didn't really want to go? Imagine being there for seventy years!

Quest

The rulers of Babylon can be traced right back to the days of Abraham. They were always around and were trading partners with Israel and Judah over the years. After they defeated the Assyrians and the Egyptians, it was pretty easy to defeat Judah and Jerusalem. The prophets Jeremiah and Ezekiel assured their people that God was using the Babylonians as part of His judgment upon them, and that they should not fight against them, but instead they should humble themselves before God and He would eventually let them return home once again. It was during their time in Babylon that God's people began to worship Him once again and to remember the Laws of Moses, the historical remembrances and celebrations. They began once again to seek the Lord and separate themselves from the pagan worship around them. It's important to pray about everything and to trust God even when we don't understand what's going on. He knows everything, including the future and He knows how to teach us and what's best for us in every circumstance. God is good at accomplishing His plans.

Quiet Family Prayer

God gives us wisdom and often helps us understand what He's doing, but we need to trust Him whether we understand or not. Ask God to take care of every detail of your lives and to help you trust Him no matter what.

Quiet Times

Younger Kids: Read and talk about Romans 8:28–29 with your parent. Thank God that He loves you and knows what you need to learn. He'll work out everything in your life as you trust Him.

Older Kids: Read and think about Romans 8:26–32. God knows your past, your heart, your future, what you need to learn, what His plan for you is and how best to get you there. He has no desire to keep things from you—He hears your every prayer, but like a good parent He wants to give you His best. Ask God to help you trust Him in everything.

DAY 1: PARENT CONNECTION

THIS WEEK'S TOPIC: DANIEL

The book of Daniel is great to go through with your family. As you do, your family will learn that we can trust God to help us do well in school and in our careers as we follow Him. He does this not only to bless us but also to show others how He blesses those who trust Him. You'll also see how Daniel experienced God through dreams and visions and how God used that to bless others. Of course with the stories of the Fiery Furnace and the Lion's Den, your family will learn about what God can do when we're bold and uncompromising in our faith. And finally, Daniel was a great man of prayer and we can learn a lot about communicating with God by taking a look at Daniel's prayers.

Tips

When we talk about guidance in prayer and/or listening prayer, some think we are to listen for God speaking to us. This is not necessarily true (although God can communicate in any way He sees fit). It's simply praying, knowing that God will direct you by His Spirit and therefore asking Him to, slowing down a bit and perhaps being silent as you keep one ear to God and what He's putting in your heart. Read Ephesians 6:18 to your kids and tell them that God wants to guide them in their prayers. Tell them that as they talk to God and wait, God will bring someone to mind. When that happens, they should start to pray for that person and pray what comes to mind. (This should of course be in line with God's will as revealed in His Word.) The Ephesians verse says to keep alert—we can do this as we pray listening, and when we're with other Christians watching, listening, and perhaps asking for things to pray about. If you're new at this, don't worry; God will always help you do what He asks you to do. Try it this week when the topic comes up—even if it takes you time to learn to get in-step with God's Spirit. You can never go wrong praying in accordance with God's Word for His people.

DAY 2: DANIEL AND FRIENDS

Read: Daniel 1

Quick Start

Do you think it is important to do well in school? Why or why not?

Quest

Back in the Old Testament days, there were a lot of battles between nations and Judah was right in-between a lot of important nations. Egypt, Assyria, Babylon all took turns ruling the region. Daniel and his friends were captives in Babylon after Judah was defeated and some of God's people were carried away. King Nebuchadnezzar liked to bring the brightest and best young people to his capitol, teach them his language, his culture, and put the best of them in leadership positions. We have already seen how God can make good things come from bad situations and this was the case with Daniel and his friends. Because they honored God in how they lived, God blessed them. The king found these four young men ten times more intelligent and competent than all the rest. This put them in the exact right place for God to use them strategically just at the right time. Daniel and his friends are great examples of how God can give us wisdom and understanding and help us do well in our studies when we trust and follow Him. He can also use how well we do to put us in the right place.

Quiet Family Prayer

Ask God to help each of you to do well where you work or go to school; to give you favor, wisdom, and understanding. Ask Him to help you be an example of how God can help you do well in your schooling and career.

Quiet Times

Younger Kids: Read the story of Daniel and his friends at school. Ask God to help you understand, learn easily, and do well at school. He'll help you like He helped them.

Older Kids: Read Daniel 1 again. Sometimes we think that how we study or the marks we get are unimportant and only affect us—not true. God can use how well we do to show others how He helps and blesses us as we trust and live for Him. He can also use it to open doors for us and put us in places where we can affect people and circumstances for Him. Ask God to give you a heart to learn and do well and to help you like He helped Daniel and his friends.

DAY 3: NEBUCHADNEZZAR'S DREAM  169

Read: Daniel 2:1–19, 25–30, 46–49

Quick Start

What is the strangest dream you have ever had?

Quest

Sometimes dreams are so vivid and realistic that they can wake you up from your sleep and leave you a bit startled. Nebuchadnezzar was so shaken by his dream that he was going to kill all the "wise men" if they could not tell him what he had dreamed and tell him what it meant. Just as Joseph could not have imagined being sold into slavery and going to prison would put him in the right place to impact the king of Egypt, Daniel never would have thought being stolen from his homeland and forced to live in another country would have been part of God's plan all along. God gave Joseph and Daniel both the ability to interpret dreams, and both of them knew it was not them, but God who could explain the dreams. Just as the king of Egypt recognized that God was with Joseph, so the king of Babylon saw God was with Daniel and gave him responsibility over the whole province of Babylon. Daniel found places of honor for his three friends and they all lived far better than if they had stayed in Jerusalem. Isn't God amazing? Next time you find yourself in a tough situation, start looking around to see what God has in mind for you.

Quiet Family Prayer

Both Joseph and Daniel stayed close to God and trusted Him to help them experience Him. Ask God help you do the same.

Quiet Times

Younger Kids: Read the story of Daniel and the king's dream. The king's dream was about Jesus and God's kingdom. Ask God to help you know more about His Son and His kingdom.

Older Kids: Read all of Daniel 2. The kingdoms after Babylon were Medo-Persia, Greece, and Rome; the great stone in the dream is Jesus and the final kingdom, God's kingdom. This event happened and was recorded more than six hundred years before any of these kingdoms (other than Babylon) existed. Daniel's faith in God was shown in that he asked for time to seek God (v. 16) before God showed him anything. Ask God to give you faith like Daniel's, to trust that He'll reveal Himself to you in His own way.

DAY 4: THE FURNACE

Read: Daniel 3

Quick Start

Put a candle in the middle of the table and feel the heat it can give.

Quest

There are few young people in the Bible that have shown such an incredible commitment to God. When the people of Israel saw how big the people were in the Promised Land, they turned and ran. But these three friends stood firm in their commitment to God knowing the king could easily order their execution, and he did. Heating the furnace seven times hotter than normal caused the men who threw them in to die too. But what an incredible statement, "Our God is able to deliver us from the furnace, but even if He doesn't we will not worship your gods." They were willing to gently but firmly stand up for what they believed causing the king to fly into a rage. They knew their God was far greater than any king and they were willing to pay the ultimate price to serve Him and Him alone. How different from the kings of Israel and God's people in the wilderness who liked to complain about everything! Shadrach, Meshach, and Abednego got to not only experience an incredible miracle, they astonished the king who became very afraid of the power of their God.

Quiet Family Prayer

We have a chance to stand up for what we believe every time someone questions our faith, makes fun of us or wants to see that God is real in our lives. Ask God to be with you, like He was with these men, giving you courage, wisdom and words. You're never alone!

Quiet Times

Younger Kids: Read the story of the Fiery Furnace in your own Bible. God was with these young men as they stood up for what they believed. Jesus is with you always. Ask Him to help you when you tell others about Him.

Older Kids: Read Acts 3:1–8; 4:1–30. When we speak up with courage so others can hear and believe, God will show up like He did in the furnace and shake things up like He did in Acts. Let Acts 4:30 be your prayer, now and every time you have a chance to lovingly speak out about your faith. It'll seem tough at first; but as you experience God helping you, it'll get easier.

DAY 5: THE LION'S DEN

Read: Daniel 6:1–23, 25–28

Quick Start

Have you ever seen a lion or a tiger, seen their teeth and claws and heard them roar?

Quest

Many kings liked to keep lions around. Sometimes moats were dug around castles and ferocious beasts were kept down there so no enemies would dare try to cross them. But keeping the mouths of the lions shut and their paws on the ground was easy for God to do. We can learn much about prayer from this story. First, Daniel could have kept praying but hidden it, but Daniel knew that our relationship with God is to be an example to others so they can know God too. Next, Daniel didn't just pray when he felt like it or even just once a day. He made it a habit to stay close and talk with God about everything, three times every day. Notice too, that when Daniel knew the document had been signed, he didn't go to God begging or complaining; he went to God thanking Him and trusting Him. As a result God rescued Daniel, and the whole kingdom heard that the God who Daniel served was to be honored. Daniel was a man of integrity with great personal convictions and character because he was a man of prayer, who knew, served, and trusted God.

Quiet Family Prayer

Talk about Daniel's prayer life. Ask God to help you learn and grow in prayer, to help you know and trust Him more and to be an example to others.

Quiet Times

Younger Kids: Read the story of Daniel in the Lion's Den in your own Bible. Daniel's prayer life and love for God helped him do all that he did for God. Ask God to help you have that kind of relationship with Him—He will because of what Jesus did for you.

Older Kids: Read Daniel 6. Daniel's accusers knew that he was so consistent in and adamant about prayer that he wouldn't quit—that's how they knew their plan would work. Amazingly though they didn't seem to connect Daniel's devotion to God with his success. Ask God to help you make the connection and to help make your time with Him the foundation of your success in every area of life.

Read: Daniel 9:1–22

Quick Start

When was the last time you saw an angel? Do you think God sends His messenger angels to the earth today (read Heb. 1:13–14)?

Quest

The prayer of Daniel shows his heart for God and his compassion towards his people. Much like Moses pleading on behalf of his people in the wilderness, Daniel pleads to God for his people and the city of Jerusalem that are both in ruins. Although Daniel was a righteous man, in fact God says he is "dearly beloved," he includes himself in the prayer of repentance along with his people. If anyone had been faithful to God all of his life, it was Daniel. Daniel shows that when we pray for others, we are to pray humbly without judging, knowing that we also need God's grace and help. There are only a handful of leaders in the Bible that had such a heart for their people that they would spend time, a great amount of time, praying and going without food, and humbling themselves before God for the benefit of their people. Paul taught (Eph. 6:18) that we are also to pray for God's people. He says that we are to allow God's Spirit to direct us and we are to be watchful (with our eyes and our hearts) as to who needs prayer and follow God's Spirit and humbly pray for those Christians.

Quiet Family Prayer

Because of Jesus all God's children are "dearly beloved" and God loves it when we pray for each one. Pray together for other Christians that you know who may need prayer. Ask God's Spirit to guide you in prayer.

Quiet Times

Younger Kids: Talk to your parent about the Christians (friends or family) you know and how you can pray for them. Simply ask God for help and pray what comes into your heart for them.

Older Kids: Read Daniel 9:1–22 and Ephesians 6:18. God knows what each Christian that you know is going through and what they need. Spend some time praying for them and ask God to guide you in your prayers. Your prayers make a difference—if they didn't, God wouldn't ask you to pray for them.

DAY 1: PARENT CONNECTION

THIS WEEK'S TOPIC: THE RETURN

In reestablishing His people in the Promised Land, God seemed focused on several key issues that we can learn from. It all started with Daniel's prayers from which we learn how important it is to believe and pray God's Word. From the first great leader of God's returned people, Zerubbabel, we learn the importance of putting God's agenda first in our lives. From the first high priest, Ezra, we are reminded of how important it is to learn and grow in God's Word. From the Governor Nehemiah we learn how important it is to be guided by God in the midst of trouble and opposition. Finally through the last three Old Testament prophets, Haggai, Zechariah, and Malachi, we're reminded that the Israelites problem was a sin problem and that God was setting the stage to send His solution to that problem into the world.

Tips

The Bible from its beginning to its end assures us that it contains the very words of Almighty God. But it doesn't just stop there, letting us believe that merely knowing that is enough, it repeatedly calls us to love it, read it, meditate on it, know it, believe it, obey it, and act on it. We're told that doing so is necessary because our thoughts and therefore our lives are to be transformed by it, that God uses it to guide us and give us wisdom, that it's our weapon against the enemy, that it's necessary to instruct us in all things and to bring us to maturity in Christ. In truth we cannot know God, truly understand our salvation and walk in it, unless we both know and consistently feed on and grow through the reading, studying, and understanding of God's Word. The devil knows that the easiest way to win a fight against us is to keep us from picking up our sword. Our children need to know that a chapter a day will not keep the world away. Pray and ask God—by His grace—to help you instill a love for His Word in your children and an understanding that their Bible is not a book to just spend some regular time in to get heaven points—it's a life changer and knowing it is as essential as a sword is in a sword fight.

DAY 2: SEVENTY YEARS

Read: Jeremiah 25:1–11; 29:10

Quick Start

Have you ever reminded your parents of something they said they'd do? Have you ever used Bible verses in the same way with God?

Quest

The prophet Jeremiah foretold of the 70-year reign of the Babylonians and how God's people would return after that. When the Babylonians were conquered, Daniel read Jeremiah's book and figured out that the seventy years was up. Daniel believed God's Word and began to pray for God's people and their return to their homeland. He was old now and had seen a whole generation of God's people grow up in Babylon. God knew what it would take to get His people to listen so that He could bless them. In seventy years God's people had stopped worshipping idols. They also must have finally realized that they needed to teach their people and their children God's Word so they wouldn't forget. They developed a whole new system of local religious leaders and places called synagogues to help. Shortly after Daniel prayed, the new king, King Cyrus, allowed God's people to start going home. As they began to trickle back, synagogues were opened and the religious leaders, scribes, Pharisees, and Sadducees began to teach and guide the people. It was a new beginning in Israel and hopefully the people would never again reject God.

Quiet Family Prayer

Daniel studied and obeyed God's Word. But he also did another very important thing; when he read God's will in Jeremiah, he believed it and prayed it. Ask God to help you learn how to believe and pray what His Word says about you.

Quiet Times

Younger Kids: Read Ephesians 6:1–3 with your parent. Be like Daniel and believe and pray these verses—that God would help you listen and obey and that you'd get the life He promised.

Older Kids: Read Philippians 4:8–9. Daniel knew that if God's Word tells us to do something, then we can and God will help us. Pray these verses asking God to help you believe and do them. Memorize verse 8 and quote it whenever you need to push away wrong thoughts.

DAY 3: ZERUBBABEL

Read: Ezra 1:1–2:2

Quick Start

How do you feel when you finally come home after a long trip away?

Quest

In the first year of Cyrus, king of Persia, Zerubbabel (also known by the Persian name of Sheshbazzar) led the first group of Jews, numbering 42,360 (Ezra 2:64), back to Jerusalem and began to rebuild the temple that lay in ruins. The work was hard and there was opposition to the rebuilding efforts by others in the area, but Zerubbabel was determined to finish his task. The building stopped for a number of years because of opposition and God's people got busy with their lives. The prophet Haggai prophesied that God's blessing was being withheld from their lives because they were building houses for themselves and ignoring God's house (Hag. 1:9). The people responded immediately and got back to work despite the opposition. When they did, God promised His blessing and also removed the opposition. When the temple was at last completed, Zerubbabel's last act as the leader of his people was to organize the celebration of the Passover (Ezra 6:22) in Jerusalem for the first time in a very long time. Zerubbabel served God faithfully and we can see his name listed in the lineage of Jesus (Matt. 1:12).

Quiet Family Prayer

Jesus told us that we're to seek God's kingdom and His righteousness first and that when we do He'll take care of us (Matt. 6:33). Ask God to help you make your priorities line up with His priorities and thank Him for His blessings.

Quiet Times

Younger Kids: Read Matthew 6:33 with your parent; God wants us to put Him first so that He can love, guide, teach, and bless us. Ask God to help you put Him first and receive His love.

Older Kids: Read Isaiah 44:28–45:13. Isaiah prophesied about King Cyrus, called him by name, and predicted exactly what part he'd play in God's plan about 150 years before Cyrus became king. If God can predict and do this so easily, how easy is it for Him to take care of our every need, as we trust Him and put Him and His kingdom first in our lives? Talk to God about this.

DAY 4: EZRA

Read: Ezra 7:7–10; Nehemiah 8:5–8

Quick Start

Which of all your coaches and teachers were your favorite ones and why?

Quest

Many believe Ezra the scribe wrote the book bearing his name, the book of Nehemiah, and the books of Chronicles helping us to understand the history of God's people. But Ezra was also a priest who helped restore proper worship at the temple and among God's people. Ezra helped the people understand that they had to separate themselves from those who were not Jews so they would be holy for God. Ezra knew they needed to stay away from those who would take them away from God. Ezra was a highly competent administrator, a godly priest, and a wise leader. He knew God and God's Word, and he taught it to the people so that they would know how to love and follow God. God's people had gotten in trouble in the past because they had forgotten to learn and teach God's Word; Ezra wanted to make sure that didn't happen again. God always knows the best persons to lead His people.

Quiet Family Prayer

Read Hebrews 5:12–13 and 1 Peter 2:2 together. As God's people today, it's still vital that we learn and understand His Word—it's the only way we can know God and what He wants for us and grow as Christians. Ask God to help you make knowing Him through His Word a goal for your life.

Quiet Times

Younger Kids: Read 1 Peter 2:2 with your parent; we need milk to make our bodies grow and we need God's Word to help our inside selves grow. Read your favorite Bible story and ask God to help you learn and grow as you do.

Older Kids: Read and think about Romans 12:1–2, Ephesians 4:20–24, and Colossians 3:8–10. God calls us to be transformed; so that we know Him, live His way, and receive His blessings. We do that by learning His Word and cooperating with God's Spirit as He changes the way we believe and think. In this way we put off the world's ways and we put on the new person God has created us to be. God has promised that He will wonderfully teach and transform us, but we must cooperate and learn His Word. Ask God to help you understand and do this.

DAY 5: NEHEMIAH

Read: Nehemiah 2:1–9

Quick Start

Can you think of a time when doing the right thing was very hard to do?

Quest

Nehemiah was fearless. He had been a well-respected government official, but he gave all that up to go back to Jerusalem and to organize physical labor. He was the right person for the job; he was a man of strong character and he was gifted at motivating and leading the people. He was undaunted by the massive amount of work that had to be done and he easily handled the many attempts to stop the work. He had a secret weapon though; read Nehemiah 2:4 again. Whenever Nehemiah faced an opportunity or a problem he quickly and quietly prayed and trusted God for wisdom. His problems and enemies came from within and without; they tried to attack the city, intimidate and discourage the workers, kill Nehemiah, tell lies about Nehemiah, threaten Nehemiah and more. But each time Nehemiah knew what was going on and knew exactly what to do because he trusted God to guide him. He finished building the wall and also led God's people with God's wisdom, reminding them that they needed to serve God and follow Him and treat each other with love and fairness. Together with Ezra they helped the people recommit their lives to God and renew their covenant with Him.

Quiet Family Prayer

Perhaps James was thinking of Nehemiah's habit of silently praying in each situation when he told us to ask God for wisdom whenever we need it (James 1:5). Ask God to help you develop Nehemiah's wonderful and helpful habit and encourage each other to practice.

Quiet Times

Younger Kids: Read the story of Nehemiah in your Bible storybook. Isn't it wonderful that such a great person who did great things had such a simple secret? Talk to God about the things that you could use His wisdom for.

Older Kids: Spend some extra time and read the book of Nehemiah. You can learn a lot about godly leadership. Consider and pray about how Nehemiah responds in each situation. Ask God to help you learn from Nehemiah's example.

178 DAY 6: NEW PROPHETS LOOK FORWARD

Read: Haggai 2:6–9; Zechariah 9:9–10; Malachi 4:3

Quick Start

Can you remember a time when you could hardly wait for something special to happen that you were really looking forward to (birthday, concert, sleepover, etc.)?

Quest

Haggai, Zechariah, Malachi were the prophets who spoke to God's people after they had returned from captivity—their books are the last three in the Old Testament. Haggai got after the people for building their own houses and not God's. Zechariah called the people to renew their covenant with God. He also accused them of following in their ancestor's footsteps because they were mistreating each other. Malachi came last. The people were wondering why God was not blessing them and he helped them understand why: the priesthood had become corrupt, worship had become insincere and routine, the people mistreated each other, divorce was common place, and God was not being put first in even the simple things like tithing. God's new people were up to old tricks. But all three of these prophets also talked about the Good News. Remember God's plan from the start was to work with Abraham's descendants to bring the Savior into the world. Only Jesus could solve the sin problem and God was setting the stage for His arrival.

Quiet Family Prayer

God's people thought they had a blessing problem, but what they had was a sin problem. Thank God that in Jesus you are free from the sin problem; you can know Him, obey Him, and be blessed by Him.

Quiet Times

Younger Kids: Read the stories in Matthew 13:44–45 with your parent; Jesus let us know that we need nothing except Him. He loves us, forgives us, changes us, helps us, and takes care of us. Ask Jesus to help you trust Him for everything.

Older Kids: Read Hebrews 13:20–21 and 1 Thessalonians 5:23–24. The price Jesus paid doesn't just get you into heaven—it supplies everything you need to know Him, walk with Him, and be blessed by Him. Thank God He has taken care of the sin problem and the blessing problem. Pray these verses and ask God to help you in any area that you're struggling in.

DAY 1: PARENT CONNECTION

THIS WEEK'S TOPIC: ESTHER

To this day the Feast of Purim is still celebrated in Israel. The Bible book of Esther tells the story behind the day and the celebration. But, of course, the book is far more than a history lesson or a reason to party. This week, while reading Esther, your family will learn that God calls us all to be an example to others in speech and conduct. We'll discuss Esther's secret to having favor with God and people and also how making selfish choices will lead to ruin, while making unselfish choices will actually turn out better for us. We'll dig into the meaning of the proverb, "He who digs a pit, will fall into it." And finally, as we leave the Old Testament behind, we'll talk about what the Israelites consistently got wrong and how God wants to gather us a hen gathers her chicks; all good reasons to celebrate. Enjoy Esther!

Tips

Read Hebrews 4:1–3. We need to be careful that we don't let our kids think that reading the Bible is merely about hearing stories with lessons and learning what we are supposed to believe. Jesus is the Word (John 1:1) and He said His words are spirit and life (John 6:63). God's Word is powerful in its ability to work in us (Heb. 4:12) and it will always accomplish God's purpose (Isa. 55:11). The author of Hebrews wrote that the first generation of Israelites failed to enter the Promised Land because they didn't put their faith in God and believe what He said. Joshua and Caleb, when pleading with the people, told them that they could do anything God wanted them to do because God would be with them (Num. 14:6–9). When you read the Word with your children, help them understand that its God's Word to them and it's full of God's power; whatever it says is true and whatever God requires of them He can and will help them do because He is with them, just like Caleb and Joshua said. With each devotional time, challenge your family to mix faith with everything you learn and pray believing that God will accomplish His will in you and in your lives.

DAY 2: THE FEAST

Read: Esther 1

Quick Start

What's the best party you've ever been to? What made it so special?

Quest

When a king throws a party, everyone wants to come and have fun. Amazing buffet tables covered with exotic food, incredible entertainers, acrobats, and music as well as special features like getting to see all of the king's riches from the treasury and special objects of beauty from his palace. Queen Vashti was a vision of beauty in her royal robes, and the king wanted to show her off to the people. Vashti declined her husband's request and she refused to come. Her decision led to her losing her title as queen and a search began for another beautiful woman to replace her. God used the situation to put a much more responsible woman next to the king, one who God would use to save His people from certain destruction. Sometimes we want to be the leader, or have more, or to be in a special position all because of the good things we get—but Jesus reminded us that with blessing comes responsibility (Luke 12:48). One of the responsibilities that come with every privilege is to use your position of responsibility wisely and graciously.

Quiet Family Prayer

God teaches and prepares us so that we can handle the responsibilities that come with the blessings He gives us. Ask Him to help you learn and grow, and to always be a good example to those around you.

Quiet Times

Younger Kids: Read the story of Jesus washing the disciple's feet; Jesus made sure that He set a good example for us in everything that He did (John 13:12–17). Ask God to help you be a good example to others.

Older Kids: Read John 13:12–17 and 1 Timothy 4:12. Jesus said that He was the example to us. We are to follow His example and also follow His example in being an example to others. Ask God to help you realize how important your example to others is and to help you become a better and better one as you grow.

DAY 3: QUEEN ESTHER

Read: Esther 2:1–11, 15–23

Quick Start

What is the greatest challenge you have faced so far in your life?

Quest

Esther was an unlikely candidate for queen. She was an orphan being raised by an older cousin. She and her guardian Mordecai had a grandfather who was taken captive to Babylon by King Nebuchadnezzar. They were foreigners trying to make a life as best they could. When Esther was chosen to be a part of the group of women from which the king would choose a new queen, she was probably quite excited, but also very cautious because she did not know how the king would respond to her being a Jew. God knew her grandfather would be exiled to Babylon, and just like with Daniel and his friends, God was going to use Esther and Mordecai for His glory. But even though this was God's plan for Esther, she was wise in how she carried herself. She paid attention to the people who were in charge of her—she even asked for advice. Esther never once thought she knew better and ignored the advice of wiser people—she listened and learned. An unlikely choice became queen because she had God's favor and used God's wisdom.

Quiet Family Prayer

A wise and successful person knows that a young person has potential and should be given opportunity when they see that they listen attentively and learn. Ask God to help you learn and live Esther's secret.

Quiet Times

Younger Kids: Read the story of Esther in your Bible storybook. Do you see how Esther listened to Mordecai and the people in the palace and followed their wisdom? Ask God to help you learn to listen to learn.

Older Kids: Read Proverbs 3:1–8. Did you notice that the Scripture says (again and again) that Esther found favor with the people who knew her? She was probably taught God's recipe for favor from Proverbs 3 by Mordecai. Verse 4 is about God's favor and the other verses show you how to get it. Notice that verse 7 says that you're not supposed to consider yourself wise—which means—always be ready to listen and learn. Make each of these verses a prayer asking God to help you with the recipe for favor with Him and with people.

Day 4: Haman's Plot

Read: Esther 3:1–11; 4:1–17; 5:1–8; 7:1–8

Quick Start

What do you do when you are afraid about something?

Quest

Haman was a powerful man who had the king's attention. Whatever Haman advised, the king would do. Haman wanted to find a way to get rid of Mordecai; it was disrespectful for him not to bow. But why stop with just Mordecai? Why not wipe out all of his people? The only problem with Haman's plot was that he did not know Queen Esther was also a Jew, and he did not know how powerful God is. God had already anticipated Haman's evil schemes and had two of his faithful servants ready for the challenge. The most famous verse in Esther is 4:14, "Who knows whether you have come to the kingdom for such a time as this?" We don't always understand God's plans, but when He reveals them to us we need to decide if we are going to obey Him or not. We will come to a crisis of belief and will have to choose faith over our fears. Fortunately Esther trusted that God knew what He was doing, and that He had been a part of every circumstance she had been through. Esther's trust in God eventually led to her people being protected and saved from destruction.

Quiet Family Prayer

If Esther had started making selfish decisions, God would have had to use someone else but she didn't. Ask God to help you trust Him and make the right choices so that He can use you to help in His plan.

Quiet Times

Younger Kids: Read one of the stories about Joseph from your Bible storybook. Can you see how Joseph and Esther's right choices got them where God wanted them? Thank God that right choices lead to good places, and ask Him to help you keep making them.

Older Kids: Read chapters 3–7 of Esther. As you read compare the choices of Haman to the choices of Esther and Mordecai. Haman's choices are all about himself, his feelings, his desires, and they all lead him to ruin. Our heroes' decisions are all about serving God, serving others, and acting wisely—which all lead to God's will and blessing. Ask God to remind you and help you with each choice, big and small, to choose well.

DAY 5: GOD INTERVENES

Read: Esther 8:1–5, 9–11, 15–17; 9:1–3

Quick Start

Have you ever fallen into a big hole that you couldn't get out of?

Quest

It is never smart to fight against God. The same ruthless, murderous plot that Haman hatched against Mordecai and the Jews was reversed and happened to Haman and all those who hated God's people. Instead of Mordecai being killed, Haman was. The signet ring and position of honor given to Haman by the king were both given to Mordecai, and Mordecai was made governor over Haman's property and household. Although the first evil decree could not be rescinded, a second decree was issued to allow the Jews to protect themselves and fight against anyone who would try to destroy them. Only now everyone was on Esther and Mordecai's side and the enemies of the Jews didn't stand a chance. The Feast of Purim was established in commemoration of Esther's intervention in Haman's plot and God's protection of His people. For thousands of years Haman has been remembered as an enemy of God's people who was destroyed by his own hatred and the hand of God. Proverbs 26:27 teaches that if you dig a pit (a trap for others), you'll fall into it yourself. It's no wonder Jesus taught that we should treat others how we'd like to be treated—because we likely will be treated as we treat others.

Quiet Family Prayer

Be quiet for a minute and think of all the things that you've done to others that you wouldn't want done to you—quietly ask God to forgive you. Pray together as a family and ask God to help you always treat others well.

Quiet Times

Younger Kids: Read and talk about the golden rule Luke 6:31 with your parent. Ask God to help you remember and live the golden rule.

Older Kids: Look up, read, and pray about each of these verses: Esther 7:10; Matthew 5:44; 7:12; Proverbs 26:27–28:10; and Galatians 5:13–15.

DAY 6: 400 YEARS

Read: Malachi 3:1; Luke 13:31–35

Quick Start

Have you ever seen chicks run and hide under their mother's wings when she calls?

Quest

Malachi prophesied about Jesus but four hundred years would pass before He was born—the same amount of time His people had been slaves in Egypt. God's people had many difficult struggles during this time but they stayed in their homeland. Although world power shifted a few times, by the end of this period Rome was ruling most of the known world including God's people and the same problems Malachi addressed had not been dealt with. The position of high priest went to the highest bidder and worship was still routine, obligatory, and meaningless. The Jews were waiting for the Messiah, hoping He would free them from the Romans. But God sent Him to free people from their sin so that He could finally truly be their loving, caring God and they could truly be His obedient people. What the Jews failed to see was that if they had listened to the prophets and obeyed and trusted God, He would have taken care of them and the Romans and all who came before the Romans would not have ruled over them. So when Christ came, many of the Jews didn't know He was the Messiah—as usual they had been seeking what they wanted instead of seeking God and letting Him care for them.

Quiet Family Prayer

We are God's children and He wants to gather us like a hen gathers her chicks, protecting, caring for, and loving us. Ask God to help you let Him gather you.

Quiet Times

Younger Kids: Talk about what Jesus said about a hen and chicks. He told us why His people always had so much trouble—they wouldn't come to Him, listen and trust. Ask God to help you be like a trusting little chick.

Older Kids: Read Luke 13:31–35 Abraham believed in God, that He was good and could be trusted to care for him and do what He promised—so he sought, loved, and obeyed Him. Abraham let God gather him—a simple message that most of his descendants missed. God and the message haven't changed but we have God's Spirit in us, helping us get it and get it right—talk to God about this.

DAY 1: PARENT CONNECTION

THIS WEEK'S TOPIC: TWO PROMISED BABIES

Angel visits, the birth of John the Baptist, Jesus born in Bethlehem, the Good News announced to Shepherds and visiting wise men—sounds like Christmas. However, as we all know, the truths in these stories should impact us 365 days a year. This week you'll take your family through these stories and perhaps learn some surprising facts and the answers to some interesting questions like: God can do anything, so why does He use angels and people? How does John the Baptist's message affect us today? Why did God choose Bethlehem? Why was the Good News announced to shepherds? And how did foreign wise men know about Jesus and when He'd be born? If it's summer time, consider digging out the Manger Scene to get you in the mood.

Tips

When we were writing this devotional, God (again and again) wonderfully used circumstances in our lives to help point to what (from His Word) He wanted written. Now we believe that God wants to use your family's circumstances to take His truths from this book and into your lives. Consider David—he was passionate about living and experiencing not only God's Word but also God Himself. David experienced God anointing him with the Holy Spirit, choosing Him, strengthening him to fight, protecting him, inspiring him to write Psalms, giving him wisdom, directing him, moving through circumstances, answering his prayers, disciplining him, revealing His presence to him, and speaking to him. David experienced all these things as he lived his life loving and serving God. He learned from God's Word but then He learned to live God's Word as God showed up in his day-to-day circumstances. So here's the tip—pray that God will do the same for your family and then watch. As you have your devotional time, God may remind you of things that happened or were said recently that wonderfully fit the lesson—lovingly bring the example up and use it in your devotional time. As well, when you leave each devotional time, watch for circumstances that naturally reinforce what you just learned. When that happens, stop and point it out and discuss what God is doing and teaching. You have God's Holy Spirit and God wants your family to experience Him and grow like David did.

DAY 2: ANGEL VISITS

Read: Luke 1:5–38

Quick Start

If God were to send an angel to you, what do you think he would say to you?

Quest

Malachi said that God would send two messengers—now four hundred years later it was time and God sent angels to the people who would become the parents of the two very special sons. Both Mary and Joseph (Matt. 1:20) had personal visits from an angel, as did Zacharias, John the Baptist's father. God was going to do something extraordinary and it called for a special angel messenger to go and talk with these people and answer any questions they may have. We see God using angels in the Bible from the Garden of Eden to the future return of Jesus to this earth, without interruption. They appear in dreams, in visions, and in person, as either an angel or disguised as a regular person. Jesus talked about children having angels (Matt. 18:10); the Bible says that angels are sent out by God to minister to His people (Heb. 1:14). God uses angels to deliver messages, protect His people, to fight spiritual battles and more. Did you know that God can do anything He wants to do all by Himself—He doesn't need anyone else? Yet God uses angels and lets them be involved in what He's doing. It is the same with people—God blessed Mary, Joseph, Zechariah, and Elizabeth by choosing them to help in His plan. He still uses angels and people for extraordinary assignments today.

Quiet Family Prayer

Thank God for choosing to use both angels and your family for His purpose. Ask God to bless you by using each one of you in His plan for this earth.

Quiet Times

Younger Kids: Read the story about Mary getting visited by the angel Gabriel and Matthew 18:10 with your parent. Thank God that He's looking after you and He even uses angels to do it.

Older Kids: Read Luke 1 and Hebrews 1:14; 13:1. Throughout the Bible we see God using both angels and people to help in His plan. Angels serve God with us. If you're ever going to experience an angel, it'll likely be while you're doing something for God. Talk to God about angels and being part of His plan.

DAY 3: JOHN'S BIRTH

Read: Luke 1:57–66, 80

Quick Start

Do you know what the job of a "town crier" was in medieval times?

Quest

Malachi mentioned God would send someone to prepare the people for the coming of the Lord (Mal. 4:5). Often before a king would come through a city or town, people would run ahead of him to clear the streets to make way for the king or prepared for the king's arrival. John was sent to prepare the hearts of the people for the coming Messiah. Like Malachi, John called the people to repent of their sins and to start living God's way. John lived in the wilderness, ate insects and honey, and wore animal skins for clothing. He may not have looked or smelled very good, but like other prophets before him, he had an important message from God. Jesus said that John the Baptist was the greatest prophet of them all (Luke 7:28), perhaps because he was the way-maker for Christ, the one who got to introduce Him. And perhaps because today John's message still prepares people's hearts for an introduction to Jesus; he told people to repent and be baptized and look to Jesus who would save them from sin, give them His Holy Spirit, and help them live God's way (Acts 2:38). What a great message to give!

Quiet Family Prayer

John the Baptist was unusual but God often does things differently in order to get people's attention. Let God know that you're willing to do whatever He wants you to do, even if it's not what everyone else expects.

Quiet Times

Younger Kids: Read the stories of John the Baptist in your own Bible. What John taught is still for us today. Ask God to help you please Him and live His way in everything you say and do.

Older Kids: Read Luke 3:8–14. Some of the Jews started to think that they were right with God just because they were God's people. John shook things up by telling them that God expected His people to live His way. This message is the same today—Jesus died so we could become God's children AND so that we could live God's way. Pray that God's Spirit in you would help you live the way God wants His children to live.

DAY 4: BETHLEHEM

Read: Luke 2:1–7

Quick Start

Where do you come from?

Quest

Bethlehem is called the City of David with the old Hebrew name meaning "house of bread." It is where Rachel was buried, where Ruth settled with Boaz, where David grew up and where Samuel anointed David as king. Micah (5:2) prophesied that this sleepy little town would "bring forth a ruler in Israel." Today Bethlehem has a large church built over the site of a small cave where tradition says Jesus was born. God has always loved to use small things to show His greatness. Out of this "house of bread" came Jesus "the Bread of Life" who would rule the hearts of men, women, boys, and girls right around the world generation after generation. This town played an important role throughout the history of God's people and today is remembered worldwide as the birthplace of Jesus. But it is not the city, town, or village that is important; it is God's activity in that place that makes it special. Every home and every city can become a place where God does mighty works if the people there will trust Him and serve Him with all their hearts. Bethlehem did not make Jesus famous; Jesus made Bethlehem famous.

Quiet Family Prayer

Remember Gideon? God uses the little things so that people will know that what was accomplished was accomplished by God. Pray and give yourself and everything you have, even the smallest things, to God for His use.

Quiet Times

Younger Kids: Read the story about Mary and Joseph traveling to Bethlehem. It seems like a big story now but to Mary and Joseph it was a difficult trip that they probably didn't understand or want to make. Ask God to help you trust that He's taking care of you even when things don't go the way you want them to.

Older Kids: Read Luke 2:21–38. Simeon and Anna were just two regular people but they faithfully loved and served God with all their hearts. God blessed them and used them, and their contributions not only encouraged Jesus' parents but have also blessed billions of people who have read about them. Ask God to help you understand that He sees the bigger picture and to help you trust Him with your life.

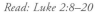
DAY 5: THE SHEPHERDS

Read: Luke 2:8–20

Quick Start

Most animals have some way of defending themselves from predators. What defense does a sheep have?

Quest

Bethlehem is about six miles southeast of Jerusalem and surrounded by hillsides. It was a very ordinary night when the announcement of the Messiah's birth came. What was surprising was that God sent angels to announce the birth of His Son to shepherds. But David spoke of God being his Shepherd (Ps. 23:1) and Jesus would later say, "I am the Good Shepherd . . . {who} lays down His life for the sheep" (John 10:11). And when John the Baptist saw Jesus he said, "Look, the Lamb of God who takes away the sins of the world" (John 1:29). How can Jesus be the Shepherd and a lamb? Jesus always was and is God the Son, which makes Him the Shepherd. But Jesus also came to the earth and was born as one of us—so He also became a sheep. Not just any sheep though, He was the Lamb that the Passover Lamb pictured. So Jesus is the Shepherd who laid down His life for the sheep and the Lamb that died to take away the sins of the world. Jewish tradition tells us that Passover lambs were raised in special flocks around Bethlehem. When one was born it was wrapped in cloth to protect it so that it could be used as a sacrifice. These shepherds were likely in charge of the Passover lambs. So when they were told about the Savior (the Passover Lamb), born in Bethlehem, wrapped in cloth, they understood.

Quiet Family Prayer

Thank Jesus that He's the Lamb of God who died for you and your Shepherd who looks after you!

Quiet Times

Younger Kids: Read the story of the shepherds. Even though Jesus was God the Son He came here to die for you! Thank Him for what He did for you.

Older Kids: Read Psalm 23:1; John 10:10–15; John 1:29; and 1 Corinthians 5:11. Jesus, who is eternally God the Son, became one of us and became the Lamb of God so that He could be our Good Shepherd forever. Thank Him for all He did for you!

DAY 6: THE WISE MAN

Read: Matthew 2:1–12

Quick Start

Have you ever played hide and seek? Where was your favorite place to hide?

Quest

We don't know how many wise men there were; the number three came from the three gifts mentioned. There was likely a large caravan worthy of a kingly visit (1 Kings 10:2) since their arrival stirred up all of Jerusalem (v. 3). The Bible doesn't say exactly where they came from, but many think they were from Babylon/Persia where Daniel had lived and been one of their chief wise men for many, many years. They were very familiar with the prophecies of the coming Messiah (probably from Daniel's book which prophesied when the Messiah would come) and were confident that when the star appeared that the prophecy had come true. Daniel's prophecies showed that this king would rule an eternal kingdom that would crush all other kingdoms (Dan. 2:44). No wonder they were there to give gifts and were astonished that no one in Jerusalem seemed to know anything about it. They had traveled at great personal expense and offered expensive gifts. Their determination was rewarded—they had found the Messiah, the only Son of God, and the King who would rule humankind forever. God said, in Jeremiah 29:13, "And you shall seek Me and find *Me*, when you search for Me with all your heart." This is still true today.

Quiet Family Prayer

We should never take God's blessings and our salvation for granted. Ask God to help keep your faith new, keeping you always seeking Him and bringing Him gifts.

Quiet Times

Younger Kids: Read the story of the wise men in your Bible storybook. Ask God to help you to be like them—willing to do whatever it takes to know and follow Jesus.

Older Kids: Read 1 Kings 10:1–9 and Matthew 12:42. Jesus praised a foreign Queen because she traveled in search of wisdom. Like Sheba the wise men came from far away but what they searched for and found was greater. Ask God to help you desire and search for what's greatest (Matt. 7:1, 8).

DAY 1: PARENT CONNECTION

THIS WEEK'S TOPIC: JESUS GROWS UP

This week we read about Jesus' childhood and preparation for His public ministry. Your children will learn to listen to others because God often uses people around us to speak to us. They'll learn that the Bible records some things about Jesus' childhood so that Christian kids can learn from His example. They'll also learn about baptism through Jesus' baptism and about resisting temptation from the story of Jesus' temptation.

Tips

This week we spend two days on a very remarkable story. When Jesus was twelve (Luke 2:41–52), Mary and Joseph took Him to Jerusalem and lost Him. They were frantic! To understand why, we need to remember that God had them flee to Egypt once because Herod was trying to find and kill Jesus (and children were actually killed). That Herod was dead but his son was ruling and he was almost as crazy as his dad was. So they took the Messiah (at twelve years old) to where Herod lived and lost Him. Can you understand why they were upset? However, when they finally found Him, they showed restraint and demonstrated great parenting. They could have flown off the handle and vented their frustration at Him but they didn't. Mary said (v. 48), "Son, why have you treated us like this? Your father and I have been anxiously searching for you." Even with everything she had gone through for three days, Mary stopped herself and sought to hear what was going on in her son's head before she proceeded. It turned out that Jesus thought His parents knew where He was. As our children are growing up, many of their mistakes come out of ignorance or from the fact that they're not in the habit of thinking things through yet. A large percentage of our children's misdeeds need to be met with patient teaching and training not discipline and the way we know which is needed is by calming ourselves and asking questions. A child who is treated this way will believe he's trusted and that his motives are assumed to be right and will respond well to teaching and training. Ask God to help you stay cool and ask a Mary question first in every circumstance.

DAY 2: MARY AND JOSEPH RETURN

Read: Matthew 2:13–15, 19–23

Quick Start

Do you ever find yourself speaking differently at school than you do at home? Why?

Quest

Nazareth was where Joseph lived and where he planned to make his home with his new family. He was a carpenter by trade and although Nazareth was a small town, Galilee was a good area. As Mary and Joseph raised their son, they never forgot the angels coming to them, the wise men's gifts, the shepherds finding them in the stable, and the scary time hiding from King Herod in Egypt. They watched as Jesus grew up wondering what God would do. It was here in Nazareth that Jesus preached His first recorded sermon in their synagogue (Luke 4:16), but He was rejected and almost killed by the crowds who were deeply offended by His message. They knew Him as the carpenter's son, not as the Messiah or even a rabbi. One way that God speaks to us is by encouraging godly people around us to tell us the things that we need to hear. When we realize this, and if we're wise, we start to listen more carefully to what our friends and family say to us, listening and learning. When we don't listen, we become like these people in Nazareth who missed an incredible blessing from God. God can and will use each one of us to speak to others.

Quiet Family Prayer

Another way we can be blessed by God through the people close to us is when they pray for us (James 5:16). Take turns praying a simple prayer for one another.

Quiet Times

Younger Kids: Read 1 Thessalonians 5:11 with your parent; when we use our words to encourage and help others God can use them. Ask God to help you to always speak helpful and encouraging words.

Older Kids: Read and think about 1 Thessalonians 5:11; Colossians 4:5–6; and Ephesians 4:29–32. When we speak in a way that our words honor God and help and encourage others God will start to use our words. Give God your mouth and your words and ask Him to help you speak His way and to use your words to encourage and help others.

Day 3: Jesus Missing

Read: Luke 2:41–50

Quick Start
Have you ever lost something that was special to you? What did you do?

Quest
Jesus knew from an early age that He was different from the other children. He probably worked hard for Joseph in the carpenter's shop, but He also was eager to get to synagogue school each day and study the Scriptures, particularly the prophesies about the Messiah. With the help of the Holy Spirit, He diligently applied Himself to knowing God and understanding God's Word. The religious leaders were amazed at Jesus' understanding and He was only twelve. When His parents finally found Him (three days later), He was still engaged in conversation about God. His reply to His parents' question tells us that He knew there was a special plan for His life, "Did you not know I must be about My Father's business?" This should be the statement of all God's children. Jesus is our example and the Bible records this story so that kids would have an example to follow. Knowing God and learning God's Word with the Holy Spirit's help isn't just for adults—it's for God's kids of all ages.

Quiet Family Prayer
Thank God that we have Jesus as an example and ask God to help you by His Holy Spirit get to know Him and to help you know and understand His Word.

Quiet Times
Younger Kids: Read the story of Jesus as a boy. Jesus was the example for every Christian kid. You too can learn and grow so that you amaze your teachers and pastors; ask God to help you.

Older Kids: Read Matthew 19:13–15; Acts 2:37–41; and John 14:26. Jesus said that His kingdom was for kids. Peter said that the Holy Spirit was for kids. Jesus taught that the Holy Spirit would teach us and help us know God and His Word. Jesus was the first kid who grew up with God as His Father and the Holy Spirit as His Teacher and Guide. He is the example for all Christian kids who (thanks to Him) have God as their Father and the Spirit as their Teacher and Guide. Ask God to help you follow in Jesus' footsteps and learn and grow—God wants you now!

DAY 4: JESUS OBEYS

Read: Luke 2:46–52

Quick Start

How much of growing up is about learning new things and how much is about playing and having fun?

Quest

We can learn much about Jesus' childhood from these verses. Some may think after reading the story of Jesus going missing that He did whatever He wanted. But Luke makes it clear that Jesus obeyed and submitted to Mary and Joseph as He grew up, which shows us that sometimes misunderstandings happen between parents and children but what counts is that kids listen, keep learning, and do their best. Verse 52 tells us about how Jesus grew up. As He grew physically bigger and stronger (in stature), He also grew mentally (in wisdom), and spiritually and socially (in favor with God and man). He was a regular kid who probably spent time doing chores, learning about carpentry, helping out in His neighborhood, going to school, and doing His homework as well as spending time just playing and having fun. But He didn't just *do* those things; He learned and grew while He was doing them. With God's help He got smarter and wiser in everything. He got closer to God as He learned God's Word and He grew socially so everyone in the community thought well of Him. He was every Christian kid's example of how to grow up.

Quiet Family Prayer

Growing in every area of life never stops. Ask God to help you grow physically, mentally, spiritually, and socially every day.

Quiet Times

Younger Kids: Read and talk about Luke 2:40 with your parent; this verse talks about Jesus when He was younger. Pray this verse asking God to help you to be filled with wisdom and that His favor (that's Him loving and helping you) would be on you.

Older Kids: Read Luke 2:52 again. As Jesus grew, He grew stronger, smarter, and wiser. He grew closer to God and He grew socially, getting better at relationships and loving and helping His friends, family, and community. How? Whether you're playing, working, in a class, reading your Bible, or just hanging out with friends and family, pray, listen, and learn. Trust God and ask Him to help you learn and do well in every part of your life.

DAY 5: JESUS BAPTIZED

Read: Matthew 3:13–17; Romans 6:1–11

Quick Start

Do you know what baptism is and why people do it?

Quest

Most people would not have thought anything of it when Christ was baptized, but there was something different about His baptism than other people's baptism. First, John was only baptizing those people who repented of their sins (Matt. 3:11), but Jesus had no sin. Second, John was right, he should have been baptized by Jesus, but it was God's will that Jesus be baptized, in order to demonstrate God's plan for making us His righteous children. Jesus' baptism pictured what God sent Him to do. Just like Jesus went down into the water, He would die for our sins and be buried, and as He came up from the water so He would be raised from the dead (Luke 12:50). Just as Jesus was baptized to show what He would do, we are to be baptized to show what that means to us. When we go into the water, we show that we believe Jesus died in our place and that our old life and sin is buried, forgiven, and forgotten. When we come out of the water, we show that we believe we are going to live a new life of obedience to God. When Jesus was baptized, God spoke and the Spirit descend upon Jesus as a dove. When we're baptized, we also show that because of what Jesus did, we believe that God is pleased with us and that He has given us His Spirit to help us live our new life.

Quiet Family Prayer

Talk about baptism. If you are baptized, thank God for all that it means. If you're not baptized, but you'd like to be, talk to God about it (and tell someone at your church).

Quiet Times

Younger Kids: Read the story of Jesus' baptism. Look at how God the Father, God the Son, and God the Holy Spirit were all present at the same time. This is what it is like when we ask God into our lives. Thank God for being with you right now.

Older Kids: What do you think Romans 6:1–11 is saying to you? Ask God if there is something you need to know. If you've never been baptized and you want to be, then talk to your parents and someone at your church about it.

DAY 6: JESUS TEMPTED

Read: Matthew 4:1–11

Quick Start
How long can you hold out before you take a candy from a candy bowl?

Quest
People are not normally tempted by something they dislike. They are only tempted with things they have thought about having or doing. Eve became easy prey to Satan in the garden because she looked at the fruit on the Tree of the Knowledge of Good and Evil and desired it (Gen. 3:6). Satan helped her do what she already wanted to do. In Jesus' case, Satan met his match. Though Jesus may have thought about power, wealth, or physical necessities, there was nothing more important to Him than loving His Father and doing God's will. Some think Jesus could not have sinned, but the Bible says that He was tested in every way as we are (Heb. 4:15). We too can pass the test of temptation when we choose to love God above everything else. We can also learn another secret to resisting temptation from Jesus. Satan always lies; so every time the devil spoke, Jesus used God's Word to speak the truth. Satan made Eve question God's Word but He couldn't get Jesus to do the same. You can easily recognize the devil's temptations; anytime you hear God or any part of His Word being challenged or doubted, that's likely him. When that happens pray and the Holy Spirit will remind you of the truth (John 14:26) so you can speak it.

Quiet Family Prayer
Ask God to help you use Jesus' temptation secrets; to love God more than anything else and to use His Word (with the Holy Spirit's help) against the lies.

Quiet Times
Younger Kids: Read Matthew 4:11. God sent His angels to take care of Jesus. We can count on God to always care for us when we need His help. Thank God for loving you so much that He even sends angels.

Older Kids: Read Ephesians 6:10–18; we are to resist the devil. Notice in verse 17 that the weapon we are to use against the devil is God's Word—just like Jesus showed us. Ask God to help you get to know His Word better, so that you can recognize and defeat lies with the truth.

DAY 1: PARENT CONNECTION

THIS WEEK'S TOPIC: JESUS AND THE DISCIPLES

It's discipleship week. Since Jesus chose very ordinary (and all very different) men to be His disciples, we can learn much about being His disciples today from reading about their selection and lives. Matthew 28:19 records that Jesus called His disciples to show others how to be His disciples and as a parents we are the primary point-people for making disciples of our children (Eph. 6:4). This week's devotions will help you teach your kids what being a disciple of Jesus is all about. Jesus is still selecting and calling each of His disciples (as Christians, that's us) and He has a remarkable and completely unique journey mapped out for each one of us. There's only one way to the Father, but there are as many ways to serve Christ as His disciple as there are Christians.

Tips

We're not just different because of our upbringing and choices, God created each one of as unique (Ps. 139:13–16). Anyone who has children can testify how that uniqueness comes packaged. God has also made us similar in many ways so that we can understand our differences and relate to one another. As parents it's good to do some reading about the patterns of similarity God has created in us so that we can respond to and raise each of our children individually. There are patterns in personality types (Read Dr. John Trent's children's book *The Treasure Tree*), patterns in the way we give and receive love (Read Dr. Gary Chapman's children's book *A Perfect Pet For Peyton*), patterns in learning styles (Cynthia Tobias's book *The Way They Learn*), and patterns in the way God gifts and calls us (see Rom. 12:3–8 and 1 Cor. 12:22–31). We're also affected by our sex, our heritage, our birth order, and much more. God made us uniquely and calls each one of us to a unique relationship with Him in Christ. And because of that, there is no cookie-cutter for what a disciple of Christ looks like and does. So the more you understand your child's uniqueness, the better equipped you'll be in guiding them in their response to God's calling. Also understanding these things will help you with the most often asked question about our children's behavior "WHY?" We highly recommend the aforementioned books.

Read: John 1:35–42; Matthew 4:18–20

Quick Start

Where is the farthest you have ever gone on a journey?

Quest

Andrew was a seeker of God. He had been a disciple of John the Baptist and when John pointed to Jesus as the "Lamb of God" Andrew decided to become a follower of Jesus. He was so convinced that he brought his brother Simon Peter to Jesus, and both were called into Christ's service. They were fishermen by trade on the Sea of Galilee, where Jesus would later calm the storm and cause them to bring in a huge load of fish. Peter would become very prominent and together with the two brothers James and John would be the "inner circle" of disciples. These were the first men Jesus called as disciples and their lives would forever be changed. Though we have great respect for them now, they were just ordinary men doing their daily jobs when Jesus called them. Although there were only 12 original disciples, every Christian is also called to be Jesus' disciple (Matt. 28:19). Jesus has never given His role as Lord, Teacher, and Master to anyone else. Jesus disciples us (teaches, trains, and transforms us) through His Holy Spirit who is in each of us; using what we learn from His Word, the church we attend and good Christian friends and family to help us learn, grow, and do His will. What a joy to know when we place our lives into His hands, just like the disciples, we will embark on a fantastic journey with Jesus.

Quiet Family Prayer

Thank God for making each one of you a disciple of Jesus. Ask Jesus to help you listen, learn, and grow daily as His disciple.

Quiet Times

Younger Kids: Read the story of Andrew and Peter becoming disciples. Jesus specially chooses each one of us to be His disciples—just like He did with Peter and Andrew, and He's excited about our journey with Him. Talk to Jesus about you being His disciple.

Older Kids: Read Luke 5:1–11. Peter, who did great things as one of Jesus' disciples, didn't think he was good enough to start with. He soon learned that Jesus starts with ordinary and even broken people and loves, teaches, trains, and transforms them into extraordinary people. Are you just curious about Jesus or are you really a disciple?

DAY 3: PHILIP AND NATHANAEL

Read: John 1:43–51

Quick Start

Is there anyone who is almost exactly like you?

Quest

Philip never forgot that day when Jesus found him and called him as a disciple. He ran straight away to find his friend Nathanael declaring that he had finally found the Messiah. Nathanael wasn't so easily convinced. He was skeptical of anyone who came from the town of Nazareth. But once He met Jesus and heard Him speak, there was no turning back. God made each of us. He made us special and unique and He knows each one of us. Jesus knew exactly what to do and say with Nathanael and with each of His disciples. Peter was noisy and up front and Andrew liked to stay in the background and be supportive (John 6:8; 12:22). Philip followed easily and Nathanael took more convincing. We're all different but God made us that way and Jesus knows each one of us. Jesus wants a personal relationship with you that is special to Him and you. Sometimes we don't know the right things to say to others about Jesus. We just need to pray for them and pray that God will give us wisdom and the right words to say. Jesus knows exactly what each one of us needs.

Quiet Family Prayer

Thank God for making you unique and for wanting a special relationship with you. Also pray for people you know who need to meet Jesus and ask God to give you His wisdom and words for them.

Quiet Times

Younger Kids: Read the story of Philip and Nathanael. God had a unique blessing for Nathanael. As you follow Him, He wants to give you unique blessings as well. Ask God to help you receive His blessings.

Older Kids: Read John 1:43–51 again and Genesis 28:10–22. Nathanael was the first disciple to call Jesus the Son of God. In response to Nathanael's faith Jesus gave him a special blessing that he would have recognized. God doesn't have favorites; He loves us all the same. However, He does bless and treat us all uniquely because He made us all different and wants a unique relationship with each of us. Ask God to help you receive His special blessings for you, as you trust and follow.

DAY 4: JAMES AND JOHN

Read Mark 1:19–20; 9:2; 10:35–45

Quick Start

When was the last time you were picked for a team?

Quest

James and John were brothers and they were fishing partners with Simon Peter and his brother Andrew. They were nicknamed; "Sons of Thunder" (Mark 3:17) and many people believe their mother Salome was the sister of Jesus' mother Mary making them cousins to Jesus. James and John, along with Peter, were close friends to Jesus and were selected to experience some things that the others missed. The Bible tells us that James was the first of the disciples killed for his faith (Acts 12:1–2) and that John was probably the youngest. Early on in Jesus' ministry James and John asked to be put in important positions. Jesus let them know that they had it all wrong—the most important one is the one who serves and puts the needs of others first. God had a reason for Peter, James, and John to be close to Jesus but it wasn't because they were any more important. God gives us greater responsibilities, as we trust Him more and faithfully follow, but to Him and Jesus each of us and the tasks that God gives us is just as important no matter how big or small—what's important to Jesus is that we trust and obey Him and serve others.

Quiet Family Prayer

Ask God to help you trust and obey Him in every task whether it's big or small. And look for opportunities to serve others on His behalf.

Quiet Times

Younger Kids: Read and talk about Mark 10:43–44 with your parent. Ask God to help you serve and love others the way He wants you to.

Older Kids: Read Ephesians 3:17–18. John referred to himself (in his gospel) as the disciple Jesus loved (John 21:7, 20). John didn't call himself the disciple who Jesus loved more than any other—we read that in and we shouldn't. John probably chose this nickname to focus on and remind himself of Jesus' great love for him and to show us that we should do the same. Jesus doesn't have favorites—no matter who you are and what He has planned for you, you are the disciple Jesus loves. Ask Him to help you understand how much He loves you.

DAY 5: MATTHEW

Read: Mark 2:13–17

Quick Start

Who do you think would make the best disciple—a fireman, a banker, or a teacher? (Answer: all of them)

Quest

Matthew was different. In fact some of the disciples may have had trouble trusting him at first because he worked for the Roman government. Tax collectors had a reputation for being dishonest and for collecting more money than necessary in order to get rich. Jesus saw something different in Matthew. When Jesus called him, Matthew threw a big party and invited his friends to meet Jesus, which caused quite a stir among the religious leaders. They were appalled that Jesus would even associate with "sinners" but helping sinners was the reason Jesus came in the first place! Jesus loves and died for everyone and He accepts each one of us the way we are when we come to Him. Then He makes us new and begins to disciple us and use us where we are. We should be careful not to be like the religious leaders and judge other Christians—instead we should love and encourage others knowing that we're all loved just the same. Jesus disciples were regular people and they understood this. Most of them worked in the marketplace and had connections in the business world. When they found Jesus, they began to help other regular people do the same.

Quiet Family Prayer

Ask God to help you accept, love, encourage, and pray for all of those who follow Jesus and thank God for loving and accepting you.

Quiet Times

Younger Kids: Talk about Matthew. He celebrated when Jesus chose him to be His disciple and wanted others to share his joy. Tell God how thankful and excited you are to be loved by Jesus and chosen to be His disciple.

Older Kids: Read Romans 14:1–12. It seems that our set-point is to think that all who are different from us or who follow Jesus differently are not right. The truth is God made us all different and that none of us are perfect. God wants us to love and accept each other despite our differences. Even with those who are clearly in sin, God asks us to help them with a gentle spirit (Gal. 6:1–3). Ask for God's help with this.

DAY 6: THE TWELVE

Read: Matthew 10:1–10

Quick Start

What have you done that involved a great cost to you (time, energy, money) but was well worth it?

Quest

The disciples were sent out to demonstrate the truth and the power of Christ to the Jews while Jesus was still here. Wherever they went they were to preach about God's love and forgiveness, heal the sick, cleanse the lepers, raise the dead, and cast out demons. This may have been hard at first for some of them to do, but this was their training time. God gave these men to Jesus (John 17:6–19) as disciples and Jesus taught them everything they needed to know to carry out their mission after He was gone. One of them would drop off the team (Judas) but the rest all stood firm and were faithful to the end. The second time Jesus sent His disciples out, He told them to go and make disciples of all nations (Matt. 28:19). The disciples became the apostles. Jesus had taught them how to follow Him and then told them to go teach others how to do the same. That's still what we are to be doing; becoming His disciples and then helping others do the same. Being a disciple is a privilege and a responsibility, one that each person has to take seriously (Luke 14:26–27, 33). The cost may be great, but the rewards are much greater (Matt. 19:29).

Quiet Family Prayer

Pray together and ask God to help you know what it is to be a disciple of Jesus and to become a true disciple so that you can help others do the same.

Quiet Times

Younger Kids: Read the story of Jesus choosing His disciples. Jesus' disciples were just ordinary people who met Jesus—but meeting Jesus changed them and they changed the world. Ask Jesus to change you so you can help change the world.

Older Kids: Read Mark 8:31–38. In verses 32–33 Jesus rebukes Satan when Peter gives his opinion. What follows is Jesus teaching about what it means to follow Him; we must put our ideas, opinions, and plans aside and trust, learn, and follow—knowing that God will take care of us, our lives and our eternity. He wants our all, so He can gives us His; talk to God about this.

Day 1: Parent Connection

This Week's Topic: Jesus Heals

This week we take a brief look at Jesus' healing ministry. The takeaway lessons from every part of Jesus' ministry are incredible and this week we'll be helping you better establish your family in the understanding of God's love for us and His willingness and ability to act on our behalf when we believe. We'll also see that truly believing is a big part. Everything God has for us is by His grace (free gift) through Jesus Christ and the only way we can receive His grace (in any form, for anything) is by faith (Rom. 4:16) in Christ. Every time we pray we come to the throne of grace (Heb. 4:16). We'll be seeing that God wants us to believe even when we can't see what's happening and what Jesus meant by "Only *keep* believing." We'll look at how persistence demonstrates faith and see that God truly wants to care for us and answer our prayers, as we trust Him.

Tips

One of the great stories that we'll be looking at this week is the story of the synagogue leader, Jairus and his daughter (Mark 5:21–43). Jairus's daughter was on death's doorstep when he heard that Jesus was nearby. He ran, fell at Jesus feet, and kept begging Him to come and lay hands on her. Each time he begged he told Jesus that it was his daughter that was sick. It seems universal that when a parent is urgently asking for help for one of their children, everyone stops, listens, and helps because we know the importance and passion of the plea—we know the love a parent has for their child. Jesus agreed to come but was interrupted by a woman who had suffered for twelve years and who was completely healed. When Jesus heard her story He said to her, "Daughter, your faith has made you well." While Jairus stood there waiting and the crowd was still feeling for the man who was pleading for his daughter, Jesus (and this is the only recorded time Jesus used this word) called this woman, "daughter." It seems that God let us know here that we are not the only ones who are passionate about the needs of our children—God loves and cares for us passionately! Help your children this week understand that God is their heavenly Father who loves them greatly and who hears their prayers and wants with all His heart to help them and to demonstrate His love in their lives. Faith is essential for receiving His grace and faith flourishes when we understand God's love for us in Christ.

Read: John 4:46–54

Quick Start

What kind of instructions does your father or mother give you that they expect you to carry out?

Quest

Here is a curious story. Jesus had come to a small town of Cana where He had done His very first miracle, and a wealthy man sought Him out that had a sick son back at home in Capernaum, the town where Jesus often stayed. This father begged Jesus to come back to Capernaum and heal his sick son because he was afraid his son would not live through the illness. Jesus saw the desperation in the eyes of this man and told him not to worry because his son was just fine. Jesus did not go to where the boy was, He did not touch the boy to heal him or even see the boy. Jesus just healed him. The man believed what Jesus said, went home to find his son was healed of his illness, and the whole family placed their faith in Christ as the Messiah. One sentence uttered by Jesus changed the lives of the whole household (which usually included the servants as well). Jesus was doing what He said His Father had asked Him to do (Luke 4:18).

Quiet Family Prayer

Jesus chastised those who were listening because they needed to see signs and wonders before they believed. Then He gave a wonderful example of what it means to have faith in God even when you can't see anything happening. Pray and ask God to help you have stronger faith so that you can believe He's working even when you can't see it.

Quiet Times

Younger Kids: Read the story of the nobleman's son being healed. God wants us to believe He loves us and hears and answers us when we pray. Ask God to help you trust Him before you see His answers.

Older Kids: Read John 20:19–29 and notice verses 25 and 27. Jesus showed Thomas that He is God—although Thomas didn't see Jesus, He was there when Thomas spoke about not believing unless he saw. Then Thomas believed not just because he saw Jesus but because Jesus showed him that He was always with him. Thank Jesus for always being with you.

DAY 3: JAIRUS'S DAUGHTER

Read: Mark 5:21–24, 35–43

Quick Start

Which is harder to believe—that you can feed 5,000 people with $10 or that you can bring a dead person back to life?

Quest

Jairus was a ruler at the local synagogue. He had heard about the wonderful things Jesus was doing and his daughter was deathly ill. So when Jairus heard that Jesus was down by the lake, he ran down as quickly as he could and he bowed down humbly on his face before Jesus' and begged Him to come heal his daughter. He wanted Jesus to lay his hands on her to make her well just as He had done for so many others. Jesus followed Jairus home but as they were going the bad news came that his daughter had already died. Jairus was torn. He wanted to believe Jesus could heal, but maybe this was too big. But parents will do anything for their kids, so he believed when Jesus said "Do not be afraid, only believe." His faith was rewarded and his daughter was raised from the dead. God's people had not seen the power of God among them for generations, but now the time had come for them to know God's love, plans, and purposes. The healing Jesus did was proof that God had sent Him and was using Him in mighty ways.

Quiet Family Prayer

The original language shows that Jesus told Jairus, "Only *keep* believing." God answers our prayers because of His love through Christ. We can't earn His grace—so the "only" thing required is to believe and to "keep believing." Ask God to help you "only keep believing."

Quiet Times

Younger Kids: Read the story of Jairus. Jairus loved his daughter so much that he'd do anything. We are God's children and He feels the same way. Ask your heavenly Father to help you always trust His love.

Older Kids: Read Mark 5:21–43. Jairus passionately asked Jesus to come and heal his *daughter*. Jesus followed but was interrupted by the woman who touched Him. Jesus called the woman *daughter*. That's the only recorded time that Jesus called someone that. Perhaps Jesus was teaching Jairus that He and our heavenly Father care for their children too (Matt. 7:11). Thank God for how much He cares and how willing He is to help.

DAY 4: EPILEPTIC BOY

Read: Mark 9:14–27

Quick Start

Sometimes we must be on guard against those who try to manipulate us for their personal gain. Who do you trust the least?

Quest

This father was beside himself. No one had been able to help his son, not the doctors, the synagogue rulers, religious leaders, no one. This was his only son and he was desperate for help. There are several things that are significant about this event. First it demonstrates a father's love for his son, and Jesus' willingness to help. Second, it shows that it is okay to have doubts when we come to God (Mark 9:24) because He is big enough to help us overcome doubts. Third it talks about different kinds of unclean spirits that must be confronted by faith and the power of God (Mark 9:29). In any case, Jesus was clearly more powerful than anything the devil can do, and He was spiritually ready to handle facing His enemies and those who try to destroy His people. The Bible says that the enemy comes to "steal, kill and destroy" but Christ came so we could have abundant life (John 10:10).

Quiet Family Prayer

Thank God that Jesus came to destroy the works of the devil and when we resist him in the name of Jesus, he flees from us (see Luke 10:19; Acts 4:30; 16:18; Phil. 2:10; Heb. 2:14, James 4:7; 1 John 3:8).

Quiet Times

Younger Kids: Read John 10:10 with your parent. The devil is like a bully who is afraid to pick on people when their big brother is there. Jesus is like your big brother and He's always with you protecting you.

Older Kids: Read Acts 19:11–17. The seven sons of Sceva tried using Jesus' name like magic words—it didn't work. We use Jesus' name because we understand who He is, that He's defeated the devil and has all authority. We love Him and have faith in Him so His name is both meaningful and powerful and using it reminds us that He's always with us. Ask God to remind you of Jesus' presence and name when you need Him. (Read the verses listed under today's "Quiet Family Prayer.")

DAY 5: BLIND BARTIMAEUS

Read: Mark 10:46–52

Quick Start

Who is the most stubborn person you know? Do they usually get what they want?

Quest

Bartimaeus is a funny fellow. He just couldn't keep quiet when people told him to because he wanted to see Jesus. People kept telling him to stop yelling for Jesus, but this was his one opportunity to find the man who could give him back his sight. So he yelled even louder! Jesus loves persistent people because it means they have faith that He can help them. In fact, when Jesus healed the man He said, "Your faith has healed you." How many people do you think were not healed because they didn't have enough faith in Jesus? How wonderful for Bartimaeus to be able to see once again. He must not have stopped calling out even after he was healed because now he would have proclaimed praises to God for his sight. Jesus must have laughed when He saw how excited Bartimaeus was and how determined he was. This story is important for us today to be reminded that persistence and faith are important ingredients for the power of God to be displayed. It may take more than one quick prayer for God to act on our behalf.

Quiet Family Prayer

Persistence shows you have faith because you wouldn't persist if you didn't believe you'd get what you were asking for. Pray about the things you've been persisting in prayer about and tell God you're persisting because you believe.

Quiet Times

Younger Kids: Read the story of Bartimaeus. Bartimaeus asked for mercy—that means he wasn't persisting because he thought that he deserved to be healed but because he believed that Jesus is good. Thank God that He answers our prayers because He is good and He loves us.

Older Kids: Read Joshua 14:6–15. Caleb asked for the land where there were giants and fortified cities because He had faith in God. Blind people are usually careful about where they put their things but Bartimaeus "threw off his coat" and jumped up. Faith doesn't have a backup plan. Both Caleb and Bartimaeus *knew* that God would help them. Pray that God would help you trust Him like that.

DAY 6: LAZARUS

Read: John 11:1–44

Quick Start
What is the hardest thing you have every tried to do?

Quest
Jesus had raised other people back to life, but never one that had been dead for four days. This was perhaps a picture of what Jesus was about to do for us (vv. 25–26). He took away death's power and when we become Christians the death of our body becomes just a step into eternal life (John 5:24). We don't know all that was going through Jesus' mind at this moment, but He became very upset and sad, and at one point began to weep. Maybe it was due to the sadness of those around him. It may also have been due to the unbelief of God's people. God wants to love and care for His people so much, but they just wouldn't trust His love and follow Him (Matt. 23:37). Jesus knew that even though He was showing God's great power and love for His people, that the religious leaders' response would be to try and kill Lazarus and to kill Him (John 11:53–54; 12:10)— that's sad. It was a joyous day for Mary and Martha though; they trusted God and had their brother Lazarus returned to them. There should never be any question about God's love and His willingness and ability to handle our problems when we read the story of Lazarus.

Quiet Family Prayer
It makes God and Jesus sad when we don't trust Them to help us. Before you start praying, thank God for His great love for you and ask Jesus to help you believe that God hears and answers you.

Quiet Times
Younger Kids: Read the story of Lazarus. Jesus loves you a lot and wants to help, just like with Mary, Martha, and Lazarus. Thank God for sending Jesus and ask Him for any help you need.

Older Kids: Read John 11:1–44 again. Replace the people and problem in this story with yourself and your family or friends and a real situation that you're praying about. This is how we should picture our lives; Jesus right with us, feeling what we feel, wanting God's best for us and encouraging us to believe; helping us understand that our way and timing may not be His, but that He'll work it out amazingly as we trust and obey. Use this story to talk to God about your situations.

DAY 1: PARENT CONNECTION

THIS WEEK'S TOPIC: JESUS PERFORMS MIRACLES

Jesus did some amazing miracles and although they're almost beyond comprehension they're packed with practical lessons for us today. Here's the summary of this week's miracle lessons: All of us are called to make the salvation of others an exciting priority in our lives. You can trust God to care for you in and through every problem and storm. When we follow God's plans for us, we demonstrate our faith and God shows up to help. Everything is possible to the one who believes, and God wants your mouth to be like a fruit tree that produces good fruit. Have a miraculous week!

Tips

We have two brief tips for this week. First it's important to make a short connection between the stories about Jesus and your children's life and an even shorter connection between them and Him. These stories from long ago can naturally feel a long way off—but they're not. Help your children understand how close and relevant they are to them by: affirming the historicity of the events—Jesus actually lived. Let your children know about Israel today and how people travel to see the places where these stories took place—go online and show them pictures. Also Jesus knew His words and deeds would be written down (Matt. 26:13) and read by Christians around the world, so what He taught was for us today as well. Most important, Jesus came so that He could be with us and in us by His Spirit forever—His Words aren't just those of a stranger, they're those of our Lord and God who is right here with us teaching us and helping us understand.

Second, family mottos can be a powerful behavioral transformation tool. For example, this week we'll be learning about the importance of using our words to build others up. You'll be reading, discussing, and praying Ephesians 4:29 as a family. In that moment, when everyone agrees that speaking kindly is the best way to speak, work together to make up a family motto that you can all remember and use to remind and encourage each other. Something like: "Our words aren't lies or dirt, and they never hurt; they're helpful and kind, all of the time." Then when the moment arises you merely need to cheerfully quote the motto to bring everyone on side. Try it.

Day 2: A Load of Fish

Read: Luke 5:1–11

Quick Start

Jesus wanted to make His disciples fishers of people. What does that mean?

Quest

Few things will impress fishermen more than a huge load of fish. When it comes, it's usually the perfect combination of being at the right place at the right time and doing everything right. Peter was an experienced fisherman and he knew his fishing grounds—this wasn't the right way, time, or place. But they obeyed Jesus and put their nets into the water. When they began to pull the nets in, they were so full that more help was needed to bring in the load. The fisherman knew that this was miraculous. They had done everything wrong yet the catch was so huge that they were astonished. It was so miraculous that Peter fell afraid at Jesus feet. This was one of the first of Jesus' lessons for the four fishermen about being His disciples. He wanted to leave an impression; first He wanted them to realize that they didn't need to fish anymore; Jesus was well able to meet their needs. Jesus wanted them fishing for people. Also in the years ahead He wanted them to remember that He caused the fish to come when they obeyed Him and He would do the same with people (John 12:32); only Jesus can change hearts. These four disciples are known around the world today because they said "Yes" to Jesus that day.

Quiet Family Prayer

All of us are called to make the salvation of others an exciting priority in our lives. Pray for those you know who aren't yet Christians. Ask Jesus to bring them to the net.

Quiet Times

Younger Kids: Read the story about the big catch of fish. Let God know that you're willing to go fishing for people with Jesus.

Older Kids: Read Luke 5:1–11 and 2 Corinthians 5:17–21. God wants us to help reconcile people. Jesus started teaching the disciples about being fishers of men by using their boat; showing that He could use them where they were, with what they had. Then He showed them that by following His simple directions they would experience God. Let God know that you're willing to help now in any way you can and ask Jesus to teach you how to fish.

DAY 3: CALMING THE SEA

Read: Mark 4:35–41

Quick Start

What are the most powerful words you can think of?

Quest

The disciples had seen Jesus heal the sick, raise the dead, and cast out demons but they had never seen the forces of nature bow to Him. They were so caught off guard that the Bible tells us they were actually terrified. The disciples knew the Bible stories, these kind of incredible miracles were done by people like Moses and Elijah; plagues, parting seas, making the sun stand still and calling fire down from heaven. The disciples were starting to understand who Jesus really was. He was not just a smart teacher or a good healer—He was the Messiah and the Son of God. God was doing these things through Jesus (John 14:10) to get their attention and help them believe (John 10:25, 37–38). The disciples also learned another important lesson about following Jesus—God can and will take care of the things that are beyond our control. After Jesus calmed the storm he asked them, "Why are you fearful? Do you still have no faith?" Through His Spirit Jesus is with all of His disciples today and He's given us His peace and told us not to worry or be fearful (John 14:27) as we walk with Him.

Quiet Family Prayer

You can trust God to care for you in and through every problem and storm. Ask God to help you keep your faith and your calm in every storm.

Quiet Times

Younger Kids: Read the story of Jesus calming the storm. Jesus is with you—those aren't just words! He's actually with you now, right there, loving you and listening to you. Thank Him that He's always there to help you.

Older Kids: Read Acts 27:1–28:10. When Jesus calmed the storm, He had told the disciples to cross the lake (Mark 4:35). In Paul's story God tried to warn Paul's captors about the storm but they didn't listen. It's not only important that we trust God to help us through problems but that we trust Him for direction to start with. Ask God to help you get into the habit of praying before you make decisions instead of after the trouble starts.

DAY 4: LOAVES AND FISHES

Read: Matthew 14:13–21

Quick Start

If you were to plan the perfect day, what would it include? If Jesus appeared in the room, and wanted to help, could He come up with an even better plan? Why?

Quest

The story of Jesus multiplying the loaves of bread and fish to feed five thousand men plus women and children (probably 20,000 people) was so impressive that it is the only one of Jesus miracles included in all four of the Gospel books. Jesus had compassion on the people and decided to feed them. He also wanted to teach another lesson to His disciples. They needed to see the difference between their plans and His plans. The disciples wanted to send the people home because they didn't think there was any way they could feed them. God knows everything, can do anything, and owns everything so His plans are usually bigger than ours. When we follow His plans, we demonstrate our faith and God shows up to help. It is always important to check with the Master before we determine our plans. "A man's heart plans his way, but the LORD determines his steps" (Prov. 16:9). The disciples were glad they went with Jesus' plan instead of theirs because they were able to see the power of God at work.

Quiet Family Prayer

Talk about the areas in your lives that could use God's direction. Now go ahead and ask Him for it.

Quiet Times

Younger Kids: Read the story of the miraculous feeding. Did you know that the loaves and fishes came from a boy (John 6:1–14)? God can use even the smallest things to help His kingdom. Let God know that He can use you and everything you have.

Older Kids: Read Matthew 14:13–21 again; the disciples actually showed great faith in this story. They followed Jesus' instructions and got the huge crowd ready to eat before they knew where the food was coming from. Then they started serving it before there was enough. The easiest way to show God our faith is to simply start doing what He asks us to do trusting Him to do the rest. Talk to God about applying this in your life.

DAY 5: WALKING ON WATER

Read: Matthew 14:22–33

Quick Start

Would you have tried what Peter tried or would you have remained in the boat?

Quest

Mark's account of this story indicates that Jesus intended to walk by (Mark 6:48) but stopped when they saw Him. Walking on water still seems to be the ultimate challenge. The only person to have done it successfully is Jesus. Well, Peter also walked on water but he wasn't nearly as successful as Jesus. Jesus was held effortlessly by His faith, Peter was held up as long as he believed and looked at Jesus. But when he started thinking about the wind and doubted, what started as an adventure quickly turned into terror. Jesus took this opportunity to teach the disciples another lesson that He'd been trying to get them to understand; "Everything is possible to the one who believes" (Mark 9:23). Following God's plan, believing and keeping our eyes on Jesus, is the recipe for taking the "im" out of the "impossible." When we start looking at the troubles we are facing or the distractions around us, we can quickly sink and find ourselves crying out to God for help. Thankfully, Jesus is always with us and ready to catch our hand; but what He'd like us to do, is to ask for help keeping our eyes on Him and believing, before we start to sink.

Quiet Family Prayer

A simple but profound prayer today—ask God to help you grow in faith and in seeing Him as the God who does what we often see as impossible.

Quiet Times

Younger Kids: Read about Jesus walking on the water. When you live trusting in and following Jesus, nothing is impossible. Thank God for His wonderful plan for you.

Older Kids: Read Matthew 14:22–33 again. What makes more sense faith or doubt? Peter could see that Jesus was walking on the water and then he actually did as well. Then he looked at the wind (which was also making waves) and stopped believing. So here's the question, what did the wind and waves have to do with it? Could Peter walk on the water if it was calm? Ask God to help you see sense in believing and nonsense in doubting.

DAY 6: WITHERED FIG TREE

Read: Mark 11:12–14, 20–26

Quick Start

Do you know what fig bud is? What is the most exotic fruit you have tasted?

Quest

Jesus was hungry and spied a fig tree. It wasn't the time for figs but it was the time for the buds, which are edible. There was nothing when Jesus came, only leaves, nothing of value. So He spoke to the tree and it withered. Many have tried finding a deeper meaning from Jesus' action but let's just look at a lesson he taught His disciples. Jesus used His words to say what God wanted Him to say, always. Jesus taught His disciples that what we say is important, just like praying, what we believe, what we do and even the attitudes of our hearts (Mark 11:25). God wants to transform us in every area of our lives (Rom. 12:2) including the way we speak. In another place Jesus said, "I am the vine; you are the branches. The one who remains in Me and I in him produces much fruit, because you can do nothing without Me (John 15:5). Jesus expects to see us bearing fruit because like the vine helps the branch bear fruit, He helps us. The fig tree left an impression upon His disciples who later understood how important our words are. After Jesus went back to heaven the disciples used their words to bear much fruit: to teach, encourage, build up, heal, and bless others.

Quiet Family Prayer

Read Ephesians 4:29 together. God wants us to use our words to love and build each other up. Ask God to help you, by His Spirit, with your words.

Quiet Times

Younger Kids: Read the story of the fig tree. God wants your mouth to be like a fruit tree that has good fruit. Ask Him to help you to always say kind and helpful words.

Older Kids: Read James 3. James says that a fig tree should bear figs not olives (v. 12). No one can tame the tongue on his or her own; we can only do it with the Lord's help—and He's ready to help. Make a decision to use your words for God and ask Jesus to help you transform the way you talk.

DAY 1: PARENT CONNECTION

THIS WEEK'S TOPIC: JESUS OUR TEACHER

We've been learning from Jesus' life and example and from His healings and miracles. This week we'll look at what He taught about prayer, love, being born again, the kingdom and following Him. Your family will learn to talk with their heavenly Father about everything, that to love God and share the love of God with others are the two most important things we can do. They'll also learn what happens when we become God's children, how to live as a part of His kingdom and what it means to "deny ourselves and take up our cross." This week is packed with life-changing stuff!

Tips

Have you ever noticed that God designed the family as a classroom? The important basics for everything that a child needs to know are hidden in lessons learned at home. For example, hidden in the family topic of "chores" are lessons in community involvement, doing your part and work ethic. Hidden in the idea of respecting and obeying your parents are the lessons in being a law abiding citizen, a good employee, and an obedient child of God. Today we'd like to talk about the classroom hidden in sibling relationships. God meant for our children to learn how to get along with their peers, be a valuable member of each team, church and community, be a great friend and an amazing spouse by learning how to get along with their siblings. The Bible doesn't just tell us to love each other, it spends a great deal of time teaching us how to do that. Our children need more than just being told to "Get along!" They need to be taught and trained how to practically love each other in each situation so that they are prepared for life by what they learn at home. This week when the topic of Jesus' teaching on love comes up, take the opportunity to discuss making learning to love each other a priority in your household. Once everyone has agreed to the program, prayerfully watch for training opportunities (disagreements, fights) and spend some time showing your kids how they could have solved the problem more peaceably.

There's a helpful six-part article series under the heading "Sibling Rivalry" called *What the Bible Says about Sibling Rivalry* on the website ChristianParentingDaily.com. It provides practical hints and helps that you may want to read before your family discussion.

DAY 2: PRAYER

Read: Matthew 6:5–13; Luke 11:1–4

Quick Start

Can you say the Lord's Prayer from memory?

Quest

Jesus taught His disciples (and us) how to pray. One of the ways He taught them was by using a simple prayer example that included: praising God, praying for God's kingdom and His will, asking Him for the things we need, asking Him to help us get along well with others so our relationship with Him would not be hindered, and asking for God's protection and intervention in our life. He was teaching us to talk with God from our hearts about anything and everything. Jesus used a simple prayer to help people move away from repeating the same prayers and from "fancy" prayers some people pray to get noticed by others. The Lord's Prayer is a great unity prayer that believers can pray together, but God loves simple prayers from the heart—ones that sound like a child coming to his or her father telling him how great and wonderful he is, letting him know their concerns and needs, and finding out what is on his heart and mind for his children to do. Jesus prayed often because there was a lot He needed to know from His Father. It should be no different for us. The Lord's Prayer reminds us that we need to talk with our heavenly Father often, about everything and from the heart.

Quiet Family Prayer

Say the Lord's Prayer together; then take turns saying one simple prayer from your hearts about anything you'd like to talk to God about.

Quiet Times

Younger Kids: Read about Jesus teaching about prayer; it's okay to pray the same prayers sometimes—but remember prayer is about really talking to God in your own words, in your own way. Also remember to be still and listen between your prayers.

Older Kids: Read John 11:41–42 and 1 John 3:18–23; 5:13–15. Jesus knew that the Father loved Him and always heard and answered Him. John says that we can have the same confidence when we love God and others and we seek His will with the Holy Spirit's help. Ask God to help you have this confidence in prayer.

DAY 3: LOVE

Read: Matthew 22:34–40

Quick Start

Name five things that you absolutely love!

Quest

Many people like to quote "God is love" from 1 John 4:16, but we need to remember that verse 18 says, ". . . we are as He is in this world." God wants us to show His love to the world by loving Him, people, and even our enemies (Luke 6:35). Love is the one thing that is supposed to characterize Christ's followers (John 13:35). Where God's presence is, true love will be present and apart from God no one would know what real love is. We have seen over and over in the Bible what happens to people when they reject God. They become evil, selfish, proud, corrupt, and violent towards others. When love is present no one is selfish or arrogant, but in humility other people's needs are cared for, no one wants to hurt others, and God is honored. When we love God and those around us, we demonstrate God's nature and fulfill our Lord's requirements for His people. Love is not just a wonderful feeling we have, it is a demonstration to others that Christ lives in us and that we belong to Him. To share the love of God with others is one of the most important things we can do.

Quiet Family Prayer

Read Philippians 1:9–11. The Bible says that we are to learn and grow in love. Ask God to help you learn and grow more and more in how to truly love Him and others—He will; Jesus died so that you could bear this fruit.

Quiet Times

Younger Kids: Read about the two greatest commandments. One of the ways that God helps kids learn how to love is by helping them learn with their siblings. Ask God to help you learn how to love them better.

Older Kids: Read Ephesians 3:14–21. We are to be rooted and firmly established in love. When we learn more about God's love and then walk in it, we will understand even more. When we continue to grow like that, we'll end up being filled with all the fullness of God. Wow! Pray these verses for yourself and your family.

DAY 4: BORN AGAIN

Read: John 3:1–18

Quick Start

Do you know how a butterfly becomes a butterfly?

Quest

Jesus tells us that we must be born again to see the kingdom of God. We were born physically in order to experience this world—all the trees, lakes, people and animals—but we need to be born spiritually in order to experience the kingdom of God. One birth happens when a mother gives birth; the other happens when we believe that Jesus died for our sins (Rom. 10:9–10). Remember, when Adam and Eve ate the forbidden fruit? God told them that they'd die that day. They didn't die physically; they died on the inside. God created us to be His children and to be connected to Him—sin broke that connection for Adam and Eve and for everyone else born from them. Jesus died so that we could be forgiven and reconnected to our heavenly Father. It's a free gift—we just need to tell God that we believe in Jesus and ask Him to forgive our sins. When we do we become alive on the inside, the Holy Spirit comes into us and we become God's children—that's being born again. We also become Jesus' disciples and He starts teaching us how to live God's way. If you have not given your life to Christ yet, today would be a great day for you to be "born again" (John 1:12–13; 10:28).

Quiet Family Prayer

If you've never been born again, simply tell God that you believe in Jesus and ask Him to forgive your sins. Then thank Him for Jesus and the Holy Spirit who will help you learn and live as God's child. If you're already born again, thank God for His great gift!

Quiet Times

Younger Kids: Read the story about Nicodemus. Like being born, being born again is very real. God washes away your sin, makes you new and comes to live in you. You know in your heart it's real (Rom. 8:16). Ask God to help you experience Him more.

Older Kids: Read Ezekiel 36:25–27; 37:1–10. Ezekiel prophesied about being born again. God showed Ezekiel that without being born again and having His Spirit, we are like a pile of dead bones. Thank God that you are part of an exceedingly great army who will live with God forever!

Day 5: The Kingdom

Read: Matthew 4:12–17, 23

Quick Start

What nationality are you? Which country would you love to visit?

Quest

Jesus teaches about the kingdom of heaven or kingdom of God about forty times in the book of Matthew alone. He wanted to contrast the difference between the kingdom of the world and His Father's kingdom. He also wanted His followers to know how they should live as a part of His kingdom, and what is theirs as members of the kingdom. It is said that Jesus took three years to help His disciples understand what it meant to be a part of the kingdom of God, but the truth is, it's an eternal kingdom that's amazing and huge and the more we seek it (Matt. 6:33), the more we'll keep learning about it and experiencing it. *Kingdom* refers to the rule or authority of a powerful person. God's kingdom is not of this earth, it's in the hearts of His people. We take the kingdom of God wherever we go as His people. We bring with us all the power, authority and provision of our King and are able to see His rule and might shown in the circumstances around us. Never forget you are already in His kingdom and under His authority as a believer. This thought will comfort and empower you to trust and obey your Lord wherever you go.

Quiet Family Prayer

Part of the Lord's Prayer is: "Your kingdom come." That's praying that it spreads and grows as we preach the "gospel of the kingdom" and bring more people in. Pray some "Your kingdom come" prayers.

Quiet Times

Younger Kids: Read Colossians 1:14. Thank God that you have been safely transferred into the His kingdom and you're taken care of there by your King, Jesus.

Older Kids: Read Colossians 1:9–14. God has rescued you from the kingdom of darkness and transferred you into the kingdom of His Son. Now God will do for you (by His grace and as you trust Him) all the things Paul prays in verses 9–11. Pray these verses for yourself.

DAY 6: FOLLOWING HIM

Read: Matthew 16:24–27

Quick Start

Have you ever joined an organization where you had to agree to follow their rules?

Quest

Some people want to decide how they will follow Jesus, but He is the only One who is allowed to set the terms. Some people talk like they are Jesus' followers, but He knows who the true followers are; they are the ones who actually "deny themselves and take up their cross." This means placing our lives; all our dreams, goals, and aspirations into Jesus' hands and giving Him permission to decide what is the best use of our talents and gifts and what our future will look like. Remember, it started with Eve—instead of her trusting in God's love, she let the devil trick her into thinking that she should run her own life. That's like a two-year-old living on his own; we don't even know what will happen tomorrow. God loves us and wants the best for us and He knows everything. From the beginning He has just wanted us to trust Him. Jesus gave His life to save us from Adam and Eve's sin and now our lives are His and He wants to teach us to trust, listen, learn, serve, and grow. That's why Jesus said that if you lose your life and follow Him you'll find your life—because He loves you and will guide you into God's best. Eve tried to keep her own life and she lost God's best. It is a relief to let Jesus be our Lord and God be in control.

Quiet Family Prayer

Read and discuss Luke 6:46 together. Ask God to help you make the right choice (the one Eve got wrong) and trust your Lord and Master Jesus to teach you and guide your life.

Quiet Times

Younger Kids: Read the story of Eve being tricked by the snake. God loves us and wants the best for us—we can always trust Him. Ask God to help you to trust and obey Him.

Older Kids: Read your favorite Bible story. It doesn't matter which one you chose, the message is the same; when we trust, seek, learn from and obey God (believing He knows best and wants the best for us), things work out now and in eternity. Put your entire life in His loving hands.

DAY 1: PARENT CONNECTION

THIS WEEK'S TOPIC: JESUS TEACHES PARABLES

The Wise Builder, the Treasure and the Pearl, the Good Samaritan, the Sheep and the Goats and the Vine and the Branches—all well-known parables that people have been mining life-changing truths from for 2,000 years. Here are some of the truths you and your family will be digging out this week: How God helps us through life's storms. Jesus gave His life for us and He asks us to do the same. We are to take the time and initiative to do things that we wish others would do for us. If we truly believe in Jesus, then the way we live our lives will change. Jesus wants to guide and teach us with His Holy Spirit helping, strengthening, and changing us from within so that we learn, grow, and follow.

Tips

After hearing something from the Bible many times over, we can (if we don't know better) grow "hard of hearing" (Matt. 13:15) "Oh, I've heard that before." But God told Joshua that meditating on His Word day and night would be the key to His success (Josh. 1:8). God's Word is living and effective and able to change us but only as it goes down inside us (Heb. 4:12). It will make us complete and equip us for every good work but only as we are taught and trained by it (2 Tim. 3:16–17).

God uses His Word to progressively save our souls but only as it's implanted in us (James 1:21). The Bible contains God's very words and they are as packed full of truth—they weren't written for us to just hear and mentally assent to but to become part of us.

The same verses have been used to teach dozens of different and biblically valid lessons. No matter how many times you've heard something from the Bible, the Holy Spirit is able to teach you more and/or more deeply from it. God's words are not ordinary words; God uses them to powerfully and continually reveal truth to us and transform us into Christ's image. Help your kids understand this and to love and value God's Word. One way to do this is to pray before each Bible reading, thanking God for His amazing Word and asking Him to teach and transform you. Also teach them to think and pray about the Bible whenever they read it and to trust God's Spirit to teach them.

DAY 2: WISE BUILDER

Read: Matthew 7:24–29

Quick Start

Challenges are great for helping us learn about ourselves and about the world around us. What is one of the biggest lessons you have learned through a challenge you have had to face?

Quest

There were two builders and there were two houses. One house stands firm when the storms come and the other house crashes to the ground. None of us want to be in the house that crashes to the ground when the storms come, we want to be nice and cozy by the fireplace. But this story really isn't about houses; it is about people's lives. It is about what we base our life on, what the foundations are in our beliefs and about whom we place our faith in. Those who know God, believe in Him, love Him, and try to please Him by living His way, will have God's hand of protection around them when difficult times come. They have His wisdom, strength and His people to help them. Those who have only themselves to rely on and their own wisdom and strength will not be strong enough in themselves to face the challenges when they come and they could quickly loose everything in the end. Jesus' stories always had practical applications to real life—and they always left people with a choice to make. Are you confident that you are ready to face any trial that may come your way?

Quiet Family Prayer

We all face challenges, but God has promised to help us through them with His strength and wisdom. Ask God now to guide you through any challenges your family is facing right now.

Quiet Times

Younger Kids: Read the story of the Wise Builder: Remember David fighting Goliath (1 Sam. 17). What a huge challenge for a young boy to face! But God was strong through David and defeated the giant. Ask God to help you always face your challenges with His help.

Older Kids: Read Psalm 18. You may have already faced some tough challenges in your life (can you name them?) but can you see how God helped you through them in the past? Are you stronger because of them? Ask God to help you live His way and to trust Him to help when things seem tough.

Day 3: The Treasure and The Pearl

Read: Matthew 13:44–46

Quick Start

What is the most expensive object in your house? Is there something you have that you would not sell at any price?

Quest

If you have ever watched or been to an auction, you understand how people can force the price of something far higher than it's worth when they bid against one another. But when someone has to have something, they can sometimes go to extreme measures to get it. Jesus teaches that some things are worth giving up everything you have to obtain it. Some call this the cost of discipleship. Peter said, "Look, we have left everything to follow you. So what will there be for us?" (Matt. 19:27). Jesus promised him all those who had given up everything to follow Him would receive back one hundred times more as well as receiving eternal life. The man who bought the pearl could sell it for more than he paid for it. The man who bought the field could have sold the treasure found in it for far more than the field was worth. For followers of Christ, there is nothing we could give up that would ever be worth more than what Christ offers in return.

Quiet Family Prayer

Thank God for giving us salvation through His Son Jesus Christ. Ask Him to help you value your relationship with Him above everything else this world has to offer.

Quiet Times

Younger Kids: What do you treasure the most of all you have? Do you know you are more special to God than anything in this world? He wants to be that special to you too. Read John 3:16 and thank God for all he has done for you.

Older Kids: What would you be willing to die for? Read Matthew 13:44–46 and John 3:16. Jesus says you are what He was willing to die for. Can you say your relationship with Him is more valuable to you than anything else?

DAY 4: THE GOOD SAMARITAN

Read: Luke 10:29–36

Quick Start

When was the last time you stopped to help someone in need that you did not know? Or went out of your way to help someone you know?

Quest

The Samaritan was the last person in the world that the Jews would have expected to be the good guy in the story. They were not surprised that the two religious leaders walked on by, but to have an enemy show kindness was very unusual. The story would have made them very uncomfortable because they were not used to being kind to their enemies. What they really didn't like was when Jesus said, "You go and do the same." This story is not just about being nice, it's about going above and beyond what others will do, to go the second mile (Matt. 5:39–44), to pray for enemies and do good to those who hurt you. We are ALWAYS to act in love towards others. This does not mean let people walk all over you or take advantage of you, but to treat each person with respect and dignity just as you would want to be treated yourself. Jesus reminds us that as we treat others, we are actually treating Him (Matt. 25:40). How have you treated Christ lately?

Quiet Family Prayer

There are needy people all around us who need our help and our love. Ask God to show you a family this week that you can help as a family.

Quiet Times

Younger Kids: Read the story of the Good Samaritan and Luke 6:31. What does this mean to you? How could you do this for your parents or friends this week? Ask God to show you a person who He wants you to help.

Older Kids: Read Luke 6:31 and 10:29–36 again. Two of the three people did not stop to help. Would you have stopped? "Doing unto others as you would have them do unto you" means taking the initiative to do things that you wish others would take the time to do for you. Ask God to open your eyes to see where He wants you to help others this week.

DAY 5: SHEEP AND GOATS

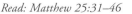

Read: Matthew 25:31–46

Quick Start

Have you ever had to pick weeds from a garden or flower bed? What did you do with the weeds once they were pulled out?

Quest

Some people believe that if they don't do too many bad things or if they are a nice person, God will let them into heaven. Being nice or good were not God's requirements; believing in His Son is. Believing in Jesus and seeking to please Him will turn you into a good person and cause you to want to do good things for others. But it starts with trusting your life to Christ. Those who allow Jesus to direct them to be a blessing to others, to continue the same kinds of things Jesus did when He was on earth, will find they will be admitted into heaven. Those who did not live for Jesus, but lived for themselves will find the gate shut when they get to heaven and they will be sent away to everlasting punishment (Matt. 25:46). God looks at our hearts to see who it belongs to, whether it belongs to Him or to this world. We cannot earn God's approval or our entrance into heaven, but if we truly believe in Jesus then the way we live our lives will show it. Living a life that is pleasing to God is not always an easy thing to do, but Jesus has promised to help us as we trust Him, and we know God rewards faithfulness, now and for all eternity.

Quiet Family Prayer

If we have given our lives to Christ, we are His sheep. Remember even though God has forgiven and accepted us as His children we don't become perfect overnight—children learn and grow. Ask God to help your family grow and live lives that are more and more pleasing to your Good Shepherd.

Quiet Times

Younger Kids: Read the story of the Sheep and Goats and 1 John 3:7. Ask God to help you learn more about loving others and to help you always be kind to others.

Older Kids: Read 1 John 3 and Romans 12:2. Our actions start in our mind first. Ask God to help you renew your mind so that your thoughts and feelings to others are always loving, understanding, and kind.

DAY 6: VINE AND BRANCHES

Read: John 15:4–14

Quick Start

Have you ever tried to fix a broken flashlight only to realize the batteries were dead?

Quest

This metaphor is one of the most important ones that Jesus taught. Jesus said, "Without me you can do nothing" (John 15:5). We cannot please God using our own wisdom and our own strength—we must learn to "abide" in Christ. This is crucial to the Christian life. Abiding in Christ allows God's Spirit unlimited control of our life, our thoughts, our emotions, and our actions so that everything we do and say (just like Christ) will bring glory to God. He does not want to control us like robots, rather to guide us and teach us like a Master does with his student—and His Holy Spirit helps, strengthens, and changes us from within so that we can. Our role is to trust and rest in Jesus' ability to teach, guide, and transform us so that we can be so in tune with Him that we function as one person, not two. Christ wants to have the same kind of relationship with us as He had with His Father (John 10:14–15; 17:21) so He can send us out in the same way His Father sent Him out (John 17:18) and people's lives will be transformed by the love of God flowing through us (John 17:23).

Quiet Family Prayer

Ask God to help you truly understand what it means to abide in Christ and to learn to let Him live in you (Gal. 2:20).

Quiet Times

Younger Kids: Read John 15:5 again. Apple trees bear apples. Lemon trees bear lemons. Christian means "Christ like" so what fruit should a Christian bear? Ask God to help you bear Jesus fruit inside and out.

Older Children: Read Galatians 5:13–25. What fruit do you think God wants to see from your life? Ask Him to guide you to cooperate with Him as He works in you.

DAY 1: PARENT CONNECTION

THIS WEEK'S TOPIC: JESUS OPPOSED

This week we talk about how the wicked and jealous leaders in Jerusalem plotted to stop Jesus by trying to trick and trap Him, and how every attempt backfired until they found a willing betrayer. Even though His enemies were hounding Jesus and He knew His betrayal was in the works, He continued to please God and provide a wonderful example for us. He taught us how we are to treat those who mistreat us and about God's mercy and forgiveness. He truly demonstrated that God did not send His Son into the world to condemn the world, but that the world through Him might be saved.

Tips

Jesus taught that we are not only to forgive those we love, but also our enemies. Not only are we to forgive our enemies, we're also to love them and show them kindness. You may have heard some say that Jesus taught using exaggeration to prove that God's standards are higher than what we can achieve. If that's true, then how much of what Jesus taught can we simply ignore? Jesus never once said that He was teaching the impossible. In fact He asked, "Why do you call me 'Lord, Lord,' and don't do the things I say?" (Luke 6:46). And Jesus told His disciples to teach others to observe *everything* He commanded them (Matt. 28:20). What Jesus taught would be impossible to live if we were left in our sin, or forgiven and then left on our own but neither is true. Read Ezekiel 36:25–27. The prophet was foretelling what God would do through the cross. In Christ we are cleansed from sin and the idols of this world that would distract us. We are given a brand new heart and spirit and our old heart of stone (our stubbornness, unwillingness, indifference and rebellion) is removed (2 Cor. 5:17). Then God puts His Holy Spirit within us and commits to cause us to follow and obey (Phil. 2:13). Jesus didn't just die to squeak us into heaven, the price He paid included freedom from sin and a total rebuild on the inside, complete with the Holy Spirit, so that we have the ability to learn and grow and actually obey everything Jesus taught (Heb. 13:20–21). Jesus taught what seemed impossible because what He was about to do for us was incredible! We as parents need to know this so that we not only raise the bar for our kids (in example and teaching) but also so that we teach them that by God's grace, Christ's work and the Spirit's help they are able to live a life that pleases God—Jesus already paid the price for their success.

DAY 2: WOMEN CAUGHT IN SIN

Read: John 8:3–11

Quick Start

In your own thoughts, quietly think of an embarrassing moment when you made a mistake.

Quest

The Jewish leaders who disliked Jesus were trying to trick Him. If Jesus had agreed that this woman should be stoned then He would have broken Roman law. If He said that she shouldn't be stoned, then He would have broken the Law of Moses. Jesus enemies thought that they had Jesus trapped. But when they threw her to the ground at Jesus' feet, they did not realize that they had brought her to the only person who could truly forgive her of her sins so that she wouldn't need to die. Jesus saved her life and gave her a new future. "Go and sin no more," Jesus said. He wanted her to repent, which means to turn and walk away from her sin and walk a new path that would be pleasing to God. Her accusers were sinners too, and fortunately for her, they listened carefully to what Jesus said. Another time Jesus said "For God did not send His Son into the world to condemn the world, but that the world through Him might be saved" (John 3:17). This woman experienced God's forgiveness and we all get to see just how compassionate and caring Jesus really is towards us all. He even treated the accusers with dignity and prevented them from needlessly taking someone's life. Jesus didn't care about the trap. He cared about the people and saving them from the destruction that sin causes.

Quiet Family Prayer

Read 1 John 1:9 and take time to silently ask God to forgive you for anything that you haven't already talked to Him about. Ask for His help to go the other direction—He'll help you.

Quiet Times

Younger Kids: Read Proverbs 28:13. Being quick to see that you're wrong and apologizing for it helps you learn and grow and have a better life. Ask God to help you be QTR (quick to repent).

Older Kids: Read Psalm 25. Sin leads to destruction, and living God's way leads to blessing, guaranteed. But because of what Jesus did, even when we blow it, we can be instantly forgiven and given the help and strength we need to make the right choices. Ask for God's help to make right choices.

Day 3: Taxes to Caesar

Read: Mark 12:13–17

Quick Start

Do you ever find yourself making more promises than you can keep?

Quest

Over and over again the wicked leaders tried to find something they could use to get Jesus in trouble so they could stop His ministry. But there was nothing Jesus did that was against the law or offensive to God. It would be hard for most people to do exactly the right thing all the time—never be unkind, never stretch the truth, always love and always keep every promise etc. But that was what Jesus did. He wanted His every word and deed to be pleasing to His heavenly Father. In order to please God like that we need to learn God's Word so we know how to please Him. We also need to trust Jesus to help us learn and understand and trust God's Spirit to change us from the inside out. Paul taught that God works inside us, helping us want to do his will and helping us to do it (Phil. 2:13). As we cooperate with God's growth plan it pays off with the respect of the community and blessings from God. People like Abraham, Moses, Daniel, and David all had special titles like, "Friend of God," "Most humble person on earth," "Beloved by God" because of their good character. God wants to help us grow so that our inside thoughts and our outside actions are both pleasing in His sight.

Quiet Family Prayer

Jesus told them to give back to Caesar the things that are Caesar's, and to God the things that are God's. We belong to God. Ask God to help you live for Him and cooperate with His growth plan for you.

Quiet Times

Younger Kids: Read the story about the wicked leaders trying to trick Jesus. Pray and tell God that you know that you are His and thank Him for loving, teaching, and helping you.

Older Kids: Read 2 Peter 1:1–11. When Peter first walked with Jesus, he had a lot of growing to do. He found out how to grow in Christ by God's grace and by God's Spirit working within him (vv. 2–4). Ask God to help you learn more about what Jesus did for you and to help you grow by God's grace and power like Peter did. (See *The Power of the Resurrection* and *The Power of the Cross* by Henry Blackaby.)

230 DAY 4: JESUS CLAIMS TO BE GOD

Read: John 8:57–59; 10:30–33; 14:8–12

Quick Start

Can you think of a situation where loosing is actually winning?

Quest

The one thing that disturbed Christ's enemies more than anything was His claim to be "one" with the Father. But when He used the name of God, "I AM" for Himself, they were furious. No one was permitted to say such a blasphemous thing and live—unless, of course, it was true. Jesus also claimed to be God when He allowed people to worship Him such as His disciples and those who had been healed or forgiven (Matt. 14:33; 15:25; 28:9, 17; Luke 24:52; Mark 5:6). Jesus was letting us know that He is far more than a good teacher, a prophet, or a miracle worker—He is God. While on the earth He acted as a man who was just as human as the rest of us—God's power flowed through Him to accomplish God's will, just as it does through us when God uses us. But Jesus has always been and always will be God the Son—He created us (John 1:1–3). Christ's enemies didn't believe it and they wanted Him dead. They had no idea that they were being used by God to accomplish His will. Jesus came to the earth to willingly lay down His life as a sacrifice for us. No enemy can prevail against God's plans.

Quiet Family Prayer

Jesus wanted us to be as close to Him as He was with His Father (John 17:22). This means being mindful of His presence in us with the help of God's Spirit. Ask God to help you grow more and more sensitive to His presence.

Quiet Times

Younger Kids: Read the story of Moses and the Burning Bush and John 8:58. "I AM." Jesus created us and He left heaven to be one of us and to die for us. Wow! That shows how much He loves us! Thank Jesus for what He did for you.

Older Kids: Read John 8:57–59; John 10:30–33; and John 14:8–12 again. Some people believe that Jesus was just a prophet or a wise man or good teacher. However, He claimed to be God; if He was lying then He wasn't good, and if He was mistaken then He wasn't wise or a prophet. If Jesus was a good and wise man, then He is who He claimed to be—God. Thank Jesus for being who He claimed to be.

Day 5: Leader's Plot

Read: Luke 19:47–48; Mark 14:10–11

Quick Start

Who is the strongest most powerful person in the world that you know of?

Quest

Christ's enemies were at a loss as to how to get rid of Him. They couldn't trick Him, they couldn't find any accusation against His character or actions, and there were always so many people around Him so they couldn't just arrest Him without causing a great commotion. But what luck! One of Jesus' own disciples was willing to betray Him late at night when no one would be around to see it. It would only cost them thirty pieces of silver, money well spent to get rid of this trouble-maker Jesus. Jesus' enemies thought they were so smart. If they had just read the prophecies written hundreds of years earlier, they would have known He was going to be betrayed by a friend (Ps. 41:9; Zech. 11:12–13), beaten and spit upon (Isa. 50:6), that He would be crucified (Ps. 22) and be raised from the dead (Ps. 16:10) and be called the Son of God (Ps. 2:7). They didn't realize that all this time they were fighting against God, not just a popular man named Jesus. All their plans and plotting were no less effective than Pharaoh's attempt to keep the slaves in Egypt or Joseph's brothers' attempt to get rid of him. The enemies of God's people are the enemies of God, and there is no one who can stand against the power of God.

Quiet Family Prayer

Jesus asked God to forgive the ones who put Him on the cross (Luke 23:34). Ask God to always help you forgive and pray for those who mistreat you (Matt. 5:44).

Quiet Times

Younger Kids: Read Luke 6:27–36. Jesus has already been kind to everyone. He died for the whole world—some of them just don't know it yet. Ask God to help you remember that, just like Jesus, you need to be kind to all.

Older Kids: Read Acts 16:23–34. When you're kind to everyone, God can rescue you and use your kindness to help others learn about Jesus. Ask God to show you what He sees and what you are to do to bring even those who aren't kind to you, to Christ.

DAY 6: JUDAS

Read: Luke 22:47–48

Quick Start

How does it feel to be forgiven for something you did and have your guilt taken away?

Quest

Many have speculated about Judas and what his motivation could have been for betraying Jesus. Some think he was selfish and greedy pointing to the fact that he kept the money bag. Others think that perhaps he was tired of waiting for Jesus to usher in His kingdom and he thought he could force Jesus into doing a big miracle to defeat His enemies. Then He and His disciples could rule over Jerusalem and the nation. We don't know for sure, but we do know that Judas regretted what he did in the end (Matt. 17:3). But regretting our sins or feeling guilty is not enough. We need to ask God for forgiveness. Judas' name is forever known as the betrayer of Christ. He had walked with Jesus for three years and saw the incredible things Jesus did and how God used Him in mighty ways. But Judas did not surrender to Christ as Lord and in the end all was lost. Failure is a part of life, but God allows us to repent and be forgiven if we choose to be. When you realize that you've sinned, don't just regret it and feel guilty, go to God immediately. Because of what Jesus did, God will forgive you instantly and wash your sin and guilt completely away.

Quiet Family Prayer

When we repent God forgives us and cleanses us from the sin and the guilt. It's the devil who wants to condemn us for things God has already forgiven and forgotten. Ask God to help you learn from the past and live for Him in the future.

Quiet Times

Younger Kids: Read Psalm 103:11–13. When we ask, God forgives us; then He washes the sin away and forgets it. Thank God for forgiving your sins and making you feel close to Him again.

Older Kids: Read Psalm 103 and Romans 8:1. Guilt can tear you apart on the inside. That's why God not only forgives us, but cleanses us from the sin and the guilt, forgets it, and gives us a fresh start. We need to accept all of that when we ask for forgiveness and move forward with God's help. If anything that you've been forgiven for is still bothering you, ask God to help you let it go completely—it's forgiven and forgotten.

DAY 1: PARENT CONNECTION

THIS WEEK'S TOPIC: JESUS AND THE CROSS

Every part of the Bible is important but since the central theme of the entire book is Christ and what He came here to do, these next two weeks are of vital importance. As Paul pointed out, if Christ has not been raised, our faith is worthless and we are still dead in our sins (1 Cor. 15:17). This week we'll be looking at and learning from the Passover, the Lord's Supper, and Jesus' arrest and brief time before Herod and Pilate. We'll also be discussing what Jesus suffered and accomplished on the cross and we'll close the week discussing Jesus' burial and now empty tomb.

Tips

Read John chapters 14 and 16. "Jesus is in our hearts." What does that really mean? It's important that our children understand that these words are much more than an abstract theological concept. When Jesus called His disciples, they left everything and they rightly understood that their call as disciples was a permanent change in occupation. So when Jesus started talking about leaving and returning to the Father, they were justifiably confused. However, Jesus assured them that not only would He continue to disciple them but that it would get better. Jesus explained that He (through the Holy Spirit) was going to come and live inside them and continue to teach them, train them, encourage them, comfort them, and help them, but now in a very personal way. In Revelation 3:20 Jesus says, "Listen! I stand at the door and knock. If anyone hears my voice and opens the door, I will come in to him and have dinner with him, and he with Me." In context Jesus is talking to Christians. Jesus lives inside us not as a theological concept but as our Lord, Savior, Guide, and Teacher and He wants us to respond to Him, trust Him, walk with Him, and let Him live in us (Gal. 2:20). Teach your kids that Jesus is truly with them and inside them. He knows how they think and feel and He's there ready to help them, teach them, strengthen them, and lead them. They can simply talk to Him and ask Him for help anytime. As they learn to trust Him and look to Him more and more, He'll make Himself more and more real to them (John 14:19–21). We have it better than the disciples did when Jesus walked here on the earth because He's in our hearts.

DAY 2: THE PASSOVER

Read: Luke 22:7–23

Quick Start

What types of things do you celebrate with your family?

Quest

Remember when the Passover was established back in Egypt after the last plague? The angel of death would "pass over" any house that had the blood of a lamb painted on the doorframe. At that time, the Passover was a picture of what Jesus would do one day. Jesus was God's Lamb that was sacrificed for our sins. Because of His shed blood, we no longer have to face God's punishment for sin. When we are born again, we are taken out of the kingdom of darkness and placed in God's kingdom (Col. 1:13). Jesus was crucified during the Passover to help us understand this. The Lamb of God was slain as a sacrifice for humankind's sin. When Jesus died, the heavy curtain in the temple that separated people from God's presence was torn open (Mark 15:38). God tore it to show us that we now have direct access to God through Christ. Instead of the Passover, today we celebrate the Lord's Supper. The bread we take represents Jesus' body that was broken for us, and the wine, his blood that was poured out for us. When we take communion (or observe the Lord's Supper), we remember what He did for us: His great love for us caused Him to take our punishment (Isa. 53:6) so that we could be forgiven and live for God.

Quiet Family Prayer

Spend a few minutes quietly remembering what Jesus did for you. Take turns saying a prayer of thanksgiving for what you appreciate about God's great love and what Jesus did.

Quiet Times

Younger Kids: Read Psalm 95:1–7 with your parent. There are many ways you can show God thankfulness: shouting, singing, and/or kneeling. Choose a special way to let God and Jesus know you are thankful.

Older Kids: Read 1 Corinthians 11:23–32. During communion we remember what Jesus did and express thanksgiving—but we also need to check ourselves. Jesus died to make us new so that we can (with His help) live a life pleasing to God. Communion is a good reminder that we need to be following Jesus and letting Him teach and change us daily. Ask God to show you in your heart where He wants to help you grow.

DAY 3: JESUS ARRESTED

Read: John 18:1–11

Quick Start

What do you think when you pass by a car that has been pulled over by a police car?

Quest

Jesus was ready for the religious leaders and the guards that night. He knew they had come to take Him away. He knew His disciples would all flee out of fear for their own safety, He knew that He was going to endure a lot of pain and suffering for the sins that other people had committed. His arrest was the beginning of the end of His life on the earth. He had prayed earnestly asking God if there was another way (Luke 22:39–46), but there was no other way and Jesus wanted to do His Father's will. So He waited for them to arrive with their swords, lanterns, and their brutal temple guards. When they came, He made it clear that they would be unable to take Him unless He went willingly. And He went; no resistance, no complaint, just a determination to see this through to the end for our sake and theirs. Although He was completely innocent, this was all part of His Father's plan to redeem a lost world and to defeat the powers of sin, death, and hell once and for all. So much was at stake and no one but God and Jesus really understood what it all meant.

Quiet Family Prayer

What do you think about when you think of Jesus being arrested for your sins? What difference should that make in your life today? Ask God to help you understand how much it cost Him to offer us salvation.

Quiet Times

Younger Kids: Read the story of Jesus' arrest. Getting blamed and punished for something you didn't do is awful. Tell Jesus today how much you love Him for taking the blame for your sins so you can be God's child.

Older Kids: Read Matthew 26:36–46. Jesus knew something about prayer that His disciples didn't then; prayer isn't just about words. When we spend time with God, He strengthens us on the inside (Eph. 3:16) and prepares us for what's coming (John 16:13). Have you ever put aside an hour to spend with God in the Bible and in prayer? Make that your daily goal and ask God for His help getting there.

DAY 4: PILATE AND HEROD

Read: Luke 23:1–25

Quick Start

How close have you been to a famous person?

Quest

Although Pilate and Herod were two of the most powerful men in the land, they played a very small role in the story of Jesus. Jesus primarily came for His people, the Jews. Along the way He spoke with Samaritans and Roman centurions and people from other regions, but for the most part Christ's ministry was limited to the region surrounding Galilee. Both men had heard of Jesus for some time and Herod had even wanted to see Jesus perform a miracle. If they expected a show, both men were sadly disappointed. He is the King of kings and the Lord of lords and did not answer to them and, in fact, He did not even answer their questions. Sadly, both men only wanted to keep the peace in their land and were not particularly interested in justice, but even they could see that Jesus was not guilty. They initially refused to condemn Jesus, but then they gave in to the political pressure of Jesus' enemies. They both talked with the Son of God, the promised Messiah, their Creator, but sadly they did not realize who it was who stood before them.

Quiet Family Prayer

Jesus, the King of kings, God's own Son, and our Creator and Savior, loves you and is with you right now. Take turns praying and saying to Him what you would say if you could see Him.

Quiet Times

Younger Kids: Read Matthew 28:20 and Philippians 4:13. Jesus is always with you. He knows how you feel and what you're going through and He knows what's best. Herod and Pilate didn't know who was with them, but you do. Ask God to help you walk and talk with Jesus everyday.

Older Kids: Read Matthew 11:29; 28:20; John 14:23; Philippians 4:13; and Colossians 3:17, 23–24. Since Jesus is always with us, strengthening us, teaching us, and helping us, it makes sense that we should look to Him in everything we do and then do everything with His wisdom and help. Herod and Pilate didn't know who was with them, but you do. Ask God to help you walk and talk with Jesus in everything you do.

Day 5: Crucified

Read: Luke 23:26–43

Quick Start

When was the last time you gave something that was very special to you to someone else?

Quest

Many think dying on the cross was the defining moment in Jesus' life. Actually, thousands of people have died on crosses. David and Isaiah in Psalm 22:1–18 and in Isaiah 53 foretold the cross. They described in detail what Christ would go through. It was a cruel way to die, but so much more was going on than the suffering of crucifixion. Christ was made to be sin (2 Cor. 5:21) for us, and God put on Him the full penalty and suffering for all of our sin (Isa. 53:4–10). The sun failed for three hours (Luke 23:45) while Jesus bore God's judgment against sin, and that was more suffering than anyone has ever suffered (Isa. 52:14). Jesus never cried out or complained about any of the physical torment but when He was made to be sin for us He cried out with a loud voice, "My God, My God, why have you forsaken Me?" (Matt. 27:46). Jesus always called God His Father but here He called Him "My God." For our sakes Jesus suffered God's displeasure so that we could call God our Father and be His loved children forever. Yet all this was not His defining moment. That came three days later.

Quiet Family Prayer

Thank Jesus today for taking your place so that you could have a relationship with His Father.

Quiet Times

Younger Kids: Read the story of the cross and John 3:16. Jesus died because He loves you and wanted you to become God's child. Thank God for loving you so much.

Older Kids: Read 1 Corinthians 1:30; 2 Corinthians 1:20; Hebrews 2:14; 1 Peter 3:18; 2 Peter 1:3–4; 2:24; and 1 John 3:8. Jesus died so we could be forgiven but He also accomplished so much more than that for us. He brought us to God, gave us His Spirit, bore the effects of sin, broke sin's power, and destroyed the devil's works, provided everything we need for life and godliness—and the list could go on for pages. Ask the Spirit of God to make you aware of God's presence as you read His Word and ask Him to help you learn more about what Jesus did for you.

DAY 6: IN THE TOMB

Read: Luke 23:50–56; John 19:38–42

Quick Start

Have you ever stopped to read the names and dates on tombstones?

Quest

There were many tombs mentioned in the Bible—the tombs of Abraham, Jacob, David, and many of the kings. But the most famous one is empty. It was borrowed from Joseph of Arimathea. Joseph and Nicodemus, who were followers of Jesus, bravely asked Herod for the body of Jesus that they might anoint the body with spices and bury it before the Sabbath when they couldn't do it. It was a very sad time for all of Christ's followers because their Lord was dead. Even though Christ had told His disciples several times that He would be killed, buried, and come to life again after three days (Matt. 16:21), they didn't seem to have believed and/or remembered; His enemies remembered though (Matt. 27:63)! Today you can visit what many believe to be this famous tomb near the Garden of Gethsemane. It's not far from (John 19:42) where the crucifixion likely took place—and it's empty. The significance of the tomb is not so much that it is where Christ was buried, but that it is where Christ was resurrected just as God had planned all along. It was okay for Jesus to be buried in a borrowed tomb because He didn't need it for long.

Quiet Family Prayer

The tomb where Christ was buried is still empty today because Jesus now lives in us. Thank Him for His presence in you and how He guides you and gives you the strength you need each day.

Quiet Times

Younger Kids: Read Galatians 2:20. Jesus would have been the best hide-and-seeker ever! He escaped a tomb and now He lives in you, so you will never be alone or without help. Thank Him for His presence in you today.

Older Kids: Read Matthew 28:20; Galatians 2:20; and Revelation 3:20. Jesus isn't in the grave, He's inside us through His Spirit to love, guide, teach, and strengthen each of us as our Lord and Master. However, He wants us to respond to His knocking—loving Him back, trusting Him, and asking Him for help and guidance as we live our lives daily. Ask God to help you walk with Jesus.

Day 1: Parent Connection

This Week's Topic: Alive Again

Jesus' resurrection was the greatest victory this world has ever known! When we identify with what He did for us on the cross, we know that our old self with all its sin, depravity, and brokenness was crucified and buried with Him. However, when we identify with what He did for us in His resurrection, we see that we were raised with Him as a new creation, raised to a new eternal life in Christ—us in Him and Him in us. This week we'll talk about how Jesus lovingly walks with us as our Master in this new life. He disciples us, teaches and guides us, and reveals Himself to us through His Word and His Spirit within us. He has risen and He wants us to join Him.

Tips

Chocolate is great; but what Easter Sunday really provided for us is mind-boggling and our kids need to understand that. When we focus just on the cross, we know that we're forgiven and that we have a ticket to heaven. But if we stop there we tend to live our lives like everyone else does. Our commitment at baptism is not only that we'll leave the old person and old life behind in Christ's death but that we'll also rise up with Him to a new life. A new life as a new creation, as a child of God obeying Him and trusting Him to love and care for us, as a disciple of Jesus following Him and learning from Him, as the temple of the Holy Spirit allowing Him to work transformation in us and to work through us to bring God's love to others. We are called to walk as Jesus walked, partake in the divine nature, abide in Christ, and bear fruit and to walk in love, righteousness, peace, and joy and to bring glory to Him with our lives. Believing that Jesus died for us is stepping onto the road and through the entrance to God's kingdom but that's only the beginning of our journey. The resurrection is what calls us to start walking along that eternal road by grace with Jesus our Master, Friend, Guide and Example. Seeing your children born again and attending church with you is only the start of your adventure and theirs. Pray and ask God to help you understand what your life in Christ is to look like and ask Him to help you be an example and teach it to your children.

DAY 2: JESUS AND THE WOMEN

Read: John 20:1–18

Quick Start

How do you feel when someone says your name with love as opposed to saying it in anger?

Quest

Mary Magdalene, Mary the mother of James, and Salome waited until the Sabbath was over and then hurried to the tomb where Christ's body had been placed by Joseph and Nicodemus. They were going to finish properly preparing the body for burial, but to their shock the stone was rolled away and the body was missing. Then there were angels! Can this really be happening? When they said Jesus was alive, no one knew what to do but run back and tell everyone. Mary from Magdala lingered outside the tomb confused, angry, sad, and that is where she met the risen Lord Jesus face-to-face. Jesus meant everything to Mary. He had freed her from seven demons, and she had been an ardent follower and supporter of His ever since. She was one of the few people at the foot of the cross when He was crucified and now she was the first to see Him after His resurrection. As soon as He said her name everything became clear. She had thought everything was over when she saw Christ die on the cross, but instead, everything was just beginning! How exciting, how extraordinary, Christ was alive!

Quiet Family Prayer

Read John 20:17 again. Understandably, Mary wanted to hang on to Jesus and never let go again! Jesus had told His disciples that He was going back to the Father and He didn't want her or others to think that had changed. But Jesus also seemed to let Mary know that she'd be able to cling to Him in a new and better way once that happened. Ask God to help you sense Jesus' love and presence with you.

Quiet Times

Younger Kids: Read the story of the boy Samuel in the temple. Jesus called Mary by name like God called Samuel. Jesus loves you, knows you best, and calls you by name. Thank Jesus for being with you and loving you.

Older Kids: Read John 10:1–15. When Jesus called Mary by name, she instantly recognized Him. He does the same with us (vv. 3–4). He's your Good Shepherd; He's with you; He knows you, loves you, cares for you, and guides you! Spend some time thanking Jesus for His love, care, and help.

DAY 3: JESUS ON THE ROAD

Read: Luke 24:13–35

Quick Start

Have you ever gotten really fantastic news when you were very tired? What happened to your tiredness?

Quest

It had been a very confusing week. Celebrating the Passover was meaningful, but the arrest of Jesus and His crucifixion were devastating. He had done all those miracles and taught like no one had ever taught before. They didn't think the Messiah was going to die—the Scriptures said that He'd rule. To make matters worse His body was missing and some of the women said they had seen angels telling them Jesus was alive. Cleopas and his friend were probably tired and emotionally drained and they started arguing about what all of this could mean. The seven-mile walk back to Emmaus started out badly. As Jesus had often done, He interrupted His disciples' argument, but He prevented them from recognizing Him. Jesus began teaching them what the Bible really taught about the Messiah—then they understood. Then He opened their eyes and they believed. Jesus had risen from the dead and He was the Promised Messiah. They had so much energy they ran all the way back to Jerusalem. Cleopas and his friend did not recognize Jesus, but He walked with them, taught them, encouraged them, and showed them God's love. It works the same today—we can't see Jesus but He's with us loving, guiding, teaching, and encouraging us.

Quiet Family Prayer

When Jesus makes Himself real in our lives, we get excited and energized and want to tell others. He's with us (John 14:21), and we merely need to trust Him and look to Him each day. Talk to Jesus about this right now.

Quiet Times

Younger Kids: Read the Road to Emmaus story. Jesus is really with you right now even though you don't see Him. Talk to Him about helping you learn and grow.

Older Kids: Read Matthew 11:29; 2 Timothy 2:7; 3:14–17; John 14:26; 16:13; and 1 Corinthians 2:12. Jesus taught His disciples using God's Word. He does the same today through His Spirit inside us. We are His disciples and as we read His Word and trust Him, He helps us to understand and live what we read. Ask Him to teach you and read and think about these verses again, slowly and prayerfully.

242 DAY 4: PETER AND ANOTHER BIG CATCH

Read: John 21:1–14

Quick Start

If Jesus did a miracle to get your attention, what do you think it would be?

Quest

The disciples were likely not sure what would happen next. They were disciples of the Messiah, but then Jesus had been killed. But then He rose again, but now He just appeared and disappeared when they weren't expecting it. And they couldn't just find Him and ask questions like before. They probably talked about this all night long while they were fishing. In the morning they still didn't know what to do and they hadn't caught any fish. When John figured out who the stranger was, Peter plunged into the water and swam, leaving the rest to bring in the big load of fish. Peter undoubtedly had a few questions he wanted to ask Jesus. Jesus had made them a promise three years earlier. He had told them to leave their boats, follow Him, and He would make them fishers of men (Matt. 5:10). They had been taught and trained and they were going to receive the Holy Spirit shortly to give them the wisdom and power to do all that Christ wanted them to do. They didn't realize it, but God was about to use them to change the world. They just needed to wait a little while longer.

Quiet Family Prayer

Jesus had called Peter to follow Him and changed his occupation from "fisherman" to "fisher of men." But Peter needed a reminder (v. 19). We may or may not be called to full-time ministry but our primary focus in life should always be following Him. Ask God to help you follow Jesus.

Quiet Times

Younger Kids: Read the big catch of fish story. Remember the first time Jesus filled the nets? Peter didn't feel worthy (Luke 5:8). Now Peter knew that Jesus loved him no matter what, and he swam to Him with all his might. Thank Jesus for loving you SO MUCH.

Older Kids: Read Luke 5:1–11 and John 21:1–19. The first time Jesus filled the nets Peter felt sinful and unworthy. The second time Peter forgot everything and headed for Jesus. What about Peter had changed? Just this—he had learned how much Jesus loved him. Thank the Father and the Son for their grace, forgiveness, patience, and love toward you.

DAY 5: FORTY DAYS

Read: Acts 1:1–5

Quick Start

Can you imagine Jesus appearing to you? What would you talk about?

Quest

After Christ's resurrection from the dead, He showed Himself to more than five hundred people (1 Cor. 15:3–7) over a period of forty days (Acts 1:3). The Bible says "by many proofs" or very convincing ways Jesus showed Himself to be very much alive prior to going up to heaven. He could have gone to Herod and Pilate or the unbelieving religious rulers, but He chose instead to show Himself to all those who already believed in Him. He wanted to strengthen their faith and show them that He truly is the Son of God. Hundreds of people got to see the risen Lord, and it was their testimony that would convince or silence everyone else. They would willingly take the message of Christ's death and resurrection right around the world and continue Christ's work—preaching the kingdom and helping the sick, oppressed, and needy. They did that because they were convinced that Jesus was the Messiah and were changed by Him. Even though Jesus has returned to heaven and remains unseen by the world, He still reveals Himself to His disciples, who believe, follow and obey Him, but in a different way; not in body but through His Spirit inside of us (John 14:19–25).

Quiet Family Prayer

When we respond to Jesus, trust and act on what we know, He helps us learn and understand more (Matt. 13:12). The closer we draw to Him and follow, the more He'll reveal Himself. Ask Jesus to strengthen you and help you respond, so you can experience Him more and more.

Quiet Times

Younger Kids: Read the story of Jesus blessing the children. Jesus told His disciples to let the kids come to Him. Jesus loves you and wants you to come to Him and be loved and blessed by Him. Go to Jesus in prayer and ask Him to bless you.

Older Kids: Read, think about, and talk to God about every verse in John 14:19–25. Read it again and trust Jesus to help you understand. God told Joshua to "meditate" on His Word—that means to really think about it, pray about it, and to think about what it means and how to live it.

DAY 6: SOLDIERS BRIBED

Read: Matthew 27:62–28:15

Quick Start

Has anyone ever tried to tell you a lie that couldn't have been true because it made no sense?

Quest

You would think that liars would try and make their lies believable—apparently not. First of all, Roman guards weren't allowed to sleep on duty and these individuals were guarding a tomb in the night. So they would absolutely not have slept. Also a large heavy stone covered the tomb; even if they had fallen asleep, how is it that the moving of this massive stone didn't wake them up? And if they were all asleep, how did they know that it was Jesus' disciples that took the body? And if authorities knew who took the body, why was no one arrested and why wasn't the body ever recovered? Also since Roman guards who failed in their duty were severely punished or even killed; why were these ones not disciplined at all? The lie made no sense! However, the real proof that the guards lied, is that more than five hundred people saw Jesus alive and their lives were changed. Also most of the disciples (who supposedly stole the body) were martyred for their faith—would they have died if they'd known that Jesus hadn't risen? No, the disciples were killed for Jesus because they knew that Jesus died and rose again for them.

Quiet Family Prayer

Jesus called the devil the father of liars (John 8:44–47). Liars need to lie and believe lies because they don't want to believe the truth. Believers believe God's Word because we want to know the truth. Ask God to keep on teaching you truth.

Quiet Times

Younger Kids: Read Matthew 28:1–4 and 18:10. Thank God that just like angels watched over Jesus, they watch over you.

Older Kids: Read Matthew 26:51–54 and 28:1–4. Jesus said He could ask God for angels to stop the guards from arresting Him, but He didn't because He was willingly doing God's will. He proved it, when guards tried to stop Him from coming out of the tomb. Thank God for His angels who also work on your behalf (Heb. 1:14).

DAY 1: PARENT CONNECTION

THIS WEEK'S TOPIC: PENTECOST AND THE CHURCH

This week we'll look at the Great Commission and learn about our responsibility to share God's love. We'll look at the Ascension and talk about how Jesus is both with us and in heaven. We'll read about Pentecost and learn that the Holy Spirit reveals Jesus to us, transforms us into Christ's image and empowers us to carry on Christ's ministry. We'll discuss the incredible change the Spirit made in Peter and finally talk about the endless resources that we have for living and doing God's will because the Holy Spirit is in us.

Tips

The ministry of the Holy Spirit is incredibly important to our growth and walk as Christians. He is God's presence and power with us and in us and our ever-present help in everything as we live our lives here. He enables us to walk with Jesus and learn from Him. He transforms us into Christ's image and He gives us the boldness, wisdom, leading, and power we need to reach the lost. However, if we (and our children) are not aware of how He works, what He does and how He so desires to fill us and work in and through us, we (and our children) will end up walking through life without accessing His wealth of help and resources. In the Old Testament the Holy Spirit was only available for God's great messengers. Today, thanks to Christ's work, He has been freely poured into every Christian (Acts 2:17–18). And there is no kid-size version either; there is only one Holy Spirit and He's in our children ready and eager to start working. It's important that are children are not told so little about the Holy Spirit that they're left thinking that He's an eternal cosmic babysitter who's just there to prod their consciences. Take time this week to read ahead and pray. Take extra time in your family's devotions and in your discussions around the house to go deeper with your kids—helping them begin to understand the amazing resources available in the Holy Spirit. Remember as you talk and teach that we did not receive Christ by works, but by faith in God's grace, and it's the same with the Holy Spirit (Gal. 3:2–5). He is ready now to do for you and your kids all He was sent to do—not because you deserve it but because Christ paid the price for you to be redeemed and to receive His Spirit.

Day 2: The Great Commission

Read: Matthew 28:18–20; Mark 16:15–18; Acts 1:4–8

Quick Start

What is the best news you have ever received?

Quest

These verses contain Christ's last words and what He asked His followers to be doing until He comes back; to carry out the mission that He had started—to share the good news with everyone in the world. This seems like a huge task, but if one person tells another person, then both of them tell another person and so on, after twenty times, more than a million people will be told. The best way for someone to come to know Christ is to be introduced to Him by a friend. Jesus told us to "go into all the world and make disciples"! If we can't go to other countries, we can help those who can with prayer and support. However, we live in a part of the world and it is our responsibility to obey Jesus and share the Gospel with those around us. Nothing is more rewarding than helping someone you know meet Jesus and receive eternal life—what's more important than that. God has placed people in your life who need to hear the Good News. Tell them.

Quiet Family Prayer

Sometimes we pray for the salvation of people we know and God sends someone else to speak to them. Sometimes God sends us to speak with a person someone else is praying for. Pray for the people you know who need Jesus and that God will help you talk with others about Jesus.

Quiet Times

Younger Kids: Read the story about the boy helping Jesus with the fishes and loaves. You can help Jesus by telling others how much He loves them. Ask God to help you do that.

Older Kids: Read 1 Peter 3:13–16. Peter gave us tips about sharing our faith with others. First, be good; people should see the love you have for God, them, and others in your behavior. Next, honor the Lord; don't push, but also don't hide who you are and what you believe. Finally, be ready: learn Scriptures about salvation and answers to questions people ask. Be ready to talk about your own relationship with God and know that the Spirit will give you the right words. Then answer gently and well when someone asks. Ask God to help you share your faith.

DAY 3: THE ASCENSION

Read: Luke 24:44–52; Acts 1:9–11

Quick Start

Have you ever watched a helium balloon fly off into the sky until it disappeared?

Quest

Elijah was taken up to heaven in a fiery chariot (2 Kings 2:11) and God took Enoch before he died (Gen. 5:21–24), but Jesus actually died, was buried, resurrected, and then taken to heaven. It was important that Jesus didn't just disappear. His disciples needed to see Him transported up to heaven to be with the Father, where He rightfully belonged and from where He would return one day. Jesus said, "If I go away and prepare a place for you, I will come back and receive you to Myself, so that where I am you may be also" (John 14:3). One day Christ will again appear in the sky, not meek and mild, but mighty and powerful, and we will be changed to be like Him and we will be with Him and the Father forever. In the mean time we need to know that Jesus will never die again and that He'll always both be with us and with the Father; He is both God the Son and our Lord and Savior forever. He will always be in us teaching, guiding, and transforming us, and He'll always be one with the Father and stand before Him as our Savior (Rom. 8:34; Heb. 7:25). While we wait for His return and the final part of our transformation, we are to learn from and follow Him and be transformed by His presence in our hearts (2 Cor. 3:18).

Quiet Family Prayer

Jesus has made an eternal commitment to us: He'll always be with us as our Teacher, Lord, and Savior. Thank Him for His amazing love and indescribable eternal commitment.

Quiet Times

Younger Kids: Read the story of Jesus' returning to heaven. Jesus will come back to the earth one day as King of all—but He's also already with us, because we've already made Him our King. Thank Jesus for being your loving King.

Older Kids: Read 1 Corinthians 15:35–49 and Philippians 3:20–21. After His resurrection Jesus had a supernatural, spiritual body. When He comes back, all of His children will be given amazing resurrected bodies like His. Thank Jesus for the amazing eternity He has planned for us.

DAY 4: PENTECOST

Read: Acts 2:1–18

Quick Start

Have you ever been completely amazed by a magic trick?

Quest

Pentecost means "fiftieth" and was first established in Exodus as a celebration that marked the end of the grain harvest. It was when people brought to God an offering of the first fruits of their harvest. Jesus had told His followers to wait in Jerusalem for the Father's promise, the Holy Spirit, who would give them power to be His witnesses (Acts 1:4, 8) to the nations. They waited and on the day of Pentecost the sound of a roaring windstorm filled the room and God poured out His promised Spirit upon Christ's followers (120 men, women, and children). The Spirit of God had previously only empowered, inspired, and enabled God's special chosen leaders to accomplish great feats—people like Moses, Samson, King David, Elijah, and Daniel. But now, because of what Jesus did, the Spirit was given to every believer. Now each Christian would be able to have God's power, wisdom, strength, and truth flow through them. When the Holy Spirit was poured out, Jesus began bringing in the first fruits of God's harvest (James 1:18) among the nations; and 3,000 people came into the kingdom that day.

Quiet Family Prayer

The Holy Spirit is in you. His job is to reveal Jesus to you, transform you into Christ's image and to empower you to carry on Christ's ministry. Thank the Holy Spirit for doing His work and ask God to help you cooperate with His Spirit's work in and through you.

Quiet Times

Younger Kids: Read the story of Pentecost. Children were filled with God's Spirit that day. They sensed God's presence in them and saw God do amazing things. Let God know that you want to experience His Spirit working in you and through you.

Older Kids: Read Acts 1:16–18 again. Joel and Peter weren't trying to be specific about who would experience what. The Jews knew that the Holy Spirit was reserved for God's great messengers. But God showed Joel that one day the Spirit would come on everyone, even kids, elderly people, and servants, so that everyone could experience the Holy Spirit and be used by God in amazing ways. Ask God to use you and to help you experience the Holy Spirit.

DAY 5: PETER'S CHANGE AND SERMON

Read: Acts 2:14–39

Quick Start

Have you ever tried to do something difficult and surprised yourself by getting it right?

Quest

Peter had not gone to Speaker College; he was an ordinary fisherman. But when God's Spirit filled him that day, and he addressed the massive crowd, every fear and inability left him. When he was finished speaking; more than 3,000 people responded. Peter probably had no idea that he'd be preaching that day and likely wasn't prepared. Maybe he remembered what Jesus had once said, "Whenever they bring you before synagogues and rulers and authorities, don't worry about how you should defend yourselves or what you should say. For the Holy Spirit will teach you at that very hour what must be said" (Luke 12:11–12). Peter simply allowed the Holy Spirit to fill him and speak through him. God isn't concerned about what you can or can't do; He's interested in what you're willing to let Him do through you, by His Spirit. When God wants to use us, we shouldn't think about why we are inadequate or unable. We need to simply say, "Yes, Lord," and ask Him for His Spirit's help. God is able, and He will accomplish His will through us.

Quiet Family Prayer

The Peter we read about in the Bible before Pentecost and the Peter we read about after Pentecost seem like two different people. God's Spirit is in you to make a difference in your life—talk to God about His Holy Spirit.

Quiet Times

Younger Kids: Read Luke 11:11–13 with your parent; we can ask God to help us know and experience His Holy Spirit more and more. Go ahead and ask God for this and thank Him for the Holy Spirit.

Older Kids: Read Acts 2:4; 4:8, 31; and Ephesians 5:18. As Christians we have the Holy Spirit living inside us but we can be "filled" with the Spirit often. That's when He seems to get bigger inside of us, in the sense of us experiencing Him moving in us and through us—it's amazing. Paul instructs us to seek this experience and the influence of the Spirit instead of the negative influences of substance abuse. Ask the Spirit to fill you now and often and spend some time praising God (Eph. 5:19–20).

DAY 6: THE HOLY SPIRIT

Read: John 14:15–25; 15:26–27; 16:5–15 and Acts 1:8

Quick Start

If you were caught in a fight, who is the one person you would want with you by your side?

Quest

Jesus promised that He would always be with us, as our Master and Teacher, and He does that through the Holy Spirit in us (John 14:17–18). But He also called the Holy Spirit "another" Helper and talked about the things He'd help us with. After the Spirit of God was sent, He began to do all the things Christ said He would do: He empowered the believers to speak the Good News with boldness (Act 4:31), He enabled them to live victorious Christian lives (Act 6:3). He led them in all kinds of wonderful ways and even gave directions on how to run the Church (Act 13:2) and much more. God's people soon learned how to depend on the Spirit for guidance and direction, for wisdom and discernment, and for power to preach and demonstrate God's kingdom. The Christian cannot live a life that is pleasing to the Lord and minister to others without the help of the Spirit. We cannot know God's will for our lives, understand the Bible, or even pray effectively without the Spirit's help. There is no closer Friend or greater Teacher than Jesus and no better Counselor, Helper, Encourager, and Guide than the Spirit of God—and they're both with you and eager to help.

Quiet Family Prayer

Thank God for the endless resources that you have for living and doing His will because Jesus is with you and the Holy Spirit is in you. And ask Him for any help that you need right now.

Quiet Times

Younger Kids: Read Acts 2:38–39 with your parent. There's just one powerful, loving, helpful Holy Spirit and He's in you. Ask the Holy Spirit to help you with everything.

Older Kids: Read Acts 6:3–10; 8:26–40. The whole book of Acts is an amazing record of how God empowered ordinary people who became disciples of Christ with His Holy Spirit and did amazing things through them. Ask God to help you be like Stephen and Philip, full of faith and of the Holy Spirit.

DAY 1: PARENT CONNECTION

THIS WEEK'S TOPIC: THE GOSPEL

Creation, the fall, God's promise, Jesus' birth, death, resurrection and ascension, the promise fulfilled, redemption, rebirth, the gift of the Holy Spirit, our walk as Christ's disciples and life eternal—this week we sum up, start to explain and call your family to accept and walk in the power of the gospel. We'll learn that it was God's plan from the beginning to send Jesus to rescue us from the devil and bring us back to Himself. We'll examine why it had to be Jesus and only Jesus and learn that although salvation is free, we are also accepting God as our Father and Jesus as our Lord. When we do He makes us new and calls us to walk as Jesus walked and walk with Him.

Tips

If one or more of your children have never asked Jesus into their life, then this week may be their time. If they have all taken that step, then you'll be able to help them better understand their salvation. If you trust that your little ones will put their heart in His hands soon, then let us help you with a few practical tips. The first step is painfully obvious but let's cover it anyway. Start by doing the single most powerful thing parents can do for their children—pray for them, individually and everyday. Next, don't rush or push. The Bible says that Jesus is the one who draws people and that even though we help by planting and watering seeds it's God who causes the seeds to grow (John 12:32; 1 Cor. 3:7). We're not saying to put it off (2 Cor. 6:2), but to rest in Him, knowing He'll guide you and bring you and them to the right moment. Patiently, plant and water seed; present the material this week, answer questions, speak about your own experience and when you feel the time is right, ask them if they'd like to pray with you. When they're ready keep the prayer simple—the right words don't save people, God sees the heart and saves people. Rejoice with them, maybe even have a little birthday party—their salvation should be a happy, memorable occasion. Everything else you need, explanations, discussion starters, teaching, Bible verses, etc., are all provided this week.

252 DAY 2: CREATION, FALL, AND THE PROMISE

Read: John 3:16

Quick Start

What is your favorite Bible verse? Why is it your favorite?

Quest

When God created everything He declared it was good. Adam and Eve were a part of His perfect creation, but they chose not to trust Him, but to do things their own way. God had warned them that the penalty of sin was death and that day they were separated from God and died on the inside. But God had a plan. He promised them that He'd send someone to defeat the enemy that deceived them (Gen. 3:15). God worked through many people to bring His plan about and all along the way He told them about the promised Special One that He was sending. God told Abraham that one of His descendants would bless all nations. God told Moses that He'd send a great Prophet. God told David that He'd send a special King. He told His prophets that He'd send a sinless sacrifice for the sins of mankind (Isa. 53:6). Jesus, God's own Son, was the Promised One. Because of Adam and Eve's sin, everyone was born separated from God and dead inside. When Jesus, who had no sin, died on the cross, He bore everyone's sin. Now when we believe in Jesus, we are forgiven and we get born-again on the inside and become God's children again. God's plan all along was to send Jesus to rescue us from the devil and bring us back to Himself. He promised it and He did it.

Quiet Family Prayer

Now we can have the relationship with God that He intended from the beginning (John 1:12). Thank God together for His amazing plan and our awesome Savior!

Quiet Times

Younger Kids: Read the story of Jesus and Nicodemus. Thank Jesus that He died so that you could be born again and become God's child.

Older Kids: Read Romans 5:12–19 and 1 Corinthians 15:22. It doesn't seem fair that everyone became sinners because of what Adam and Eve did, until you realize that we all get to be forgiven and made right with God because of what Jesus did—fair's fair! Thank God for His incredible gift!

DAY 3: WHY JESUS NEEDED TO DIE

Read: 1 Peter 3:18; 2 Corinthians 5:16–21

Quick Start

Can you explain what a "sacrifice fly" is in baseball?

Quest

Why did Jesus need to die on the cross? Romans 6:23 tells us that the "wages of sin is death." When people sin they are under a death penalty, which means when they die they will be eternally separated from God. The only way for us to avoid the penalty of eternal death is if someone dies in our place. However, no one, no matter how great could die for anyone else's sins because they had to die for their own! You see, because we are all children of Adam and Eve we were all born with sin and separated from God. But Jesus was God's Son—God planted Him by a miracle in Mary's womb. He was born without sin and He lived His whole life without sinning once! So He was the only one who could die for the sins of others. Jesus loved us so much that He came here and willingly laid down His life as a sacrifice for our sins so that we would have everlasting life with Him in heaven. That's Good News! Many people don't know that God loves them and wants to bless them, but that's what Jesus came to show us and that's why Jesus asks us to tell others this Good News.

Quiet Family Prayer

A good parent always takes responsibility for his or her own children. God didn't look for someone else to pay the price for our sins—the Father, Son, and Holy Spirit agreed right from the start (Gen. 1:26; 3:15) to rescue us. Thank God for His awesome rescue plan.

Quiet Times

Younger Kids: Read the story of Zacchaeus. When Zacchaeus met Jesus he was changed and everyone could see he was acting differently. Thank God for making you new on the inside and ask Him to help you act new on the outside.

Older Kids: Read Romans 6. Because of Adam we were all born sinners and before we became Christians, we automatically acted like it. Now through Christ we are righteous and with the help of God's Spirit we're to act like it. Ask God to help you grow in and act like what Jesus made you, righteous.

DAY 4: BECOMING A CHILD OF GOD

Read: John 1:12; 3:3, 16; Romans 10:9–10

Quick Start

Have you ever joined a team? What were the requirements?

Quest

When you join God's team, there are no tryouts or applications to fill out. Anyone who wants can become a member of God's family and enter into His kingdom—God loves the whole world and sent Jesus for everyone (John 3:16). No one is left out! Jesus died for you, and salvation is free, you just need to ask God to forgive you because of what Jesus did—it's simple. However, we need to remember that we're becoming children of God and disciples of Jesus; that means trusting them and letting them love us, teach us, guide us and direct us into His best plan for our lives. Eve talked with the snake and made a choice not to trust God. When we accept Jesus, we do the opposite; we decide to trust God's love, obey Him, put our lives in His hands and allow His Spirit to work in us to transform us. Also, each member who joins a team must work together with their teammates. As members of God's team, with Jesus as our coach and the Spirit as our trainer, we all work together with God's help to accomplish all that He has planned. It's an exciting life with purpose and it includes having Jesus with you, God on your side, and eternal life in heaven.

Quiet Family Prayer

If you've never asked before: ask God to forgive you, Jesus to come and disciple you and the Holy Spirit to fill you and help you. If you have, thank the Father, Son, and Holy Spirit for loving you and for living in you!

Quiet Times

Younger Kids: Read the story of Jesus calling His disciples to follow Him (Matt. 4). When you accept Jesus you become His disciple and He loves and teaches you through His Spirit. Ask Jesus to make you His disciple today.

Older Kids: Read Romans 8:1–17. When you accept Jesus, His Spirit comes inside you, makes you new and begins to help you live a new life. You'll notice that even your desires change—that's God's Spirit at work. When you follow and cooperate with Him, the wonderful changes keep happening. Ask God to help you cooperate.

Day 5: All Things New

Read: 2 Corinthians 5:14–21; Ephesians 4:20–24

Quick Start

How do you feel when you get to wear brand new clothes that you really like?

Quest

When we receive Jesus, we are actually changed on the inside—made into completely new creations in a miraculous moment. First God completely cleanses us from all sin. Then He gives us a new spirit that's alive and joined completely with Him (1 Cor. 6:17). Next He takes our old hard heart that doesn't want to listen and replaces it with a brand new soft one that desires God and wants to do what's right. Then once we're all new inside, God's Spirit comes in to connect us with and help us know God our Father, help us walk with Jesus, and to help us do God's will (Ezek. 36:25–27; Jer. 31:33–34; 2 Pet. 1:3–4). But that's just the start of our journey! Brand new babies need to learn and eat and grow. It's the same thing with new spiritual babies and God wants us to get excited about and cooperate with the process; learning His Word, spending time with Him and His people, and changing the way we think, talk and behave. He made us new so we can grow up and become like Jesus.

Quiet Family Prayer

Even if you don't see it or feel it sometimes, God made you awesome on the inside. Ask God to help you grow into the amazing new creation that He's made you to be.

Quiet Times

Younger Kids: Read 2 Corinthians 5:17. When a caterpillar turns into a butterfly, it is completely transformed into something new. Thank God that you are changed on the inside like a beautiful butterfly.

Older Kids: Read Romans 12:1–2 and Ephesians 4:20–24. Part of being a disciple of Christ is renewing your mind or learning to think God's way. We do this by learning His Word and choosing (with His help) to believe it and think it. For example, if we have unkind thoughts towards someone, knowing we are to love, we push away the unkind thought and choose to be kind towards them with our thoughts. Ask God to help you with the process of renewing your mind.

DAY 6: FOLLOWING JESUS

Read: John 8:12; 10:1–18; 1 Peter 2:21

Quick Start

Who in your family do you resemble the most?

Quest

Following Jesus today is part of our discipleship process and we follow Him in two different ways. First we must learn to be like Him in our character (Phil. 2:5) and in the way we live our lives, to "walk as He walked" (1 John 2:6), to speak to others like He spoke to others, to depend on God's guidance as He did, and to serve God just like Jesus did. We can learn a lot by reading about what Jesus did and taught and by following His example and commands. When we do we become an example to others. Paul said, "Be imitators of me, as I also am of Christ" (1 Cor. 11:1). Jesus was a different person, with a different task and different circumstances than us; so the second way of following Him is more personal; it's walking with Him day-by-day as His disciple (John 14:12–21). He said He'd always be with us; He's our good Shepherd and we're His sheep. He loves, teaches, and guides us like He did Peter, James, and John but now from the inside by His Spirit. We can talk to Him, listen, learn, follow, and obey. Our goal is to be Christlike and we do that by walking as He walked and walking with Him.

Quiet Family Prayer

Jesus is right there with you wanting to help you learn and grow—talk to Him about being like Him.

Quiet Times

Younger Kids: Think about 2 Corinthians 3:18. Jesus was the most wonderful and amazing person who ever lived and God is helping us be just like Him—that's amazing! Thank God for transforming you more and more to be like Jesus.

Older Kids: Read John 15:1–17 and read verse 7 again. If we remain in Jesus (or walk with Him, obeying Him and relying on His complete work, His help, teaching, direction and His Spirit within us) AND His words reside in us (we know, believe and live God's Word), then our prayer life will work perfectly. Ask God to help you walk this closely with Jesus.

DAY 1: PARENT CONNECTION

THIS WEEK'S TOPIC: THE CHURCH

This week we take a look at the beginning of the New Testament church. On Pentecost 3,000 people were added to the church. At the Gate Beautiful Peter and John stirred things up by getting a man who had been born lame completely healed and the church swelled to around 10,000. Things were changing and the huge body of new believers needed to be taught and organized—Jesus told them to make disciples not just converts. The church and its community structure were being birthed.

Tips

We need to teach our kids about the church, it's importance, and their role in it so when they leave home they don't leave the church. Some say that the only Scripture on church attendance is Hebrews 10:25 and that we can obey this Scripture in different ways, but that's not true. The New Testament is mostly made up of letters written to churches and/or its leaders in order to help them lead their congregations. They include instructions on most every aspect of the local church; leadership, governance, discipline, structure, correct teaching, ordinances, individual involvement, even how to run a worship service! To ignore the importance of the local church is to ignore the purpose and content of the New Testament. Jesus talked about building His church (Matt. 16:18) and He's still doing it. Yes, the body of Christ is the people not the buildings but communities need structure and the Holy Spirit filled the New Testament with instructions to help us with that. Those instructions show us that the purpose of the church is for us to be taught and raised up as disciples of Christ, to encourage and be encouraged in our spiritual growth, and to get involved and support one another in the Great Commission. Yes, standing in a parking spot doesn't make you a car anymore than sitting in a pew makes you a Christian. The number one way you can teach your children the importance of church is to make it a priority: attend regularly, get involved consistently with your time, talents, and resources, learn and grow in your place in the body and support, submit to, and pray for the leadership. Your local church is God's idea, and if you and your family are following Jesus it's not an option, it's a necessity.

DAY 2: HEALING AT THE GATE

Read: Acts 3:1–16; 4:1–22

Quick Start

What is the best gift you have ever given someone?

Quest

Many people thought God had cursed this man because he was born lame. He had never played ball with his school friends and he never chased after other children playing tag because he couldn't walk, run, jump, or skip. All he knew how to do was sit by a gate of the temple and beg for money. For forty years that was what he did each day. Some would drop a few coins into his basket, others walked on by without even looking at him. This day God had a plan to change his life forever. Peter and John had no money to give the beggar but they had something far more precious. In the name of Jesus, they gave him full use of his legs for the first time in his life. Immediately he jumped and leaped, skipped, ran, and walked all for the first time. Jesus said that Satan comes to steal, kill, and destroy, but that He came that we might have life and have it abundantly (John 10:10). God didn't curse this man and Jesus wanted to give him his life back and more than that, Jesus wanted him to have His forgiveness, salvation, and eternal life. We may not always have money or time to spare, but we always have Jesus to share with people. Many people do not even know how much they need Jesus in their life or how much He loves them until someone shares Him with them.

Quiet Family Prayer

Peter and John showed us one way we can share Jesus with people. We can pray for them and when they see God answers they'll be ready to hear more about Jesus. Ask God to give you boldness and faith to pray for others.

Quiet Times

Younger Kids: Read about the lame man getting healed again. With Jesus inside us, our prayers for others are powerful. Pray for people you know that could use God's help.

Older Kids: Read James 5:13–18. James said that our prayers (we are righteous in Jesus) are powerful and that we are to pray for others. Ask Jesus to teach you to pray and to give you more boldness in praying for others.

Day 3: Prayer for Boldness

Read: Acts 4:23–31

Quick Start

Can you think of a time when you were afraid or worried about something you had to do?

Quest

The religious rulers were amazed at the boldness of Peter and John, particularly because they were untrained and uneducated men (Acts 4:13). But they decided their boldness came from being with Jesus, another man who absolutely frustrated them because He was also fearless before them. Jesus inspired Peter and John and now they had the Spirit in them to give them courage and the right message to say each time. So they prayed to God for continued boldness to share the Good News in spite of the threats and opposition they faced. God granted them their request (v. 33) and accompanied His answer with a small earthquake. They were all filled with the Spirit of God and continued to speak the word of God with boldness. Jesus chose ordinary people to be His disciples and now God was using them to do extraordinary things. It doesn't matter who you are, how educated you are or aren't, or how old you are; if you believe in Jesus and are willing to obey Him and tell others about Him, then He'll help you and use you and do amazing things.

Quiet Family Prayer

Pray the house-shaking prayer—that God would help you speak His Word and share Jesus with boldness and power. Pray this prayer now and whenever you need it.

Quiet Times

Younger Kids: Read the story of Jesus walking on the water (Matt. 14). When Peter got afraid he sunk. In today's story Peter was filled with God's Spirit and there was no stopping him. Thank God for giving you His Spirit and ask Him to give you boldness whenever you need it.

Older Kids: Read Ephesians 6:19 and Colossians 4:2–6. In these verses Paul asked the believers to pray three things for him. Pray these things for the people you know who share the gospel and for yourself: that God would open doors of opportunity to share the gospel with others; that God would give the boldness needed and also the right words to speak.

DAY 4: THE CHURCH

Read: John 13:33–35; 17:20–26

Quick Start

What did you learn at church last week?

Quest

In John 16:17 Jesus talked about building His Church. Later, He prayed for all those who would believe in Him—that they would all be one. At the time His disciples probably had no idea what He was talking about—but Jesus knew God's plan. Today we know that Jesus' Church is all of those who have believed on Him from everywhere around the world from all time. The Bible also calls that group the body of Christ (1 Cor. 12:27). Local churches are small parts of the body of Christ, where Christians who live close by can meet together to love and support one another, encourage growth in Christ, and together help fulfill the Great Commission. The book of Acts shows how this all began. Believers were added to the church in Jerusalem and were taught and led by the apostles. As the gospel spread, groups of new believers were started in each city and leaders were taught, trained, and appointed for each church so that they could teach the others how to follow and serve Jesus. Local Christian churches today are part of Christ's church and it's God's plan that we attend (Heb. 10:25). We should take part, love and support one another in Christian growth, and help each other fulfill the Great Commission.

Quiet Family Prayer

Playing sports is boring if you're always on the bench. Likewise, church is exciting only when you get involved. Pray for your church and about ways you can all be involved.

Quiet Times

Younger Kids: Choose a favorite Bible story to read tonight. Pray for your teachers and friends at church and ask God to help you be more attentive and helpful.

Older Kids: Read 1 Peter 2:1–10, 17. God loves us as individuals but He's also called us to be part of the body of Christ. We cannot fulfill all of what God has for us without "loving the brotherhood" and letting God build us together with them into a spiritual house. Ask God to build you into His Church so that you can grow and work with others to see God's will done.

DAY 5: LEADERS AND HELPERS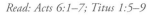

Read: Acts 6:1–7; Titus 1:5–9

Quick Start

What characteristics or qualities do you think a spiritual (church) leader should have?

Quest

The new church leaders were to be "men of good reputation, full of the Spirit and wisdom." Acts describes Stephen as "full of faith and the Holy Spirit" and "full of grace and power" and says that he "was performing great wonders and signs among the people." Philip also spoke powerfully and performed miraculous signs (Acts 8:6–7). If the rest of the men they chose as deacons that day were like Stephen and Philip, the church was very blessed. God still uses leaders in His Church and He wants them to be of good reputation and full of the Spirit and wisdom—only those who follow Christ can help others do the same. Pray for the leaders in your church to be godly and wise and to seek God's presence in their life. Seek to be like this in your own life so that one day you might also be chosen to be a leader among God's people. You may not see yourself as a pastor, but there are many other ways to help lead in the Church. Humble yourself before God and serve Him, and He will put you where you can serve Him the most effectively.

Quiet Family Prayer

Read Hebrews 13:17. We are to listen to our spiritual leaders and let them teach and help us become mature in Christ. Ask God to help you have a humble and teachable heart with your church leaders and teachers—pray for them as well.

Quiet Times

Younger Kids: Read a Bible story or verse you learned at church. Going to church can be fun but God also wants you to learn. Pray for your church teacher and ask God to help you pay attention and learn.

Older Kids: Read Galatians 6:6 and Hebrews 13:7, 17. We are to submit to and obey our spiritual leaders, support them and follow their example. We cannot possibly know them, or be known by them, well enough to be obedient to God in this unless we attend faithfully, get involved and let them know that we're interested in learning and growing. Ask God to help you become a faithful part of the body.

DAY 6: STEPHEN

Read: Acts 6:3–15; 7:51–60; 8:1–2

Quick Start

Have you ever been made fun of for being a Christian or for doing what's right?

Quest

Stephen was not one of the twelve disciples. He was just a strong believer who wanted to tell others about Jesus. The Bible describes him as being an honest man, full of the Holy Spirit, wisdom, faith, and power. He did great wonders among the people. Stephen was one of the first ordinary Christians that God used in a mighty way. He made such a big difference that he couldn't be ignored; people argued with him, lied about him, threatened him, and then stirred up a mob to kill him. But the Bible says that God reward martyrs and even Stephen's death was an encouragement for the church to scatter throughout the world as Christ had commanded them. When this persecution against Christians began, many believers decided to leave Jerusalem and they scattered all throughout the region taking the gospel with them. The killing of Stephen made Christ's followers even more passionate and now they were sharing the gospel and the church grew bigger and stronger because of it. These traveling Christians became the first missionaries to leave their homes and bring the Good News to those who had not yet heard it. Christ's Great Commission (Matt. 28:18–20) was starting to be fulfilled.

Quiet Family Prayer

Jesus knows how it feels to be persecuted and He'll always be with us in a very real way and help us even if we're just being mocked or teased. Ask God to help you never fear.

Quiet Times

Younger Kids: Read the story of Samson. The Bible says that Samson killed more Philistines in his death than he did in his life. Stephen caused more people to become Christians by giving up his life and he got to go to heaven.

Older Kids: Read Acts 7:54–60. Notice that Stephen saw the heaven open before he was attacked. Jesus and the Father knew what was about to happen and they showed Stephen personally. They stayed with him and received him themselves. Stephen fell asleep—God just took him. Jesus knows how it feels. Ask God to help you never fear persecution.

DAY 1: PARENT CONNECTION

THIS WEEK'S TOPIC: THE CHURCH

God told Abraham that He would bless all nations through one of His descendants. He chose Abraham, Isaac, Jacob, and the Jews for this purpose—to be His coworkers and to set things up so that Christ could come, walk a sinless life by keeping God's law, and go on to pay the price to redeem the nations. This week we see the church move beyond the Jewish nation and start blessing all cultures and countries.

Tips

The vast majority of kids spend most of their school years in the same school system with many of the same kids—and it becomes a large part of their personal community. Unfortunately, not as many kids spend the same kind of time in the same church community or get as involved. But God's community purpose for the church is for its members to be strengthened and supported in their faith and calling, by people who love and know them, and are loved and known by them—and that kind of community, takes time, attendance, and effort to cultivate. God is clear that our primary community and fellowship is not to be with the world but with believers (2 Cor. 6:14–18). How can we expect our kids to grow in their faith if their primary community isn't one of faith? Let's look at this practically. We are all to listen to and receive from our spiritual leaders and follow their example (Gal. 6:6; Heb. 13:17). Teens are to do this with their youth leaders and those setting an example in their church. There comes a time in every young teen's life when they naturally start looking outward to the community around them for support and answers. God designed the church community to play this role. However, if your kids are not established and involved in a church, they cannot possibly know the people there, (or be known by them) well enough for this to work and they'll look elsewhere. If you haven't started to establish this kind of community involvement at your church, pray and start this week. Don't go from 0 to 60 in a week—slowly but surely increase your family's involvement, stay longer after church, encourage friendships, attend special events, etc. You'll be very thankful that you did when you see your teens supported by a godly community when they're making important life choices.

DAY 2: PHILIP

Read: Acts 8:4–40

Quick Start

How fun would it be to have a "transporter beam" that could send you anywhere you wanted to go?

Quest

Philip is one of those people like his friend Stephen, an ordinary believer who just wanted to serve the Lord however he could. Whenever he preached about Jesus, God performed signs and great miracles (Mark 16:20). People were amazed and responded. For a long time Simon the Sorcerer had tricked the people into thinking he was powerful, but when he saw what Philip could do, he was amazed because there were no tricks. No one had ever seen the kind of power Philip had before and many people believed in Jesus. After Philip baptized the man from Ethiopia, all of a sudden he found himself in Azotus (modern Ashdod) about forty miles away! Some people wonder what really happened but the language implies that Philip disappeared and was supernaturally transported to Azotus. In two short stories about Philip we see him being spoken to by God's Spirit, talked to by an angel, casting out demons, getting the paralyzed and lame healed, performed signs and great miracles, preaching the gospel, teaching God's Word, baptizing a new believer and getting supernaturally transported by God's Spirit. Philip was a man led, controlled, and empowered by the Spirit of God, which should be the goal of every believer.

Quiet Family Prayer

The Bible says that we are the temple of the Holy Spirit (1 Cor. 6:19). He's there to connect us with, and to help us experience God. Ask God to help you experience Him through His Spirit more and more.

Quiet Times

Younger Kids: Read the story of Philip again. Philip wasn't a superhero—he was just a Christian who had a super God inside him. Thank God that you have His Spirit inside you.

Older Kids: Read 1 Corinthians 12:1–11, 27–31. Not everyone has the same calling and gift and not everyone has God's Spirit move through them in the same way. But God's Spirit will use everyone that yields to Him and desires it; in some way. Let God know that you'd like to be used to help others by His Spirit.

Read: Acts 9:1–9

Quick Start
What does it mean to have an "Aha!" moment?

Quest
Saul (his Hebrew name) or Paul was born in the wealthy city of Tarsus, the capital of Cilicia, a Roman province. Tarsus had a famous university, which Paul could have attended. His father was a strict Pharisee and a Roman citizen. Following in the footsteps of his father, Paul also became a Pharisee after learning the trade of tent-making. It seems his whole life had been focused on training, education, and preparation for serving God. The only problem was that he didn't know God. It wasn't until he came face-to-face with Jesus on the road to Damascus that Paul realized he had been going down the wrong road. In his heart he wanted to serve God, but he was doing it according to his own understanding. Paul would become one of the greatest missionaries ever and the one who God would use to write most of the letters found in the Bible. But it wasn't until Paul met Jesus and started to learn from Him and follow Him that he was able to truly serve God. He later said that he considered all his education and achievements before he met Jesus to be filth (Phil. 3:7–8). He had learned that the only thing that mattered was what Jesus did for Him; through Christ, he was forgiven and made righteous, was given God's Spirit, was made a disciple of Jesus and taught by Him and allowed to know and serve God, all by God's free gift.

Quiet Family Prayer
Before meeting Jesus, Paul was very sincere but he was very sincerely wrong. Ask God to help your confidence be in His free gift through Christ, Jesus with you and His Spirit in you.

Quiet Times
Younger Kids: Read the story of Jesus appearing to Saul (Acts 9). Ask God to open your heart and teach you through His Word and Jesus your teacher—so you can really know Him and His will for you.

Older Kids: Read Philippians 3:1–17. These verses contain Paul's heart; learn from Paul (v. 17) and pray for yourself and your relationship with God as you read.

DAY 4: SAUL AND ANANIAS

Read: Acts 9:10–25

Quick Start

Have you ever had a friend who cared enough to tell you the truth even if you didn't like hearing it?

Quest

Saul and Ananias couldn't have been more different from one another. Saul was full of hate and fury wanting to destroy Christians, Ananias was kind and godly and wanted to introduce more people to Jesus. In fact, Saul was probably going to Damascus to arrest Ananias and throw him and his family in prison. It took a lot of courage for Ananias to obey the Lord and go to Saul. But when God asks us to be a part of His plans even when we don't understand, we need to ask for boldness and go. It would have been understandable for Ananias to be nervous, but he obeyed and spoke to the most feared man among the Christian community. Saul had three days to think about his life and about what God was doing with him before his sight was returned. The day he met Ananias, Paul was able to see clearly again physically, but he was also able to see spiritually for the first time. It is always a wonderful feeling to help another person open their eyes to Jesus and become your brother or sister in Christ.

Quiet Family Prayer

This story is a good example of Jesus always being with us and sometimes in a very real way; He appeared to Paul and also spoke to Ananias in a vision. Thank Jesus for being with you and ask Him to use you to bring others to Him.

Quiet Times

Younger Kids: Read Matthew 28:20. Jesus is God and He can easily be with, teach and help every Christian everywhere all at the same time. Praise Jesus for His love and presence.

Older Kids: Read Acts 26. Paul used the story of what happened to him to tell others about Jesus. Ask God to give you the opportunity to tell others what Jesus has done for you and to help you tell it well every time. Also ask Him to continue to do good things in your life that you can tell others about.

DAY 5: PETER AND CORNELIUS' FAMILY

Read: Acts 10

Quick Start

Do you have any friends that come from other countries or cultures?

Quest

Jesus had another lesson He needed to teach Peter. This time Jesus came to him in a vision and explained to Peter that other people from different cultures and countries also needed to hear the Good News. At the same time, God sent an angel to Cornelius, a Roman commander, telling him to send for Peter. Cornelius sent his men 40 miles (63 km) form Caesarea to Joppa (modern Jaffa in Tel Aviv) where Peter was staying. God needed Peter to understand that God wanted the whole world to hear the Good News, not just his own people. Although Peter is not known for his missionary travels like Paul was, he needed to break out of his own prejudices and accept that God's message was for everyone, and that Gentiles (non-Jews) did not have to become Jews first in order to become Christians. They needed only to place their faith in the Son of God and live for Him to be acceptable to God. Sometimes we make becoming a Christian too complicated, when Jesus only asked for repentance and faith. As a child comes to a father, so we too can come to our Heavenly Father, whatever race we are, whatever place we are from—"For God so loved the world . . ." (John 3:16).

Quiet Family Prayer

Cornelius sought God and tried to please Him and God brought the gospel to him and his family. Ask God if He'd do the same for those in your life or community who have responded to God in their hearts (Rom. 2:14) but haven't received Jesus yet.

Quiet Times

Younger Kids: Read John 3:16. Can you say it from memory? Jesus died for everyone in the world—some just don't know it yet. Ask God to send people to tell them.

Older Kids: Read Acts 10 again. Can you imagine angel visits, visions, divine appointments between people who have never previously met and the Spirit of God showing up big time? God will do whatever it takes to get the gospel to someone who is seeking Him. Ask God to lead you to those who need to hear the gospel.

Day 6: The Gospel for Everyone

Read: Acts 11:1–24; Galatians 3:6–9

Quick Start

Can you guess which sport was invented in Canada, but is now popular around the world?

Quest

The Jewish people had lost track of something. When Adam and Eve sinned all of humankind was separated from God. God sent them out of the garden but He made a promise that He'd defeat Satan through one of Eve's offspring (Gen. 3:15). God loved Abraham and chose him to help with His plan. He told Abraham that He'd bless him and his descendants because He wanted to use them to bless all nations. God chose Abraham, Isaac, Jacob, and the Israelites to be His coworkers to help bring Jesus into the world so everyone could be with God again. The Jewish people forgot that and started to think that God only cared about them. God had called the Jews to be separate from the Gentiles not because he didn't love the Gentiles or have a plan for them but because it wasn't time to include them yet (Acts 14:16). Now that Jesus had come it was time for the Jewish people to complete the job God chose them to do—receive their Messiah and take Him to the rest of the world. It took a bit of convincing but the Lord got His disciples on track and they started to bless the nations with the gospel.

Quiet Family Prayer

We need to make sure we don't lose track of the same thing. God loves us but it's not just us He wants to bless. He loves the whole world and now that we know the Good News, He wants us to help spread it to others. Ask God to help you always remember this.

Quiet Times

Younger Kids: Read the story of God's promise to Abraham under the stars (Gen. 15). Thank God that He was calling Abraham to help bring Jesus into the world so we could be saved.

Older Kids: Read Galatians chapter 3. This idea is the key to understanding the Bible. God knew before He created anything that Jesus would have to come (1 Pet. 1:20) and that Christ's work would be the foundation on which humankind's eternity with Him would be built. So everything in the Bible points to Jesus. Ask Jesus to help you understand His amazing gospel.

DAY 1: PARENT CONNECTION

THIS WEEK'S TOPIC: PAUL'S MINISTRY

This week lessons from the life of Paul can probably be summed up best with some of the words that God had him write:

- "My speech and my proclamation were not with persuasive words of wisdom, but with a demonstration of the Spirit and power."
- "If I were trying to please people, I would not be a slave of Christ."
- "If God is for us, who can be against us?"
- "Imitate me as I also imitate Christ."
- "I am able to do all things through Him who strengthens me." (1 Cor. 2:4; Gal. 1:10c; Rom. 8:31; 1 Cor. 11:1; Phil. 4:13)

Tips

In Ephesians 6:1–3 Paul quotes the fifth commandment and its promise and thereby reminds us of how God wants us to motivate our children to obey Him. "Children obey your parents as you would the Lord, because this is right. Honor your father and mother, which is the first commandment with a promise, so that it might go well with you and that you may have a long life in the land."

Notice the promise. God is basically saying, "Hey kids, do things my way and your life will work better and be more blessed." God etched it in stone and let us know how to motivate children to follow Him—the same way He does. Here are a few tips to help: Don't just tell your kids about right behavior; tell them why it's best. For example, if you always tell the truth people will trust you. When people trust you, you gain friends and opportunities. When you lie the opposite happens. Bible stories are packed with this message—doing things God's way works and brings blessing. Next be careful not to threaten your kids with God, "He's watching you. He knows what you're doing!" God isn't watching them, He's with them, loving and helping them with joy, rewarding and blessing them as they respond to Him. It's God's kindness that leads us, and our children to Him (Rom. 2:4). God is love and He loves our children more than we can even imagine. He wants to reward them and do well for them, reinforcing everything you teach them about Him.

DAY 2: PAUL AND THE MAGICIAN

Read: Acts 13:4–12

Quick Start

What is the difference between a body builder and a boxer? (Answer: One has muscles for show; the other has muscles for action.)

Quest

The proconsul, Sergius Paulus, was an important person on the island of Cyprus. The Bible tells us that he was a wise and discerning man and that he wanted to hear what Paul and Barnabas had to say. When Elymus tried to prevent Sergius from believing the Gospel, Paul relied on God's power. In 1 Corinthians 2:4, Paul said, "My speech and my proclamation were not with persuasive words of wisdom, but with a demonstration of the Spirit and power." The sorcerer came face-to-face with the power of the Holy Spirit, and he was left as helpless as a child. Jesus said that He had "all authority on heaven and earth" (Matt. 28:18), and when Elymus faced Christ's servants, he faced God living in them as well. The devil wants us to feel weak by getting us to forget that we have God's Spirit in us because he loses when we remember. If there is anything that you are afraid of remember that you are never alone and that God is right there with you always, with ALL authority in heaven and on the earth!

Quiet Family Prayer

Do you remember someone else who was struck blind for being against Jesus? Paul knew that God could get Elymus's attention. Pray for people you know that are against the gospel and ask God to get their attention.

Quiet Times

Younger Kids: Read the story of Paul and the magician again. God loved Elymus and showed him that He was real. Pray for someone you know and ask God to show them that He's real.

Older Kids: Read Acts 13:4–12 and 1 John 4:16. When Paul blinded the magician, he was filled with the Spirit and doing and saying as God directed Him—it wasn't Paul's idea, it was God's. You never know what God will do when you start sharing the gospel, but you can always know that He's with you, He's working and He's greater than anything you may face. Ask God to help you experience Him more and more as you follow Him.

DAY 3: PEOPLE THINK PAUL IS HERMES

Read: Acts 14:8–23

Quick Start

Did you ever try to do something good for others that turned out just the opposite?

Quest

The only superheroes that the people of Lystra knew about were their made-up gods. So when Paul began performing miracles, they naturally assumed he and Silas were two of their gods. But their adversaries who had tracked them down quickly turned the crowds against Paul and Silas and the frenzied mob stoned Paul nearly to death. Some people think Paul died here and was raised from the dead, but even if he wasn't he was miraculously healed and got up and walked back into the city. It's a good thing they convinced the people Paul wasn't a god because they would have got the sacrifice out again when he walked back into the city. It had been a rollercoaster ride for Paul in Lystra but he knew that it's not our job to convert people. We are called to share the truth and make disciples of those who respond. Unfortunately, some people prefer the lies that they believe. We are to share Jesus and leave the results up to the Spirit of God who alone can change hearts. Paul risked his life to share the gospel, God looked after him and many received eternal life—it had been a good trip.

Quiet Family Prayer

Paul had to deal with those who refused to believe so he could reach those who would. Ask God to give you that same resolve.

Quiet Times

Younger Kids: Read the story of David and Goliath (1 Sam. 17). The people of Lystra didn't know what to do with Paul because they didn't know what they believed. Ask God to help make you strong in what you believe like David was.

Older Kids: Read Acts 14:8–23 and Galatians 1:10. The people of Lystra were pretty fickle! First Paul was someone to worship, then he was a rock target; ridiculous. But we can look like that as well, when we let our faith and behavior be affected by the people we're around. Ask God to help you be consistent in your walk with Christ.

Read: Acts 16:16–40

Quick Start

As you've become bigger and stronger, have you lost fears that you had when you were younger?

Quest

The Philippian jailer had probably heard that Paul and Silas told others about God's love and grace even though they didn't ask for any money or compensation. He heard them trust and worship their God regardless of their circumstances and finally he saw that their God was with them, caring for them and helping them. What Paul and Silas had was real, he knew it in his heart and he wanted it. In fact he wanted it for his whole family! There is something attractive about people who are authentically in love with God, who truly trust Him and who are not afraid for others to know how important Christ is to them. Paul and Silas's lives were a living testimony to the power and love of God and to His presence in their lives. They brought praise and worship to the prison where others only brought cursing and groaning. The jailer was probably impressed with anyone who was not intimidated by him or afraid of the prison, but Paul and Silas went beyond impressing him; they were courageous because they loved and served a very real and loving and powerful God. Paul wrote, "If God is for us, who can be against us?" (Rom. 8:31).

Quiet Family Prayer

The first word in verse 26 is wonderful, "Suddenly . . ." When we follow Jesus, doing in our lives what He's asked us to do and we continue to thank and praise Him for His love and help even when we don't see it, we will experience "suddenly" moments. Spend sometime praising God together.

Quiet Times

Younger Kids: Read the story of the Philippian Jailer and his family again. God loves you and He loves your family too! Pray for each person in your family.

Older Kids: Read Acts 16:16–40 and Matthew 6:19–24. Money was so important to these Philippian business people (v. 19) that they didn't care about the girl's freedom, Paul and Silas's rights, the lies they told or the fact that they were fighting against God and missing their own salvation—they were blind. Ask God to help you to never be blinded by money and stuff (Matt. 6:33).

DAY 5: PAUL'S JOURNEYS

Read: 1 Corinthians 9:19–27; 2 Corinthians 11:23–33

Quick Start

What is your greatest achievement so far?

Quest

Paul was carrying out his commission from Jesus, "to carry My name before Gentiles, kings, and the sons of Israel" (Acts 9:15). Wherever the Spirit led, Paul went. He did not know what would happen when he went and it wasn't always easy, but if it were not for Paul, the Good News would not have spread throughout the civilized world nearly as quickly as it did. Each place he went, God did amazing things, people came to Jesus and new churches were started. Paul's ministry spanned about thirty-five years and his journeys took him more than ten thousand miles (possibly much more) by ship, foot, and animal. That's the equivalent of almost half way around the earth. He started and helped at least fourteen main city churches and affected the lives of thousands. He also wrote most of the New Testament, which has gone on to help change the lives of billions. Paul is considered by many to be second only to Jesus as the most influential person in Christian history. Paul himself claimed that he did more for Christ than anyone else in his time (1 Cor. 5:9–11). He wasn't bragging though, but letting us know that great things can be done when you rely on God's grace and what he can do in you, instead of yourself.

Quiet Family Prayer

Paul said, "Imitate me as I also imitate Christ" (1 Cor. 11:1). Ask God to help you learn to trust Him, His grace, help, and power, so that you can accomplish great things for the kingdom.

Quiet Times

Younger Kids: Choose a favorite Bible character to read about. Like Paul, every great person in the Bible lived obeying God and helping others. Ask God to help you do the same.

Older Kids: Read 1 Corinthians 9:19–27. Jesus said that love lays down its life for others (John 15:13). Paul did that with all the strength, ability, and power God provided him and he never stopped till his race was done. Ask God to help you run your race inspired by Paul's example.

DAY 6: PAUL IN PRISON

Read: Acts 24:22–27

Quick Start

What does a crown mean? Is it more than just for decorating a person's head?

Quest

When we belong to Christ we are in a spiritual battle zone (Eph. 6:12) whether we realize it or not. There is a war that rages around us and we have an adversary who wants nothing better than to discourage, distract, or destroy us. The devil worked overtime to try and silence Paul, even persuading people to beat him and throw him into prison. He was in prison so much that many of Paul's letters to the churches were written while he was there. Since those letters became part of the Bible and have helped billions of people, it's safe to say that plan backfired for the devil. Jesus says that we should expect to be treated just like He was treated when He was on the earth (John 15:20). That includes the rejection as well as acceptance, harsh words as well as encouraging words, and difficulties along with the pleasant times. When we face adversity because of our faith, we're in good company with all the other faithful followers of Christ who have suffered. Also we have this confidence that our trials are temporary, Jesus will help us through each one personally, and that there is a crown that waits for us (1 Pet. 5:4) for faithfully finishing the race set before us.

Quiet Family Prayer

Paul told us what to do about the spiritual battle he described. He told us to pray (Eph. 6:18). Ask the Holy Spirit to guide you in prayer and then pray for the situations that come into your heart.

Quiet Times

Younger Kids: Read Luke 11:1. Jesus teaches His disciples to pray. He's in you and can help you with each prayer. Ask Him to teach you. Then pray about the things that come into your heart.

Older Kids: Read Philippians 4:10–14. Paul found the secret that helped him get through everything. Not contentment, but being content because he knew Jesus was really with him. Paul had experienced God taking care of him so often and in so many ways that he just rested in His love, trusting Him no matter what was going on. Ask God to help you be content in His love.

DAY 1: PARENT CONNECTION

THIS WEEK'S TOPIC: PAUL'S LETTERS TO THE CHURCHES

Paul originally meant for his letters to encourage, teach, help, and strengthen the believers in the churches of his day. But God preserved the letters so that we could use them to do the same thing in our lives and in our churches. This week we'll talk about some of the key themes that Paul wrote about: the body of Christ, its different members and the parts they're to play, the work and ministry of the Holy Spirit, and the role of both God's grace and our faith in salvation and the Christian life. Paul probably had no idea at the time he wrote his letters but they've been used by God to change the lives of billions of people.

Tips

The Bible says that God's Words are living and active (Heb. 4:12) and that they work effectively in believers (1 Thess. 2:13). Jesus said that His words are spirit and life (John 6:63) and Isaiah said that God's Words would always accomplish what they are sent to do (Isa. 55:10–11). But do we believe it concerning our kids? In parenting and talking to other parents we've discovered something amazing and really practical about kids and the Bible. We can put in much effort trying to explain God and biblical concepts to our children with little success. We attempt to boil the truths down to understandable kid-bites or we elaborate with much common sense and our kids may still not get it. But sit them down, open the Bible, and read His Word concerning the topic and discuss what His Word says and the lights go on. This seems like it should be Christian Parenting 101 but because it seems a little strange that the words of a book would be powerful, it's often overlooked. Honestly you have to try it to believe it. Do your homework ahead of time and look up appropriate Scripture passages for the topic in question, sit down, pray and start by reading. Explain what the verse says and means line for line and watch the lights come on. When you see it work, tell your friends and smile at the look of disbelief that appears briefly just before they realize it must be true. God's Word is alive and powerful.

DAY 2: PAUL WRITES LETTERS

Read: 1 Corinthians 1:1–10

Quick Start

Why do some people say "bless you" when others sneeze?

Quest

Paul started most of his letters to the churches with the phrase, "Grace and peace from God our Father and the Lord Jesus Christ." Perhaps Paul felt that these two things were what would sustain Christians more than anything else. God's grace helps us overcome sin and to become all He wants us to be. God's peace helps us rest while we're growing by giving us the assurance of His love and presence and His control over our destiny. As we grow in our understanding of God's grace, we will also grow in our appreciation for His peace (John 14:27). Paul's letters were meant to encourage believers, help them walk with the Father, Son, and Holy Spirit and to equip them for every good work. His letters also instructed them about their responsibilities towards one another in the church and how they should behave towards non-believers. Paul wrote other letters that were passed around from church to church that have been lost over time, but we have the ones God wanted us to have preserved in the Bible. Those letters are still having an impact on millions of churches today right around the world in almost every language. Paul originally meant to merely encourage, teach, help, and strengthen people in the churches of his day. But God preserved the letters so we could use them to do the same thing, for us and others.

Quiet Family Prayer

Paul spoke grace and peace as a blessing and a prayer to all who would hear or read his letters. Tell God that you receive the blessing and thank Him for His grace and peace on you, your family, and your home.

Quiet Times

Younger Kids: Read Psalm 119:33–35. The Holy Spirit inspired Paul's words so that they could be part of His word. Thank God for His Word and pray these verses in Psalms.

Older Kids: Read 2 Peter 3:14–18. Peter knew that Paul's letters were intended by God to become Scripture. Peter also talks about people who try and twist Scripture—that's when we want to change Scripture instead of letting it change us. Ask God to help you understand and be changed by your Bible.

DAY 3: PAUL WRITES ABOUT THE CHURCH

Read: Ephesians 4:1–16

Quick Start

When was the last time you made a mistake and had to try to fix what you had done?

Quest

Paul had once been the chief persecutor of the church and did everything in his power to destroy it. Now he had become the chief supporter of the church and did everything in his power to keep it going. Before, the letter he carried gave him permission to arrest Christians. Now the letters he wrote to churches were to correct their errant ways, to encourage the members to stay strong in the midst of persecution and to help them walk with the Father, Son, and Holy Spirit. He knew that to serve the church meant serving Christ, because Jesus is the Head of the church, and the members of the church are a part of His body. The church is given the Great Commission to continue His ministry while they remain on the earth. The great thing about being a part of a church is knowing that Christ is still the Head, and that He still guides the body to accomplish His will where He has placed them so that they will have an eternal impact on the lives around them. It is exciting to look around you at church at all the other people who have given their hearts and lives to Christ. What a joy it is to be able to worship our Lord together with those who also want to show their love for God and serve Him with all their hearts.

Quiet Family Prayer

Thank God for your church and spend some time praying for the leaders and also for your friends who attend with you.

Quiet Times

Younger Kids: Read Psalm 78:4–7 with your parent. God wants your parent (and your teachers at church) to teach you the Bible so you'll know God's love and trust Him. Thank God that you're being taught about Him!

Older Kids: Read Ephesians 4:1–16. Then think about verses 11–15. They explain God's purpose for you: maturity in Christ and ministry. They also explain some of the reasons you go to church: to be taught and brought to maturity and to be trained in God's purpose for you in the church so that you can help bring others to maturity. Talk to God about you and these verses.

278 DAY 4: PAUL WRITES ABOUT BODY PARTS

Read: Romans 12:4–8; 1 Corinthians 12:13–27

Quick Start

Have you ever tried to smell with your ear or touch something with your eye?

Quest

Do you know anyone whose legs don't work and they have to use a wheelchair? Obviously, part of their body is not functioning properly. The same thing happens in the church when people decide not to function as God intended in Christ's body, the church. Every member of a church has an important role to play and gifts, talents, and Spirit-given abilities to help them do it. When we tell God that we want to do our part, He helps us learn and grow up into it. We might just start by helping to move chairs or serve coffee but as we show ourselves faithful we can be given other responsibilities. Some parts may not have a title, but they still need to be done. For example, if you love to encourage people, do it on purpose with everyone you see at church. If you're a giver, pray and watch for ways to give, etc. Remember, we're all called to learn and mature in Christ—that's not just for the people whose part is teaching. Every part of the body must be connected to the head, and as we learn to walk with Jesus He helps us do our parts better.

Quiet Family Prayer

Talk about the gifts and abilities you see in each other that are helpful to others. Ask God to help you grow in your part.

Quiet Times

Younger Kids: Read Psalm 139:13–18 with your parent. God made you and gave you special gifts. They're already inside you like seeds. Ask God to help you discover and grow your talents.

Older Kids: Read Romans 12:4–8 and 1 Corinthians 12:13–27. God made you with gifts, desires, and talents that match His purpose for you—developing them will help lead you to that purpose. Sometimes we don't think that the things we're good at and like doing are talents because they're easy and no big deal. But the fact that something comes naturally is a sign that God made you that way. Ask God to help you recognize and grow in your gifts and talents.

DAY 5: PAUL WRITES ABOUT
THE HOLY SPIRIT

Read: Romans 5:5; 8:6–16, 26–27

Quick Start

Have you been in a car that ran out of gas or had a dead battery?

Quest

The Spirit of God is much more to us than gas or a battery is to a car. He facilitates everything we do in the kingdom of God. Paul wrote a great deal about God's Spirit to encourage believers. Here's some of what he taught: All Christians have God's Spirit in them. He keeps us from walking in sin as we set our minds on Him and He gives us life and peace. He puts God's love in our hearts and helps us love others. He leads us, helps us pray, and shows us that we are God's children (Rom. 5:5; 8:6–16, 26–27; 15:30). We are the Spirit's temple. He teaches us, helps us understand all that God has given us, and manifests Himself through us (1 Cor. 2:9–13; 3:16; 12:7–11). He transforms us and we have fellowship with Him (2 Cor. 3:16–18; 13:14). God's Spirit is at work within us doing great things and He fills us with His presence (Eph. 3:20; 5:18). God's Spirit is amazing and Paul taught that we should cooperate with His work—we are not to grieve Him (Eph. 4:30) or stifle Him (1 Thess. 5:19). It is a great encouragement to know that we have the Father looking over us, the Son teaching us, and the Spirit helping us every day. There's only one Spirit and He's in every Christian, uniting us all in Christ.

Quiet Family Prayer

Ask the Holy Spirit to fill you with His presence as you thank God for His great gifts and pray together.

Quiet Times

Younger Kids: Read the story of Pentecost (Acts 2). The Spirit is not just God's presence and power; He is God, a person and your friend. Thank Him for all His help.

Older Kids: Look up and read the verses about the Holy Spirit in the "Quest" section above. Pray about each verse and start trusting the Holy Spirit to do all those things in you and in your life. Memorize the verse that helps you.

DAY 6: PAUL WRITES ABOUT GRACE AND FAITH

Read: Ephesians 2:4–10

Quick Start

Can you sing the words to the song "Amazing Grace"?

Quest

The most common definition of grace is "God's undeserved favor." We cannot ever be good enough to deserve anything from God but He loves us and gives to us anyway—that's God's grace. We didn't deserve Jesus dying for us but God loved us and sent His Son anyway! When we believed that we became Christians—we accepted His grace by faith. Now that we're Christians we live and grow and receive from God by His grace (Gal. 3:2–3). Everything He's given us and will ever give us is because of what Jesus did. So everything we receive from God is by faith in His grace. God did it this way in order to guarantee everything He's promised to us (Rom. 4:16). You see, God can't always guarantee our behavior but He can always guarantee His grace. Whenever we pray we come to the throne of grace (Heb. 4:16) and we receive God's answers not because we deserve them but because of His grace in Christ. In fact, the Bible says that thinking that we can earn anything from God is falling from grace (Gal. 5:4). God's grace precedes God's involvement in our lives every time. Some describe grace as "**G**od's **R**iches **A**t **C**hrist's **E**xpense." By believing in God's grace we got saved and now we can freely receive His love the same way (Rom. 8:32). That's amazing grace!

Quiet Family Prayer

Even though we can't earn anything from God, He wants us to please Him in all we think, say, and do. We do that by believing in His grace as well because He promised to work in us and transform us (1 Thess. 5:23–24; Heb. 13:20–21).

Quiet Times

Younger Kids: Read a story of Jesus healing someone. Jesus never made people earn anything He did for them. Thank God for His love and grace.

Older Kids: Read the "Quest" and "Quiet Family Prayer" again. Look up and read all of the verses provided. Our faith in God's grace is an essential and freeing part of our relationship with Him. Ask Him to help you understand as you read.

DAY 1: PARENT CONNECTION

THIS WEEK'S TOPIC: PAUL'S LETTERS TO TIMOTHY AND TITUS

This week we examine some pretty straight forward but life-changing teaching:

- Building the kingdom of God is truly a team effort, and each person has a significant role to play.
- When we let God purify us, our lives will be filled with His presence, love, peace, joy, and blessings.
- Living and loving God's way is the surest way to introduce others to Jesus because they'll see Him living in us.
- We need to read, study, and know our Bibles and check what we're being taught against it.
- Our lives must reflect the truth of Scripture.

Tips

Jesus is the Word (John 1:1–5). And He said that His Words are spirit and life (John 6:63). The author of Hebrews told us that God's Word is living and effective (4:12); when we put it in, it goes down inside of us and renovates (1 Thess. 2:13). James called it the "implanted word, which is able to save you." Paul taught that being "renewed in knowledge" is the recipe for us being transformed into His image (Rom. 12:1–2; Col. 3:10). When we become Christians we're given a new heart with God's law written on it and Christ comes to live in us by His Spirit. When we take in God's Word, He uses it to teach us and transform the way we think, believe, feel, etc., to match what's written on our new heart, and we are steadily transformed into Christ's image.

Here's a way to help you explain this to your kids: You are an incredible super computer built by God. When you became a Christian God gave you a new hard drive (heart) and a new operating system (the Holy Spirit). In order for this super computer to be all it's supposed to be and do all it's supposed to do, you have to install the right programs for each task (God's Word on every topic). Everything works together because it is all built by the same person, as one system built for the same purpose.

DAY 2: PAUL WRITES TO
ENCOURAGE YOUNG LEADERS

Read: 1 Timothy 4:12; 2 Timothy 1:1–7

Quick Start

How old does a person have to be before he or she can be a leader? Who is the youngest leader you know about?

Quest

Timothy was a young believer that Paul considered as a "true son in the faith." He accompanied Paul on some of his missionary journeys and is listed as a coauthor on six of Paul's letters. He became a sort of apostolic representative to the churches to help guide them through difficult situations. Titus was another believer likely converted under Paul's ministry and became a very close companion to Paul. Paul mentions Titus nine times in 2 Corinthians and speaks of the encouragement Titus brought to his life (2 Cor. 7:6, 13). Titus was also given authority to guide struggling churches and Paul trusted him to establish leadership among them (Titus 1:5). Building the kingdom of God is truly a team effort, and each person has a significant role to play in helping churches move forward in the faith and in having an impact on their communities. Paul understood that the church not only needed leaders for today but that it also needed new young leaders to be trained to help so they called the current ones. Paul's letters to Timothy and to Titus are great examples of how this works and how we can encourage one another (young and old) and help one another build God's kingdom.

Quiet Family Prayer

Think of two or three young leaders in your family or church and take time to pray for them today. Thank God for raising up new leaders, and pray God's wisdom for them.

Quiet Times

Younger Kids: Read 1 Samuel 17:31–50. Even though David was a very young man, he showed great leadership skills, and later God put him over all the people as their king. Ask God to help you be a leader among your friends to help them do what is right.

Older Kids: Read all three chapters of Titus. Imagine Paul is writing to you. Can you find three important instructions to remember to do? Ask God to build into your life the character to carry out His plans for you in the days to come.

DAY 3: PAUL WRITES ABOUT PURITY

Read: 1 Timothy 1:5; 2 Timothy 2:19–22; Titus 2:11–14

Quick Start

Have you ever looked into your glass and found a bug floating in it?

Quest

The word *sincere* comes from an old word which means "without wax." Some pottery sellers would cover small cracks in their pots with wax, paint over it, and then sell it as new—cheating the buyers. Being sincere means being pure, authentic, and genuine. God is looking for people who aren't faking their Christianity or putting on a show for others. We have to be people with a pure heart, steadfast love, and have such good character that no one can raise any accusation against us. In essence we need to be transformed into the image of Christ. There is no way we can do this on our own or be perfect overnight; it's a process and God's Spirit does it in us by His grace (1 Cor. 3:18). When we make mistakes, God is ready to forgive us, teach us, and help us keep moving. When we let God purify us, our lives will be filled with His presence and His love, peace, joy and blessings—and we'll be "without wax." Your life will not only be a joy to live and a good example to others, but it'll attract nonbelievers who will want to know what you have that's so different.

Quiet Family Prayer

Read 1 John 1:9. Silently ask God to forgive you if there's something you haven't already talked to Him about and thank Him that He's cleansing and changing you.

Quiet Times

Younger Kids: Read Ephesians 6:1–3. Listening to your parents, being obedient, and talking to them respectfully is being obedient to God. God will help you do that better and better—just ask Him.

Older Kids: Read Titus 2:11–14. Jesus' work wasn't just to get us forgiven but also to redeem us from sin, cleanse us, and make us eager to do good works. Read verse 14 again—who cleanses us? Jesus is at work inside us by His Spirit, cleansing and transforming us by grace. Our job is to believe it and cooperate. Thank God that He's at work inside you.

DAY 4: PAUL WRITES ABOUT LOVING PEOPLE TO CHRIST

Read: Titus 2:6–8; John 13:33–35; Colossians 4:5–6

Quick Start

Do you know what a copycat is? Do you know what a mockingbird is famous for?

Quest

If we want others to listen to our message of God's love, we need to live and love His way. First we need to love each other, in our families and in our churches. We must also love non-Christians—even if they are hostile to the message of God's love. We should choose our words carefully, be pleasant, helpful, and kind. People can react negatively to our words, but few will resist your loving actions toward them. Many times what we do speaks more loudly than what we say, and people are always watching what we say and how we act. For some Christians, their lives cancel out their message because they want to live like those in the world, but be identified with God's people at the same time. John reminds us (1 John 2:15), "Do not love the world or the things that belong to the world. If anyone loves the world, love for the Father is not in him." We shouldn't try to show people how much we are like them; we should show them how much we are like Christ by living and loving like He did. Sometimes it's hard to love certain people, but remember: God loves us even when we don't deserve it. Living and loving God's way is the surest way to introduce others to Jesus because they can see He lives in us.

Quiet Family Prayer

Being a loving person and living a life of love is the best possible life; it also attracts others to God, because "God is love." Ask God to help you live love.

Quiet Times

Younger Kids: Read John 13:34–35. Name two ways you can better show love to others. Ask God to help you do those two things and to learn how to live love.

Older Kids: Read 1 Corinthians 13:1–8 and John 13:34–35. How did Christ show you love? How can you use His example to show love to those around you? Thank God for helping you live love and for giving you opportunities to be a blessing to others so that they can know about His love for them.

Day 5: Paul Writes about False Teachers

Read: 1 Timothy 6:3–6; 2 Timothy 3:1–10

Quick Start

What is the best trick you have ever played on someone?

Quest

Paul warned the followers of Jesus that they should watch out for evil people who distort God's Word. The devil wants to hurt God's people and to harm God's church and one of the ways he does that is by attacking God's Word, which makes sense because God gave us His Word so that we'd know and grow in the truth (2 Tim. 3:16). The devil uses false teachers to twist the Bible to mean things it doesn't mean and/or to convince people that God's Word is not important or relevant or us today. Paul tells us how to keep ourselves safe from these false teachers. First we need to read, study, and know our Bibles and check what we're being taught against it. We should never just take a teachers word for it (Acts 17:10–11). Next God has given us His Holy Spirit to help us know the truth (John 14:26; 1 John 2:26–27). We can pray and trust Jesus to show us the truth as we read and study His Word. And finally, Paul told us (in the verses you read today) how to recognize false teachers; they promote themselves, love money, they don't teach that the result of our faith is a godly life, they don't live godly lives themselves and they argue about stuff that has nothing to do with godly living and cause strife.

Quiet Family Prayer

Ask God to help you know and grow in His Word, trust His Spirit to teach you, and check what you're taught and who's teaching it.

Quiet Times

Younger Kids: Read the story of Jesus' temptation in the wilderness. Jesus had God's Spirit and God's Word in His heart to help Him beat lies. Thank God for His Spirit in you, and for help learning His Word.

Older Kids: Read Acts 17:10–11 and 1 John 2:26–27. When Jesus was tempted by the devil, He had God's Spirit and He used God's Word. Listening to godly teachers is helpful but it can never replace your responsibility to read and study God's Word and to trust Jesus and the Spirit to teach you. Ask God to help you learn and grow in His Word.

286 DAY 6: PAUL WRITES ABOUT THE BIBLE

Read: Hebrews 4:12–13; 2 Timothy 3:15–16

Quick Start

What do you think the Bible means when it describes the Bible as a living book?

Quest

We often see the Bible as a book that we must look into in order to discover the truths of God. But Hebrews says the Word of God is also looking into us and changing our hearts. As believers we must put our lives alongside the Bible to see how we match up with God's expectations for His people. Our lives must reflect the truth of Scripture. The Bible is like a bright light that reveals every corner, every space in our life and heart and mind so that the Spirit can help conform us to the image of His Son (Rom. 8:29). God has also given us His Word so that we can know about life and truth and know all the promises that are available to us when we believe in Him. Only the Bible teaches us about salvation, His Spirit, joy, peace, heaven, true wisdom, and amazing love! The more time you spend reading the Bible, the more you come to love God and appreciate all that He has provided for you. If you have ever read a Bible verse that pierced your heart or answered your questions, you understand how it is more than words on a page; it is an instrument in the hands of God to transform people's lives.

Quiet Family Prayer

Tell one another what you like best about the Bible. Thank Him for sending us His Word to help us know Him and live an amazing life in Christ.

Quiet Times

Younger Kids: Read Psalm 1. God compares us to fruit trees planted in just the right place. Reading and living the Bible helps us grow healthy fruit in our lives and helps our lives work better. Ask God to help you love, learn, and live His Word.

Older Kids: Read Psalm 1 and 2 Timothy 3:16. Do you see the contrast between those who base their lives on God's Word and those who don't? It's not enough for us to just read and know God's Word; we need to let God use it to change us so that we live it as well. Ask God to help you love, learn, and live His Word.

DAY 1: PARENT CONNECTION

THIS WEEK'S TOPIC: LETTERS FROM PETER AND JAMES

This week we look at the letters from Peter and James. These key verses nicely sum up the weeks lessons:

- "But be doers of the Word and not hearers only, deceiving yourselves." (James 1:22)
- "But the wisdom from above is first pure, then peace-loving, gentle, compliant, full of mercy and good fruits, without favoritism and hypocrisy." (James 3:17)
- "If anyone thinks he is religious without controlling his tongue, then his religion is useless and he deceives himself." (James 1:26)
- "Like newborn infants, desire the pure spiritual milk, so that you may grow by it for your salvation, since you have tasted that the Lord is good." (1 Pet. 2:2–3)
- "Always be ready to give a defense to anyone who asks you for a reason for the hope that is in you." (1 Pet. 3:15b)

Tips

This week we'll be talking a lot about what comes out of our mouths, and it would be a great time to establish some family ground rules for words used in your home. Here's your background agenda for the week: this week each time you read a verse or verses about our words (as a family or with one of your kids), make a point of starting a discussion on what the meaning of the Scripture passage is and how it should be applied in everyday household, family conversation. Then purposely move the discussions beyond theory and ideals to making family commitments together about how you are and are not going to speak to each other from that point on. At one point, get everyone to agree, that you are all going to live by the new rules and have a happier more peaceful home. Then decide on a certain signal or reminder that can be used when a family member (parent or child) forgets and starts to use their words inappropriately. Perhaps agree on a family motto and use that as a reminder (e.g., "In all our family's words, kindness, joy, and love are heard.").

DAY 2: PETER AND JAMES

Read: James 1:27; 2:17, 24; 1 Peter 2:11–17

Quick Start

What do you think when someone says one thing but does another?

Quest

James was Jesus' half brother. At first James did not believe Jesus was the Christ, but after he had time to see what God did through Him, he was convinced. Although James was not one of the twelve disciples, he was a follower of Jesus as were many others. Peter was one of the first disciples Jesus called to follow Him and he and James played a significant role in the early church. Both men wrote about true religion being more than right thinking, it has to be right doing. In other words your actions must demonstrate what you believe. If you believe in Christ, then your behavior, your generosity, your kindness and gentleness will prove it because it'll be Christ like. James reminds us to be doers of the Word, not hearers only (1:22–23). Our lives must back up what we say we believe. If we think it doesn't need to, James says we're actually fooling ourselves. Peter reminds us that we will stand before God one day to give an account of what we have done (1 Pet. 1:17; 4:5) and should have done but didn't. The good news is that in Christ, God has already given us everything we need (His Spirit in us, Jesus teaching us, His Word, God's promises and grace) so that we can learn, grow, and live godly lives (2 Pet. 1:3–4).

Quiet Family Prayer

The word *Christian* means "Christlike." Ask God to help you know Him and live for Him like Jesus did.

Quiet Times

Younger Kids: Read James 3:3–5. We can control large animals with small instruments, but our small tongue can get us in BIG trouble. Ask God to help the words that come out of your mouth to be kind and encouraging to others.

Older Kids: Read James 3:3–17. A small tongue can either cause huge problems, leave emotional scars, and hurt others, or be an encouragement, cheer others on, and be a blessing; your choice. Ask God to help you be the one who builds others up rather than tearing them down with your words.

DAY 3: JAMES WRITES ABOUT WISDOM

Read: James 3:13–18

Quick Start

Have you ever gone a direction you thought was the right way, but wasn't?

Quest

The Bible says there are two kinds of wisdom. One is from God, the other one is not. God's wisdom leads us to live a life that is pleasing to Him and that demonstrates the characteristics of Christ. Listening to His wisdom brings joy, happiness, and many blessings to our lives and home. The world's wisdom does the opposite. It produces envy, selfish ambition, deceitfulness, disorder. and every kind of evil. It is usually pretty clear by looking at people's lives which type of wisdom they are following. If someone is peace loving, gentle, merciful, and caring, you know they are following God's wisdom. If they are angry, argumentative, liars, selfish, mean, and arrogant, you know they are following the world's wisdom. There are many people who like to use whichever one they think will work at the time. When they do that, they show that they're really using the world's wisdom and trying to fake God's wisdom only because they think it'll get them what they want. James says that is like having your water faucet give both bad water and good water—it's impossible because it all becomes polluted (James 3:10–12). Water is a good analogy because you know that if bad water is coming from the faucet, then the place the water is coming from is polluted. God wants our hearts and our words to be full of His wisdom and to be a fountain of blessing.

Quiet Family Prayer

James said that if we lack wisdom we can ask God for it and He'll give it to us (James 1:5). Ask God to help you learn and grow so that your heart and tongue are full of His wisdom.

Quiet Times

Younger Kids: Read the story about Solomon's prayer for wisdom. God gave Solomon wisdom in his heart and it came out in his words and actions. Ask God to fill your heart with His wisdom.

Older Kids: Read James 3:10–12; Ephesians 4:29; 5:4; and Colossians 3:8. God's instructions are clear in these verses. Look up Psalm 19:14 and make it your prayer.

DAY 4: JAMES WRITES ABOUT OUR WORDS

Read: James 1:26; 3:1–12

Quick Start

What was the kindest thing you have said to someone? How did that feel?

Quest

The power that words have can depend on how much authority the person has. A king can send an army into battle with his words; a judge can pronounce prison time with his words and God can create a world with His words. Our words also have the ability to build up or tear down. We can bless or curse people, draw people to us or repel them from us. Some of our words will never be forgotten. Every word we say is a choice that we made. Nothing just "slips" out. What comes out of us reflects what is inside us. If our hearts and minds are centered on God, then our words will show it. If our hearts and minds are far away from God our words will also show it. Luke 6:45 says the condition of our heart determines the words we say; so the more we cooperate with learning God's Word and letting Him purify our hearts and minds, the less we'll have to be concerned about our words. Let the Holy Spirit teach and change you by drawing your attention to the words that are about to come out of your mouths. When He does, stop and change them. Make a decision today to use your words to show others that Jesus is inside your heart.

Quiet Family Prayer

Imagine if every word spoken in your home was kind, gentle, and uplifting. With God's help it's possible. Read and pray David's prayers in Psalm 19:14 and 141:3 and trust God to do it.

Quiet Times

Younger Kids: Read Matthew 21:21. Imagine a mountain jumping into the sea! If Jesus said that our words could be that powerful, we need to use them wisely. Ask God to help you with your words.

Older Kids: Read Matthew 12:36; Psalms 34:13; 39:1; 141:3; and Proverbs 13:3. Ask God to help you guard your words. Then when you feel the Holy Spirit reminding you, close your lips and ask for God's wisdom and strength before you continue speaking. The more you do it the easier it'll get.

DAY 5: PETER WRITES ABOUT GROWTH 〔291〕

Read: 1 Peter 1:13–16; 2:2–3, 11–12

Quick Start

Have you ever had a friend who was acting silly and you told them to "grow up!"?

Quest

We are born once physically and then immediately start growing towards becoming a mature adult. We are also born again spiritually, and we are also supposed to start growing towards maturity in our faith. God expects that we will not be satisfied with only "milk" or the simple things of faith, but that we would desire Him more and want to move beyond the simple to the profound things in faith (1 Cor. 3:1–3; Heb. 5:12–14). Growing up in our faith means we become more and more like Christ in our attitude and behavior towards God and others. There are certain markers we can check when we want to see if we are growing up in our faith (Phil. 2:12–13) and most of them look a lot like the fruit of the Spirit in our behavior (Gal. 5:22ff), but in our relationship with God is looks like greater dependence, increased faith, and more profound confidence in His ability to intervene in our lives and circumstances. When you're growing up, your bodies automatically grow. But you must cooperate by eating properly, sleeping, exercising, etc. Our spiritual growth is similar. God's Spirit is working in us and causing us to grow because of God's grace and promise (1 Thess. 5:22–24). But we must cooperate by learning, believing, and choosing to live God's Word, getting closer to God in prayer and letting Him change the way we think and behave.

Quiet Family Prayer

Parents, tell your children how God is growing you in your salvation right now. Ask God's blessing on your children as they grow in their love and understanding of God.

Quiet Times

Younger Kids: Read the story about the boy Jesus at the temple and Luke 2:52. Jesus was your example and He grew closer to God as He grew older. Ask God to help you grow closer to Him as you grow bigger.

Older Kids: Read 2 Peter 1:3–11. What does having a "divine nature" mean? Read the list in verses 5–7. How well are you doing in this progression? Ask God to help you cooperate with Him as you continue to grow in your salvation.

Day 6: Peter Writes about Sharing your Faith

Read: 1 Peter 2:9–12; 3:15

Quick Start

What would you do to promote an event? Would it be easier if you worked with someone who knew how?

Quest

Peter says that we are a chosen race, royal priesthood, and holy nation. When God came to Abraham, He said, "Abraham is to become a great and powerful nation, and all the nations of the earth will be blessed through him" (Gen. 18:18). God's people have been chosen to show His glory to the nations. Jesus said, "God into all the world and make disciples" (Matt. 28:18). We are chosen to complete His mission on the earth so that every person gets to hear the Good News. We cannot just expect others to do this; we all must feel the excitement and urgency of sharing Christ with others. Think about the people God has placed in your life; these people are God's assignment to you. Jesus told us to go and tell others and He showed us how to do that by being our example. He said that He could do nothing on His own and only did what He saw the Father doing. Then He told us that we can likewise do nothing without Him (John 5:19; 15:5). Jesus also said that He's the one that draws people to Himself (12:32). So we're to go and always be ready and willing to tell others; however, we're to pray and let God's Spirit direct us and inspire our timing and our words; we are His coworkers (1 Cor. 3:9).

Quiet Family Prayer

Name some friends and neighbors who you think need to hear about God's love and take some time to pray for them. Ask God to give you opportunities to be His coworkers.

Quiet Times

Younger Kids: Read Acts 8:26–39. What happened when the Ethiopian heard the good news about Jesus? Ask God to help you tell others about Jesus.

Older Kids: Read Acts 8:26–39. God was already drawing the Ethiopian to Himself, and He used Philip as His coworker. God created, knows, and loves every person. When we pray for them and talk to them, we need to trust the Holy Spirit to help us cooperate with what He's already doing in their hearts. Ask God to help you learn to be His coworker.

Day 1: Parent Connection

This Week's Topic: John's Letters

Here are some of the concepts we'll explore in detail this week:

- We can love God because He first loved us.
- Living a life of love towards others is an absolutely amazing life.
- God is now our Father, He loves us and has promised us that we can know Him and love Him.
- When we minimize sin, we minimize the death of Christ.
- Jesus defeated sin's power and the devil's power over our lives.

Tips

John called himself "the disciple Jesus loved." He was big on the topic of love. So much so that you may be tempted to call him a softy; until you read his stance on Christians who continue to sin. John was not soft on sin! If you're of the mind that the New Testament turns a blind eye to Christians sinning and that the purpose of God's grace is to cover up the fact that we're living in the flesh—you may want to slowly and prayerfully read the book of first John before starting this week's devotions. Jesus came not only to forgive our sins but to cleanse us and free us from sin. He gave us the gift of righteousness so that with His help we could open up the present and start using it. If you're hearing "works" and starting to cringe, relax. Paul taught that we got into God's kingdom through no merit of our own but by grace, and that we are to continue towards God and holiness in the same grace (Gal. 3:3). Some believe that because we cannot earn God's grace that we can continue to sin (while trying our best not to, of course). That's not scriptural and the example it leaves for our children will lead them down a wrong road. Simply put, we received the kingdom by God's grace and promise and we walk in and grow in the kingdom by the same grace and promise. Jesus defeated sin and the devil, and Jesus is now our teacher, the Spirit is working inside us and God has given us everything we need to live godly lives (2 Pet. 1:3). As you read 1 John, know he's not telling you to try harder—he's telling you to trust Him and to learn to walk in step with the power and provision of God for your transformation. It's essential that our kids understand this because it's the only way they can live an overcoming Christian life.

DAY 2: LOVING GOD

Read: 1 John 4:7–21

Quick Start

Do you love ice cream? Do you love to go swimming? Do you love your family? Is it the same kind of love each time?

Quest

When Jesus was asked what the greatest commandment of all time was, He replied that we are to love God with all our heart, soul, strength and mind (Mark 12:30–31) and the second is to love our neighbor as ourselves. John reminds us that love is the key ingredient for our relationship with God, and the key factor in our relationship with others around us. The one thing that has to mark every Christian's life is love (John 13:35). We show our love for God by keeping His commands (John 15:10), by being of one heart and mind with our fellow Christians (John 17:11, 22), by spending time with Him and seeking Him with all of our heart (Ps. 119:2), and by reading and following His Word (John 14:24). If we truly love God, He will become our highest priority and we will not let anything prevent us from worshipping Him, serving Him, and spending time with Him. Read 1 John 4:19. We can love God and others because He first loved us! In other words because He loved us and sent His Son, we were given new loving hearts and the Holy Spirit, who fills us with love (Rom. 5:5). So now we are able to know love and to love God and others. We were created for loving and being loved—we just need to grow in it.

Quiet Family Prayer

How much time do you spend with God? Thank Him that He made it possible for you to know Him and love Him and ask Him to help you grow even closer to Him.

Quiet Times

Younger Kids: Read John 21:15–17. A few days earlier, Peter told everyone he didn't even know Jesus. Here Jesus gives Peter a chance to say how much he loves Jesus. Jesus asks each of us the same question. Tell Him your answer.

Older Kids: Read John 21:15–17. We all fall short at times, but God knows we're growing and He keeps working in us and helping us move on. Jesus is with you right now. Tell Him how you feel and ask Him to keep helping you grow closer and more obedient.

DAY 3: JOHN WRITES ABOUT LOVING OTHERS

Read: 1 John 3:16–18; 4:18–21

Quick Start

What kinds of people are easiest to love?

Quest

The soldiers that go off to war are highly trained for battle. In their training they are taught how to follow orders, how to handle the stress of battle, how to stay put even when the fighting gets tough. The one thing they also have to count on is that the person on either side of them will do their duty and not run away. They depend on one another, they respect one another, and they must be willing to give their lives for one another if they need to. John reminds us that we need to love others to the degree that we are willing to "lay down our lives" for one another (1 John 3:16). If we truly loved others this much, we would not be so quick to get angry with them, or be so critical of others, or resist being inconvenienced by those who have needs. If we truly loved them, we would be eager to help, quick to sacrifice, and happy to put our schedules on hold in order to help others in need. Living a life of love toward others is an absolutely amazing kind of life that brings more rewards than you could ever imagine. That's what Jesus did for us. And it's not hard to do because we've been recreated (born again) full of love and faith (1 John 5:3–5).

Quiet Family Prayer

Family is God's practice ground for learning to love. Ask God to help you grow in love by learning to love one another. When we truly love others, only then can we truly love God.

Quiet Times

Younger Kids: Read Luke 10:30–37. Which of the three men showed love to the injured man? Ask God to help you show this kind of love and kindness to those around you even when they're not injured.

Older Kids: Read Ephesians 4:31–32. There is a huge contrast between these two verses. God says that the stuff in verse 31 "must be removed from you." Make a decision to remove them from who you are right now and ask God to help you live verse 32.

DAY 4: JOHN WRITES ABOUT KNOWING GOD

Read: John 17:3 and 1 John 1:1–4; 2:3–6

Quick Start

Do you know the president of the USA or just know about him?

Quest

Knowing God is no easy task if we think we can do it on our own. However, Jesus came and paid the price to reconnect us with the Father and help us know Him (Matt. 11:27). God is now our Father and He comes to us (John 14:23) and He has promised us that we can know Him (Heb. 8:11). If we believe this incredible promise, then we'll spend more time learning about Him and getting close to Him and growing in it. Just like any relationship, when you invest time, it gets closer and stronger. And you can count on that because God loves you, wants you to know Him and has promised it. We can know about God by reading books about Him, and hearing people talk about Him, but we can actually know Him personally by trusting His promise and responding to His love. The more we get to know God the more we'll become like Him and the more we'll come to understand His heart and His will for our lives. The greatest commandment (to love God) reflects the greatest promise and blessing we're given in Christ—to actually and truly be able to love and know and have a relationship with God; we just need to believe it and seek after our heavenly Father. It was the apostle Paul's heart desire (Phil. 3:10) and should be ours too.

Quiet Family Prayer

John said that eternal life (the purpose of it) is to know God and His Son (John 17:3). Thank God for His amazing promise and ask Him to help you walk in it by His grace.

Quiet Times

Younger Kids: Read John 14:23. Jesus and the Father are with you right now and always. They want you to get closer to them and know them more and more. Let them know that you'd like that and ask for help knowing them.

Older Kids: Read and pray about John 14:21, 23; Philippians 3:10; Hebrews 8:11; and 1 John 1:3. Knowing God is the supreme privilege anyone can have. Ask God to help you walk in this incredible promise.

DAY 5: JOHN WRITES ABOUT SIN

Read: 1 John 1:7–2:1; 3:1–10; 5:18

Quick Start

How long does it take you to say you are sorry after you have done something wrong?

Quest

It was sin that caused Adam and Eve to be cast out of the Garden of Eden, sin that caused God to flood the earth, sin that caused Sodom and Gomorrah to be destroyed, sin that forced God's people to go into exile in Assyria and Babylon, and sin that caused God to send His Son to die on the cross for us. All of the hate, crime, destruction, death, evil, sickness, poverty, etc., in the world are here because of sin! When we minimize sin, we minimize the death of Christ. He came to destroy sin's power over us and now we can live our lives without sinning. When we continue to sin (doing things we know are wrong) and do not repent, God will not bless us until we repent. If we realize we've blown it, ask God to forgive us, and help us not do that again, He forgives us immediately, cleanses us, and sets us free. When we're growing up and learning, we make mistakes and our parents teach us and help us grow. God does the same thing with us—He gradually transforms us into the image of Jesus. Its okay to not be perfect overnight, we just need to cooperate with Him as He teaches and changes us and do what we know is right. Remember, God is love, and He always comes to us in love.

Quiet Family Prayer

When we ask, our sin is forgiven and forgotten instantly and we get a fresh start. Thank God for His grace and for freeing you from sin.

Quiet Times

Younger Kids: Read Luke 15:11–24. God is just as happy with us when we ask Him for forgiveness as this father was. Thank God for being so kind and gentle with us and for loving us like He does.

Older Kids: Read Luke 15:11–24. The primary feature of this story is that a loving, waiting father rejoices over the return of a repentant son. The son is not shamed, rebuked, punished, or rejected by the father, but welcomed home in love. Thank God now for accepting you back with open arms each time you blow it.

🖐298 DAY 6: JOHN AND PETER WRITE ABOUT GOD KEEPING US

Read: 1 John 5:18–20; 1 Peter 1:5; 2 Peter 1:3–4

Quick Start

Do you try things first by yourself, or do you ask for advice from others before you start to make sure you won't fail?

Quest

John tells his readers that they can know for sure they are kept in Him. According to 1 John 5:4 we have victory over the things in this world that come against us. Temptations, distractions, challenges, and our weaknesses should all give way in our life to the indwelling power of God's Spirit in us. Victory will come to those who belong to Him as they trust and obey Him. John also says (1 John 5:18) that Jesus keeps us from sin and makes sure that the devil cannot touch us. Peter says that we are protected by God's power through faith (1 Pet. 1:5) and that His power gives us everything we need to live godly lives. By believing God's great promises we can share in the divine nature and escape the corruption that is in the world (2 Pet. 1:3–4). Peter and James knew that Jesus defeated sin's power and the devil's power over our lives. We now have new hearts that want to know God and follow Jesus and we have His Spirit, who is working in us, transforming us into Christ's image. We need to have confidence in God's promises, submit to His will and desire for us, and resist the devil (James 4:7). When we do Jesus will teach us and keep us, the Spirit will continue to transform us, God will protect us, and the devil will run from us.

Quiet Family Prayer

Thank Jesus for His incredible work and the great and complete salvation He provides.

Quiet Times

Younger Kids: Read Matthew 26:66–75. When Peter was in trouble, he should have asked for help instead of relying on His own strength—God promises to help and keep us. Thank God for protecting you and helping you grow.

Older Kids: Read 1 Thessalonians 5:23–24 and Jude 24–25. How do these verses encourage you? Do you ask God for help? Ask God to remind you of the help He promises in times of trouble.

DAY 1: PARENT CONNECTION

THIS WEEK'S TOPIC: JESUS IS COMING BACK

This week: When we are excited about His return, we may be surprised by the timing but not by Him, because we were ready and waiting. While we wait, Jesus wants us to make disciples. It has always been the desire of Jesus' heart for every person to have a chance to respond to His great love. Our job is to work with Jesus and share God's love; His job is to help, guide, and empower us, and to work in the hearts of those who hear and give them salvation. We do this looking forward to our real life in heaven and desiring to share it with others.

Tips

Read Romans 8:18–25; 2 Corinthians 4:16; Philippians 1:23; Colossians 3:1–4; Hebrews 11:8–16; and 2 Peter 3:12–13. This life is our life now, and God will love and help us through it because we're His children. However, focusing on the worst and shortest part of our eternal life with Him is not what God recommends we do. One of the reasons that we get caught up with our temporary lives here is simply because we don't spend much time focusing on what's to come. The only way we can shift our focus is to spend some more time focused on our eternal lives. Time in prayer and in the Word is a great start; but if we spend all of that time praying and studying about God blessing us in this life, we won't have tipped the scales by much. What we need to do is spend some time investigating, imagining, and anticipating the amazing future God has promised us; that's what we'll be helping your family do for the next two weeks. It's a great time to work on shifting the focus a bit. Pray that God gives your kids a revelation of the reality of heaven and the new heaven and new earth, through what they'll learn. That's important because it's hard to get excited about something you misunderstand or know nothing about and it's even harder to stay focused on something and live for it when you're not excited about it—which is why God recommends we shift our focus.

DAY 2: JESUS IS COMING BACK

Read: John 14:1–3; Luke 21:25–28; Matthew 24:37–44

Quick Start

Have you ever woken up on an important morning only to discover your alarm clock didn't go off?

Quest

There are two things that most believers really look forward to: going to heaven when they die and the return of Christ. However, many people do not seem to think Jesus will come back in their lifetime; if they did it would affect the way they lived. They just assume they will see Him when their time on the earth is finished and so they feel there's lots of time to make things right with God. Others are taking every opportunity to serve the Lord and witness to others whenever they can because they love Him and are excited about Him coming back. The truth is Christ said He would come at an unexpected time and catch people by surprise! When we are pumped about His return we may be surprised by the timing but not by Him because we were ready and waiting. It will certainly be an amazing day beyond what any of us could think or imagine. Jesus gave a parable about this describing the importance of being ready and alert (Matt. 25:1–13). We should read it, get ready and excited, and stay alert! Are you excited and ready? If you are, pray for those who may be caught off guard and see if you can help get them ready. It really is something to look forward to!!

Quiet Family Prayer

Some people fear standing before God, others are looking forward to it. Ask God to help you live every day like He's about to return.

Quiet Times

Younger Kids: Read 1 Thessalonians 4:14–18. It will be so exciting when Jesus returns. Tell God tonight that you believe Jesus is coming back and ask Him to help you be ready when that day comes.

Older Kids: Read 1 Thessalonians 4:14–5:11. The Bible says many people will be caught off guard when Christ returns and they will not be ready. If you knew that Jesus was returning in a few hours, what would you do to get ready? Jesus told us to live continually like He's about to return. Ask God to help you live that way every day.

Day 3: Jesus' Last Instructions

Read: Matthew 28:18–20; Mark 16:15–18

Quick Start

How do you feel when your teacher gives you an assignment? Do you see it as a challenge to complete, or a burden you have to bear?

Quest

When you look at the very last words of Jesus, you have to understand the importance of last words. When someone is dying or leaving on a long trip, usually the last thing they say to you is what they want you to remember and pay special attention to—those words are usually the most important words. So we need to see Jesus' last words as significant, and let those last instructions occupy our time and thinking until He returns. We don't know when the last day will be so we need to be living like Christ could come back tonight. Also we need to be prayerfully sharing the Good News with those around us and with those around the world and making disciples for Jesus, just as He commanded us to do. The really great thing is Jesus also said, "I'll be with you till the end of the age," and we can be assured that Christ will help us fulfill the Great Commission. He works with us, teaching us, training us, guiding us, gifting us, empowering us, and giving us increase. The last verse in Mark reports what happened after Jesus ascended back to heaven; it says that as the disciples preached the Lord worked *with* them, confirming the Word. Teamwork always makes the job much more fun to do!

Quiet Family Prayer

Thank God for His marvelous promises and allowing us to work with Him in bringing the Good News to the world.

Quiet Times

Younger Kids: Read Luke 24:44–53. It would be amazing to watch Jesus ascending. He will come back the same way He left one day. In the meantime He's with us in our hearts and helping us tell others about Him. Thank Him for His amazing plan and for letting you be part of it.

Older Kids: Read Matt 28:18–20 and Hebrews 5:11–14. Jesus commands us to make disciples. Of course, we must first be a disciple before we can help others be one. Ask Jesus to make you His disciple and prepare you to help others.

DAY 4: THE GOSPEL WORLDWIDE

Read: Mark 13:10; Matthew 24:11–14; 2 Peter 3:8–10

Quick Start

Name five different ways to spread a message around the world.

Quest

It has always been the desire of Jesus' heart for every person to have a chance to respond to His great love. Not everyone will respond, but everyone should have the *opportunity* to respond. Missionary efforts to share the Gospel in every language and in every tribe and nation have made great strides in the past one hundred years. Many people have given their lives to take God's love to remote places and in challenging locations, and soon the goal will be accomplished. But just as Christians are making great strides to share the gospel around the world, so too has the opposition to the Good News greatly increased. Persecutions, threats, discriminations, and all sorts of hardships await God's people, but still they persevere out of love for Christ and others. Pray for those who are making many sacrifices to tell the Good News, and ask God what you can do to help in the effort this week. Every person can go, share, give, pray, and witness where they are, and many more can still go to places where no witness has yet gone. God still asks the question today that He asked Isaiah, "Then I heard the voice of the Lord saying: Who should I send? Who will go for Us?" and may we respond just as Isaiah did, "I said: Here I am. Send me" (Isa. 6:8).

Quiet Family Prayer

In Colossians 4:3 Paul asked the church to pray that God would open doors for him to share the gospel. Pray that prayer for your family today.

Quiet Times

Younger Kids: Read Luke 7:24–30. John the Baptist was the one to prepare people for the coming of Jesus the first time. We are chosen to prepare people for the coming of Jesus the second time. Thank God for choosing you for His special purposes on the earth.

Older Kids: Read John 4:38; 17:18; 20:21. You understand we are not chosen to sit and watch but are being sent and must go to finish what Christ started. Jesus gave you an assignment; ask Him now for the wisdom, strength, and help you need to carry it out.

Day 5: God Is Working Today

Read: John 5:17, 19–20; Mark 16:20

Quick Start

Can you imagine having a job where God was your boss and Jesus was your working partner?

Quest

Jesus told His disciples that His Father was still working, and that He was also working. The fact is God has been working since the beginning to redeem lost people, and show them that He loves them. Today He's working with missionaries, people who build websites and post social media messages, book writers, radio and television people, newspaper and magazine people, and individuals around the globe to share the Good News of His great love for people. The Bible tells us that God is not willing that any should perish but that all would come to repentance and have eternal life (2 Pet. 3:9; John 3:16). Christ is coming back soon, and people need to know about the love of God. Thousands of people are accepting Christ as their Lord and Savior every day around the world. Those who share the Good News are bearing much fruit and seeing the harvest from all the spiritual seeds that were planted. Our job is to work with Jesus and share God's love; His job is to help, guide and empower us, and to work in the hearts of those who hear and give them salvation. God is always doing His part, we just need to come alongside Him and do ours.

Quiet Family Prayer

Jesus said His "food" is to do what God wants (John 4:34)! God's assignments were what kept Him going, energized, and excited. There's nothing better than to see God working and to be part of it. Ask God to create that kind of excitement for carrying out His assignments.

Quiet Times

Younger Kids: Read a Bible story that you think is really exciting. Working with God is the most exciting adventure. Ask God to help you be a good worker in His kingdom.

Older Kids: Read what you think is the most exciting story in the Bible. Imagine if you were the one God used in the story. Working with Jesus is an amazing supernatural and exciting experience—He really shows up and works with you as you follow and trust Him (Heb. 13:8). Talk to God about this from your heart.

DAY 6: LOOKING FORWARD

Read: Colossians 3:1–4; Hebrews 11:8–16; 2 Peter 3:12–13

Quick Start

What do you know about heaven? What are you looking forward to the most about heaven?

Quest

On many occasions Jesus talked about coming back to gather all the faithful ones; first those who have already died, then those who are still living. Jesus is looking forward to it and the huge party He's going to have with us! He promises to exchange our bodies for amazing ones like He has now. We'll still be us and look like us, but super and perfect like God created us to be. All of God's people since Abraham have been looking forward to what God has planned for us—living with God and Jesus in His amazing new city, being eternal and perfect, living in paradise with nothing but all of the good things God created for us. Imagine the ultimate in beauty, fun, adventure, music, laughter, joy, play, love, rest, friendship, humor, comfort, wonder, food, animals, gardens, etc. We'll even be hanging out with angels. If you think of all the very best that's ever existed or been imagined, with nothing bad, nothing hurtful or disappointing, heaven is better. In fact no matter how much time you spent imagining it and coming up with cool ideas of what heaven could be like, Jesus would smile big and say, "All that, but even bigger, more, and better!"

Quiet Family Prayer

We need to remember that our life here is so very short compared to our eternal life in heaven. Heaven is our real life and nothing here is worth trading for that. Thank God for eternal life in heaven.

Quiet Times

Younger Kids: Read 1 Corinthians 9:24–25. Paul said we should live this life like we're racing for the greatest prize ever—heaven! Thank Jesus for bringing you into the race, for being your coach, and for helping you run it well.

Older Kids: Read John 19:30; 1 Corinthians 9:24–27; and 2 Timothy 4:7–8. Paul and Jesus both, with God's help, stayed the course, finished well and had their faithfulness rewarded. Thank Jesus that He helps you stay on course, run and finish your race well, and receive your reward.

DAY 1: PARENT CONNECTION

THIS WEEK'S TOPIC: A NEW HEAVEN AND EARTH

In this final week we will talk about what God has prepared for us next. We'll talk about how each one of us will stand before the Lord. We'll talk about, the amazing new heaven and earth, what God living with us will look like, what "no more tears" means, and how in the end what God had planned from the beginning will be exactly what happens.

Tips

This is our last Parent Connection tip and we'd like to leave you with this thought. Who we are in Christ, and who Christ is in us, is the most important thing we can understand and teach to our kids. It's often said, "God made me and He doesn't make junk." We need to go much further and say, "God *recreated* me and He used Christ as the blueprint." Paul wrote that Christ in us is the hope of glory (Col. 1:27). Jesus died to have our sins forgiven and to transfer us out of the kingdom of darkness (Col. 1:13–14), to cleanse our conscience (Heb. 10:22), to destroy sins power over us (Rom. 6:6), to give us new hearts and spirits and to put His Spirit within us (Ezek. 36:25–28) and thereby unite us with God in Him for all eternity as His righteous children. We are new creations completely remade (2 Cor. 5:17). We are not what we see ourselves to be; we are who He recreated us to be. When God looks at us, He not only sees us in Christ but He sees who He recreated us to be and all we will be in Christ and He has committed to getting us there (1 Cor. 3:18). We can believe God and can begin to see ourselves as He sees us or we can let ourselves be diminished by what Jesus already paid a huge price to destroy: "You'll never amount to much." "Remember what you did?" "You're stupid, hopeless, a failure, etc." NO! God has recreated you and all your sins and failures are GONE. God is at work in you (Phil. 2:13) transforming you from glory to glory into Christ's image (2 Cor. 3:18)—all by God's grace and promise through Christ Jesus. God wants your family to know who they are recreated to be. The more you understand this and trust Him, the more He'll be able to help you walk in it. And as you do, you will begin to reflect Him in all you are and do.

DAY 2: EVERYONE GIVES AN ACCOUNT

Read: Romans 14:12; Hebrew 4:13; 1 Peter 4:5

Quick Start

What do you think God will say to you when it's your turn to stand before Him in heaven?

Quest

All throughout the New Testament, from the Gospels to the end, God warns us that there will be a day we will stand before Him to declare to Him how we have spent our time on the earth. God has always expected His people to take the initiative to love others, to make the first move to be reconciled with others, to go the second mile and stand out in the crowd for going beyond what is expected. Standing before the judge at the end of time is not for the purpose of seeing whether or not your good deeds outbalance your bad deeds, it is perhaps for the purpose of handing out rewards to those who like Paul trusted Christ not only to save them but to transform them and work through them. Paul said, "For to me to live *is* Christ, and to die *is* gain" (Phil. 1:21). He knew the secret to living a life that was pleasing to God was to allow Christ to strengthen, empower, teach, lead, guide, and direct Him—in that way Christ living in us becomes our hope of glory (Col. 1:27). In the end, we are not judged according to our deeds, though, we are judged according to whether or not Jesus was our Lord and Savior. We enter heaven because of His righteousness, not ours. We are forgiven for our sins because of His sacrifice, not ours. God is great, and God is just.

Quiet Family Prayer

Take time to thank God for Christ's work in us and through us and for us that we would be able to live with Him forever because we believe in Him.

Quiet Times

Younger Kids: Read Matthew 25:31–46. Did you know that pet sheep recognize people and animals in their lives and act differently with each one depending on their personality and need? Ask God to help you love Him and follow Him by loving others like a sheep.

Older Kids: Read Matthew 25:31–46. Notice those who took action were rewarded and those who didn't bother to get involved were punished. Christ only expects us to do what He was willing to do Himself. But we are never on our own; He is always with us, helping us, and partnering with us to accomplish His will. Thank Him now for that.

DAY 3: NEW HEAVEN AND EARTH

Read: 2 Peter 3:8–13; Revelation 21:1–2; Romans 8:18–25

Quick Start

Do you prefer something that is brand new or something that is slightly used?

Quest

New things are always fun to have. New car, new house, new clothes, new experiences, all bring with them a sense of excitement and wonder. But wow! Can you imagine what a whole new heaven and earth will look like, the place prepared for all of God's people to live and enjoy? John was having a vision of it and it was so wonderful and so incredible, he could hardly even describe it. Paul tells us in Romans that the whole of creation, the earth, animals, bugs, weather, plants, trees, etc., was all corrupted and changed because of sin. The flood also did some heavy-duty damage. God is going to recreate it so all that damage and corruption is gone. Everything will be new. There will be no more decay, natural disasters, or bad weather—everything on the earth and in the sky will function perfectly. You think this world is beautiful—wait until you see it then. The Bible says that even all of the animals will be at peace with us and each other (Isa. 11:6–9). When you really imagine it, it's hard to wait; but we all know that relaxation comes after our jobs are done and we've got work to do here with Jesus. Besides we'll only be here for a short time but we'll live on the new earth forever.

Quiet Family Prayer

Take a few minutes to talk about what you think heaven may be like. Thank God for loving you so much that He has wonderful things planned for you.

Quiet Times

Younger Kids: Read Revelation 21:1–2. The apostle John had a peek at what God has prepared for us. It will be better than Christmas, birthdays, and special vacations all in one. Tell God how excited you are. Tell Him how much you love Him too.

Older Kids: Read Revelation 21:1–2. Did you notice there will be no more sea? There will still be water just no more barriers between people. We'll all be part of the same kingdom, brothers and sisters in Christ, living together in peace. Ask God to remove any barriers like that in your life so that you can love and be loved.

DAY 4: GOD'S HOME WITH US

Read: John 14:23; Revelation 21:22–24

Quick Start

What would it be like to climb up on God's lap for a hug or go fishing with Jesus?

Quest

In the Old Testament, we first see God walking and talking with Adam and Eve in the Garden of Eden. They were sent out of the garden because of sin. Much later God made a covenant with the Israelites and made His home in the most holy place. God was with His people. When Jesus was on the earth He actually walked and talked with His disciples. When Jesus left He sent the Holy Spirit to live in us and God made us His temple. So through the Holy Spirit God and Jesus live in us and with us. In the new heaven and new earth we'll have the best of all of this. God will live with us like He did with Adam and Eve, God's Spirit will still live in us like He does today and we'll be able to walk and talk with Jesus like the disciples did when He was here on the earth. We'll truly be with Him and Him with us in every way for the rest of eternity (1 Cor. 13:12, 1 John 3:2; Matt. 26:29; Rev. 22:4–5). It is hard for anyone to truly imagine what this will all be like, but just like a loving parent does for their children, there will be some amazing surprises and incredible joys for us to experience.

Quiet Family Prayer

God loves us more than we can imagine and He made us so that we could be with Him, know Him, and be taken care of by Him forever. Wow! Spend some time thanking Him for loving you so much!

Quiet Times

Younger Kids: Read 1 John 3:1–2. Heaven will be amazing but remember we're God's child now. He loves you and wants to take care of you. Talk to Him about being His child and ask Him for what you need.

Older Kids: Read Revelation 22:1–5. Who is at the center of heaven? Who is the Lamb? We seem so powerless on the earth today, but God promises we will reign with Him forever. Ask God to prepare you now to be able to handle whatever plans He has for you now and for eternity.

DAY 5: NO MORE TEARS

Read: Revelation 21:3; Philippians 4:4–7

Quick Start

When was the last time you cried? What made you cry?

Quest

Tears tell us a lot of things. We can cry because we are hurt or sad or even when we are overjoyed or overwhelmed. The Bible tells us that in heaven there will be no more tears. God will make things in heaven so that there will never be any more reasons to be hurt, disappointed, or sad. No one will hurt you, no one will leave you, and no one will die or cause you any pain. That tells us that not all of those things we face here on the earth are from God, but from our enemy. But in heaven, our enemy will have been dealt a final blow and will never bother us ever again. We will be able to experience the same kind of relationship Adam and Eve experienced before the enemy came and ruined everything. In the world, we will have trouble, but in the presence of God, we will live in perfect peace and complete freedom to enjoy the presence of the Lord and fellowship with one another. Many people today have a lot of tears in their life, but in heaven God will wipe them all away for good. That is what our loving Father is like.

Quiet Family Prayer

In heaven pain and suffering and sadness will no longer exist. Philippians 4:4–7 tells us that today, God also helps us rejoice in the midst of suffering, walks with us when we worry, and gives us peace. Thank Him now for that.

Quiet Times

Younger Kids: Read Luke 7:37–47. This woman was crying a LOT! She was so grateful to Jesus for forgiving her sins and giving her a new life. There are tears of sadness and tears of joy. She had tears of joy. Thank God that He promises to wipe away our tears and replace them with His joy.

Older Kids: Read Isaiah 25:8; 38:5; Psalm 126:5; and 2 Kings 20:5. Tears communicate emotions when words fail. They reveal what is in our heart. But when we are in God's presence, they will no longer be necessary. Express your love for God in your prayers and thank Him for His great love for you.

310 DAY 6: GOD'S ORIGINAL PLAN REALIZED

Read: Revelation 21:5–22:6

Quick Start

Do you know what a "do-over" is? If there was one thing that you could take back or "re-do" what would it be?

Quest

Many times throughout the Bible, God started things all over again: Noah and the ark, Abraham, Jacob, Moses, the return of the captives from Babylon, and when He sent Christ to die on the cross. He originally created us in His image and planned for us to enjoy heaven on earth, but Satan tried to destroy every good thing God had done. But God knew the beginning *and* the end before He started. In the end heaven will be like a complete "do-over" of creation. Satan thought he'd wrecked it for good, but God always knew that He'd make everything new in Christ, including us and all creation. Everything will become new and we will get to experience all that God intended us to experience right from the beginning. God originally created the heavens and the earth and everything in it for us to enjoy and He was here with us. Now He will recreate it and everything in it and give it to His recreated people to enjoy and He will live there with us forever. We will live in His presence enjoying His goodness with our fellow believers for the rest of time. God can't be tricked or thrown off His plans. It is impossible to truly guess or imagine what the do-over will be like, because it will be beyond our imagining. God can do anything and He's planning to really knock our socks off with the place He has for us to live in with Him forever.

Quiet Family Prayer

Thank God for making you part of His amazing forever plans!

Quiet Times

Younger Kids: Ask your parents to find some verses talking about heaven. God loves you and has a great plan for your life and your eternity. Thank Him for loving you.

Older Kids: Read Job chapters 1–2 and 42. In many ways Job's story is the story of mankind. Things started well, Satan messed them up causing a lot of pain and suffering, and God restored things back to their proper order. Job lived for 140 years and his troubles only lasted nine months. Thank God for loving, guiding, and caring for you here but also that it's just a short time compared to eternity.

BIRTHDAY (CHILD)

Read: Luke 2:10–14; John 3:3–7

Quick Start

Happy birthday! You have made it through another year and God has some great things in store for you. Out of all your birthdays, which present has been your favorite so far? Do you know that you are actually a gift from God? You were wrapped in love and given to your family—parents, grandparents, brothers, and sisters.

Quest

Every birth is a special event in the eyes of God and is worth celebrating. When you were born, your parents celebrated; when you are "born again," there is another great celebration in heaven too. When God's Son was born, a whole multitude of angels appeared to the shepherds. They couldn't help praising God and celebrating the event, startling the poor shepherds who were guarding their flocks at night. The birth of Christ was all a part of God's greater plan to bring peace on the earth and forgiveness for our sins. When you were born, all of heaven was aware and celebrated too—because God has plans for each person who enters this world. When we choose to follow God and submit to His plans, we too can be peacemakers and ambassadors of hope. You were born with a purpose in the heart and mind of God; you can discover this purpose when you seek and search for God with all your heart (Jer. 29:11–14).

Quiet Family Prayer

Thank God for placing your son/daughter in your family and for giving them the talents and abilities they have. Ask a special blessing of God upon this child for today and in the years to come.

Quiet Times

Younger Kids: Read Zephaniah 3:17. How do you feel knowing that God rejoices over you and that He sings and celebrates over you? Thank Him today for creating you in His image.

Older Kids: Read Zephaniah 3:17. What kind of song would you imagine God singing over you? Would it be a blessing, a dance tune, a loud celebration, or a quiet reflective song? Thank Him today for all He has done for you.

BIRTHDAY (PARENT)

Read: Proverbs 16:9

Quick Start

Happy birthday! When you look back over the past year, did you accomplish all of your goals? Which ones have yet to be completed?

Quest

Every year we have in mind things we would like to accomplish. Some years we are successful in achieving our goals; other years, we don't even come close. The Bible recognizes that we like to make plans, but it also recognizes that God is sovereign over us. When we give our lives to Him, we also give Him the right to guide our footsteps. Though we may not achieve all of our goals in a year, we may have accomplished far more in God's kingdom than we ever realized; our plans often have to do with our lives, but God's goals have to do with eternity. In past generations, people used to tell others their plans by beginning or ending with, "God willing." This was a way of saying, "Here is what I am planning, as long as God's plans coincide." We should be grateful even when God changes our course, because His plans are always best for us; sometimes they include unexpected blessings and reminders of His great love for us.

Quiet Family Prayer

Reflect over the years of your life today, what are the highlights? What are the low points? Do you see how God was with you every time? Thank God for His guidance, blessing, and strength through the years.

Quiet Times

Younger Kids: Read Psalm 149:5. What are you celebrating today? Why do you think we celebrate birthdays? Think how you can honor your birthday parent this week. Thank God for them now.

Older Kids: Read Psalm 149:5. When is the last time you shouted for joy? How can you celebrate your birthday-parent this week? What special thing can you do for them? Thank God for them now.

OUR COUNTRY'S BIRTHDAY

Read: Philippians 3:20

Quick Start

What is it that makes you feel the most patriotic?

Quest

It is not difficult to be proud of your country; it is your home and what you know best. When we travel to other countries, we can appreciate new foods, smells, sights, and sounds, but often people breathe a sigh of relief when they finally return home. Every nation has its own positives and negatives, but there is one kingdom that is different; it surpasses every earthly kingdom, nation, country, and continent. It is God's kingdom. When we allow Christ to be our Lord and Savior, we take on a new identity and are adopted into a new family and culture. Our Christian brothers and sisters become our family and the priorities of our King supersede the priorities of the countries in which we were born and raised. We long for the day when we can be finally get to be with our fellow citizens in heaven and rejoice in that we are at long last home. Although we may not resemble the others there on the outside, our hearts will be the same as they were all given to Jesus long ago.

Quiet Family Prayer

Some countries are old, others are new. When was your country founded? Do you think God is being honored in your country today? Pray that the leaders of your nation will turn to God for wisdom and guidance.

Quiet Times

Younger Kids: Read Psalm 22:27. Your country is a part of who you are. Ask God how you might be a better citizen this week to represent your country well.

Older Kids: Read Psalm 22:27. What would it take for people to recognize God's rule over your nation? Ask God to show you if He is truly ruling over your heart today.

FAMILY BAPTISM

Read: Mark 1:8

Quick Start

When have you felt overwhelmed, snowed under, overcome, or gotten in way over your head?

Quest

All of those words above could also be used to describe *baptism*. In a letter written by a ship captain to folks back home, the captain describes how his ship was "baptized" during a violent storm at sea with only a few survivors. In other words, the ship sunk! Baptism symbolized death and being buried with Christ (Rom. 6:4; Col. 2:12), but we are not left there—we are raised up to new life. To be baptized by the Holy Spirit also signifies being "overwhelmed," "overcome," and completely covered by Him, so that all of our being is under His control and care. Relinquishing your rights to Christ, giving the Spirit freedom to fill, use, empower, control, and permeate all of your being is a wonderful thing; you know then that God is in complete control in your life. Then we, as Paul, can say, "For me to live is Christ" (Phil. 1:21). The challenge is not so much denying ourselves and taking up our cross as it is walking daily in the presence and guidance of the Spirit of God.

Quiet Family Prayer

Baptism represents new life—starting over. We say good-bye to old habits and old ways of doing things, and welcome the Holy Spirit to guide us to live a new life pleasing to God. Ask God to help you live a life that is pleasing to Him this week.

Quiet Times

Younger Kids: Read Matthew 3:6. Why should we confess our sins to God? Ask God to show you if there is anything in your life that is not pleasing to Him and to help you serve Him with all your heart.

Older Kids: Read Matthew 3:6. When was the last time you confessed your sins to God? Are you allowing Him to take out of your life bad habits and attitudes and replace them with thoughts and actions that are Spirit-led and directed? Ask Him to show you what He sees when He looks at you.

SALVATION

Read: John 3:3

Quick Start

After a long, bleak winter, it is always great to see the flowers, leaves, and plants come alive again. What is your favorite plant or flower to see bloom?

Quest

Only God can accomplish a person being "born again." Our role in salvation is to put ourselves in the place where God is willing to grant salvation to us. Jesus says we must "repent and believe" (Mark 1:15). *Repentance* means turning away from everything that is contrary to God's will for our lives. *Believe* means trust our lives and our future to His hands and trust that what He said in His Word is true. Salvation is something that is accomplished (Rom. 8:24), and something we are "working out" in our own lives (Phil. 2:12). He is preparing us for the day we see Him face-to-face. It is a comfort to see God working in us, because we know He cares for us, and it reminds us of His presence in our lives. You are no longer the person you were before you were saved, but you are not yet the person God will help you to become as you continue to release your life into His hands.

Quiet Family Prayer

Born again means coming alive in Christ and starting a new life with Him in the center. Ask God today to help your family place Him in the center of your home and activities each day, so others will see how important He is to your family.

Quiet Times

Younger Kids: Read John 17:3. Sometimes we think all we have to do to be saved is say a prayer. Actually, knowing God, entrusting our lives to Him, and living for Him is the right answer. Thank God for providing a way for you to know Him because of what Jesus did.

Older Kids: Read John 17:3. How would you explain salvation to someone? Have you given your life to Christ? Is He your Lord and Savior? Take time to reflect on this verse and ask yourself how well you know God and His Son Jesus.

EASTER

Read: Matthew 28:7

Quick Start

In September 2009 Ray Jasper of Niagara Falls and his wife, Robin, spent four hours mourning their son, Sgt. Jesse Jasper, after receiving a call telling them their son had died in battle in Afghanistan. Many friends sent messages of condolences that afternoon before their telephone rang. You can imagine how shocked they were when they heard their son Jesse asking what all the commotion was about! He assured them he was very much alive and that whoever had informed them of his death were very much mistaken.

Quest

The disciples were very confused. All they knew was that the man they had followed for the past three years was dead. They were afraid that they would be arrested next, so while others took care of Jesus' body, they stayed out of sight wondering what they should do. Suddenly one of the women, Mary, burst into the house saying that Jesus was actually alive! Impossible! They were startled, amazed, and overjoyed when Christ finally appeared in their midst showing them the nail prints in His hands. If Christ could even defeat death itself, nothing was impossible for Him. Nothing would ever be the same again. God's love for the world was made clear (John 3:16) and the power of the resurrection was made available for all those who believe in Him (Phil. 3:10).

Quiet Family Prayer

Easter represents the most important event in history. Has there been an "Easter" in your heart where Christ came alive in you? Thank God for raising His Son from the dead so that we could have eternal life through Him if we believe.

Quiet Times

Younger Kids: Read 2 Corinthians 5:15. What does it mean to live for Jesus? What can you do to live for Jesus this week? Thank God for loving you so much and for letting you know Him.

Older Kids: Read 2 Corinthians 5:15. Are there things in your life that you need faith—faith that God will overcome on your behalf? Put those things in His hands today and watch His faithfulness to you.

Read: 2 John 1:6; John 15:13

Quick Start

In basic training soldiers learn a lot about war: how to fight, defend themselves, follow orders, work as a team—and that sometimes they must sacrifice themselves for the sake of their fellow soldiers. If you had to choose between saving yourself or to save someone you loved, what would you do?

Quest

Jesus not only commanded us to love one another and to love God, but He showed us how to do it. Everything He did was from the standpoint of love—His treatment of widows, people caught in sin, religious leaders, disciples, seekers, and everyone else was based in His deep love for them. On Valentine's Day, we celebrate love by giving candy, cards, flowers, or other gifts to those we care about; we should also not forget to show our appreciation to God for showing us His great love. We can do that by loving others in need around us. Jesus says when we do this, we are doing it for Him (Matt. 25:40). Look for opportunities each day to show Christ's love to those He sends across our pathways.

Quiet Family Prayer

We know how to love because God first loved us (1 John 4:10). How did God show you His love today? Thank Him now for His amazing love for your family.

Quiet Times

Younger Kids: Read 1 John 4:11. How many people can you name who love you? Whom do you love? Do you think you can tell these people you love this sometime this week in a card or phone call? Tell God how much you love Him today.

Older Kids: Read 1 John 4:10. What is the difference between God's love and love shown in Hollywood movies? Which kind of love would you say you exhibit more often in your life? Ask God to help you show His love to others more.

CHRISTMAS EVE

Read: Luke 2:9–18

Quick Start

Would you describe yourself as a patient person? Would others describe you this way? How did you feel when the day finally came that you could have what you were waiting for?

Quest

The birth of Christ was foretold hundreds of years before He was born. People had looked forward to the Messiah coming for generations, and every child heard stories from their parents and grandparents about what the Messiah would do. The day of Christ's birth finally came, and only a handful of shepherds were there to congratulate Mary and Joseph. There was no fanfare of trumpets, no four-star hotel, and no national holiday, nothing that would have marked such a momentous occasion. People were so busy with their own lives they totally missed what God was doing; it is not much different today. Even those who believe in Christ can be so busy with their own interests that they miss what God is doing all around them. We often forget that the world does not revolve around us—it revolves around what God is doing in the world. As you celebrate Christmas Eve, ask God to open your eyes to what He is doing in your home, in your family members, and in the lives of those around you.

Quiet Family Prayer

Things were very different on the first Christmas Eve than they are today. Mary and Joseph could not have known all that their son would accomplish in the next thirty-three years. Ask God to help you be faithful to Him over the next year so He can do incredible things through you too.

Quiet Times

Younger Kids: Read Philippians 4:16. Christians were helping Paul when he was imprisoned by sending different gifts to him for his support. What gifts have you given this year to help support others serving God?

Older Kids: Read 1 Corinthians 12:4. God has given you gifts too. He wants you to use them for helping others and bringing glory to Him. What gifts can you see that God has placed in your life? Thank Him for the gifts and talents you have been given.

Christmas Day

Read: Luke 2:16–20; John 3:16

Quick Start

Do you know the story of Pinocchio? Even though the puppet caused a lot of trouble, do you think Geppetto, his maker, would have preferred Pinocchio had stayed a puppet or became a boy?

Quest

The shepherds, the wise men (Matt. 2:1–12), Simeon (Luke 2:25–35) and Anna (Luke 2:36–38) all had a "coming to Christ" experience before Jesus was an adult. For some, it was an undeserved privilege; for others, it was a pure honor after a long, hard search; and for others still, it was a reward for years of faithful service to God.

Each of us is given an opportunity to come to Christ too, and to have Him born into our hearts as we surrender our lives to His lordship over us. As we let Christ live His life through us, we also bring glory to our Father in heaven. Now we are able to join the Father, the Son, and the Spirit in their work on the earth as they work through us to bring joy and good news to those who have not heard of God's love.

Quiet Family Prayer

Every day we can come to Christ when we talk with Him and think about His Words to us. Think about someone you know who has not yet come to Christ; ask God to help your family have a chance to share His love with them soon.

Quiet Times

Younger Kids: Read Acts 3:3–8. What did the beggar want? What did Peter have to offer? Which was better to have? Ask God to show you what you have to give people in Jesus' name that is a blessing to them.

Older Kids: Read Acts 3:3–8. There is a difference between what the beggar asked for and what Peter gave him. We don't always know what is best for us and ask God for something different from what He wants to give us. Ask God if there is something on His heart to give you that you should ask for today.

Read: Isaiah 42:13; 2 Timothy 2:3–4

Quick Start
How many famous battles can you name?

Quest
God's people were very familiar with war. From Abraham to John's vision of Revelation, God's people have fought against evil and oppression. One chapter is devoted to listing the names of David's mighty men, known for their outstanding courage and their expert ability in battle (1 Chron. 11 and 2 Sam. 23). The apostle Paul reminds us that our battles are not always physical battles, but they are also spiritual battles (Eph. 6:12–18). The key to winning the battle is not always being bigger and stronger than your opponent; more often, it involves knowing your enemy and keen preparations. Paul tells us about the armor and weapons that are available to us as Christians, reminding us that "the One who is in you is greater than the one who is in the world." (1 John 4:4) and, "I am able to do all things through Him who strengthens me" (Phil. 4:13). We should be grateful to those who have fought for our country in the battles against oppression and tyranny. We should also be grateful to those who have gone before us to fight many spiritual battles on our behalf and for the kingdom of God.

Quiet Family Prayer
Since ancient times, the world has always had wars and battles; there can also be wars inside us when we have to choose to do the right thing or stop doing the wrong things. Ask God to help you have victory in the battles you face in your own life.

Quiet Times
Younger Kids: Read Hebrews 12:1. Have you ever run in a race with cheering crowds around you? Did it make you run faster and harder? We have many people cheering for us to be good ambassadors for Jesus every day. Ask God to help you represent Him well this week.

Older Kids: Read Hebrews 12:1. Many faithful believers have gone before us to lay a foundation for us to build upon in our own lives and ministry. How are you building on that foundation? Ask God to help you be faithful to what He has called you to do.

THANKSGIVING DAY

*Read: 2 Chronicles 30:22; Matthew 26:27;
Ephesians 5:20; Colossians 3:17*

Quick Start

Let each person say one thing for which they are grateful. Repeat this three more times.

Quest

Christians should be the most grateful people on the planet; we should regularly be thanking God for His goodness and blessings to us. Even when we cannot think of anything in particular for which we can be grateful, we can always think of the cross upon which Christ willingly offered Himself to pay the penalty for our sins. It seems so much easier to complain about the things we don't have, or criticize others for letting us down, or grumble about the weather, or gripe about not being treated fairly. This is so selfish of us. When we whine, nit-pick, or nag, we are often thinking only of ourselves. When we are grateful and thankful, we are appreciating what others have done for us. If you have ever visited an orphanage, men's shelter, food distribution center, or charity toy location, you will have an appreciation for just how much you really have. Some families always invite others to be a part of their Thanksgiving meal—particularly those who have no family nearby—because they want to share what they have with others. Are you a grateful person? Do you regularly give thanks to God and to others for their kindness towards you?

Quiet Family Prayer

Being a thankful person shows gratitude and humility towards God and others. Ask Him how He is working, even in the midst of the difficult things in your life.

Quiet Times

Younger Kids: Read Psalm 107:22. How many things are on your "thankful" list—can you come up with forty? Tell God how grateful you are to Him for all His blessings.

Older Kids: Read Psalm 100. Do you think you can memorize this psalm? Putting His word on your heart usually makes us more thankful. Ask God what verses you should start memorizing to carry with you to help grow your character and attitude.

DEATH IN THE FAMILY

Read: 1 Corinthians 15:55; Psalm 116:15

Quick Start

What would you say is better to lose or get rid of than to keep?

Quest

Funerals are often very somber and quiet events. People dress in dark colors, some people cry, and quiet music plays in the background. Two things are happening: First, people mourn the loss of a loved one; it is sad to not have that person to talk to and spend time with any more. Second, people remember the words that the Bible says about death; it is not the great enemy if we believe in Jesus—it is just the end of one kind of life and the beginning of another. Naturally we are sad that someone we love is gone, but we can be comforted knowing that we will see them again one day in heaven.

Quiet Family Prayer

There are times to sing and celebrate; there are times to cry and be reflective. God is with us in all times. Thank God for the people He has placed in your life and how they impact you. Ask Him to help you be a family that will always be remembered as helpful and kind to others in their times of need.

Quiet Times

Younger Kids: Read Matthew 5:16. When people die, they are no longer with us physically—but the memories of them remain with us. What are some good memories you have of the person who has gone to be in the presence of God? Can you thank God for having them in your life as long as you did?

Older Kids: Read Matthew 5:16. We are never guaranteed a long life, but we are promised a life of meaning and purpose if we let God guide us. How are you letting your life shine so that people will think well of you and remember you made a difference in their life? Ask God to help you use all your days to be a person of purpose and influence.

A New Baby

Read: Psalm 139:13; Jeremiah 1:5

Quick Start

What is the most difficult thing about having a new baby in your home? What is the best thing about having a baby around?

Quest

When a baby comes to a family, there is always a lot of anticipation and questions: What if the baby doesn't like me? Will I be a good big brother or sister? How much work is this going to be for me? Sometimes we forget that God has a plan for every baby and we are a part of God's plan to help that baby grow and learn and experience things in life. Moses had a big brother and sister that God used when they grew up to lead His people out of slavery in Egypt. There were four sisters who lived in Caesarea who were very important to the early church (Acts 21:9). Jesus even chose two sets of brothers to be some of His disciples. We may see a baby in a crib, but God may see an important leader one day or a great person that He will use in His kingdom. Your new baby may seem like a lot of work at first, but as they grow, they may one day be your best friend and strongest ally when you face tough times. They are a gift from God to you, but you are also a gift from God to them.

Quiet Family Prayer

Ask God to help you be a good influence on the new baby and a good example for them to follow as they grow.

Quiet Times

Younger Kids: Read Titus 2:7. Ask God to help you be a good friend and guide to the baby as he or she grows.

Older Kids: Read Titus 2:7. You probably are not going to be the perfect big brother or sister every day, but you *are* going to be a person of influence over the years. Treating younger siblings well when they are younger will lead to being good friends when they are older. Ask God to help you be a positive force in their life now.

ELECTION DAY

Read: Titus 3:1; 1 Peter 2:13–15

Quick Start

How many levels of government can you name? Do you know who is in charge of each level?

Quest

We are more likely to criticize our government leaders for not doing what we think they should be doing rather than taking time to pray for them. Being a politician can be a very challenging job, and one that requires a lot of wisdom and hard work. Praying that those who govern over you seek the Lord's guidance and that God would guide them to do what is best for the people is a wise thing to do. There certainly have been political leaders who have used their position for personal gain, but there are far more who use their position of influence for the good of families, communities, cities, and states. God used many national and local leaders to accomplish His will in the Bible, and still does today around the world. Pray for your leaders. Write them letters of encouragement and support. If you are old enough to vote, ask God for guidance during elections. Who knows—God may want you to be His instrument to govern over people one day!

Quiet Family Prayer

Regardless of the election results, God is able to work through those who govern over us. Pray for the winner and for those who lose the election, and ask God to help you be a good citizen.

Quiet Times

Younger Kids: Read Titus 3:1. You may not know who the election winners are, but pray that they will honor God in their decisions and be people who are honest and helpful.

Older Kids: Read Titus 3:1. It is not easy to work in public life as a politician; there are many challenges and temptations. Pray for your leaders to be people of integrity and strong moral convictions. Consider writing the winner of the election telling them that you are praying for them and write a Scripture verse for them to read.

Read: Proverbs 1:1–9

Quick Start

What do you think the difference is between knowledge and wisdom?

Quest

Knowledge is information, data, and facts. Wisdom is knowing how to use information. In school, we learn a lot of facts—famous names, historical dates, scientific data, and math. As we get older, we learn how to use all of these things in daily life. The Bible tells us that "The fear of the Lord is the beginning of knowledge" (Prov. 1:7) and "The fear of the Lord is the beginning of wisdom" (Ps. 111:10). As you begin your school year, ask God what He wants you to learn, and what He wants to teach you so that you will grow both in wisdom and knowledge. As Jesus grew up, the Bible tells us that He "grew up and became strong, filled with wisdom, and God's grace was on Him" (Luke 2:40) "And Jesus increased in wisdom and stature, and in favor with God and with people" (Luke 2:52). When we seek after God, we will grow both in knowledge and in wisdom as He teaches us what is important for us to know.

Quiet Family Prayer

Ask God to bring you good friends, good teachers, and show you how to be a good citizen in your class. Ask God to help you be a positive influence on others and to learn all that He wants you to learn this year.

Quiet Times

Younger Kids: Read Proverbs 2:6. Ask God to help you learn and understand important things. His Spirit is sent to be your helper and guide. Ask Him to help you to be a good student this year.

Older Kids: Read Proverbs 2:6. You will learn a lot of information, concepts, philosophies, and principles this year. Ask God what things He wants you to learn spiritually as His Spirit guides your mind and heart.

LAST DAY OF SCHOOL

Read: Ecclesiastes 3:1–8

Quick Start

You have a few months to rest from school and enjoy your summer! What three things would you like to do before school starts back again in the fall?

Quest

The Bible tells us there is a proper time for everything, and that we need to make the best use of our time so that it is not wasted on meaningless things. We can sit and play video games for days at a time and have little to show for it (except maybe new high scores); or we can choose to learn new things, develop skills, or enjoy new activities. The more experiences we have and the better we improve our skills, the greater the opportunities will be open to us in the future. There is a time to rest and relax, to party and celebrate, to learn and grow, and to work hard and to enjoy life. Use your time wisely so at the end of the summer, you will have grown into a much more exciting and competent person than you were last year.

Quiet Family Prayer

Your report card reflects both the effort you put in to your classes and how well you learned all the material that was taught this past year. Did you do your best? Thank God for the rest you have over the break from school, and ask Him to prepare you for the fall when things start up again.

Quiet Times

Younger Kids: Read 2 Timothy 4:7. You finished! Another school year is done. Congratulations! Thank God for giving you the opportunity to learn in school—many children around the world don't have schools to attend. Ask God to help you use your vacation time well.

Older Kids: Read 2 Timothy 4:7. If you are pleased with how you ended your year, thank God for the chance to learn and grow. If you are disappointed in how you finished the year, ask God to help you through the disappointment and prepare you for the year to come.

CELEBRATING AN ACHIEVEMENT

Read: Zephaniah 3:17

Quick Start

When would you say the following words: Whoohoo! Yay! Yesssssss! Alright! Uh Huh! Hoo Ha!

Quest

Did you know that God sings? Some translations of Zephaniah 3:17 say God "will sing and be joyful over you," others say He "will delight in you with shouts of joy." Either way, God knows how to celebrate with His people. Even the angels celebrate when even one person comes to salvation (Luke 15:10). Sometimes we get so caught up in our achievement and victory that we forget it was God Who gave us the ability to do what we did in the first place. He loves it when we are able to experience what He created us to do, and to take advantage of the abilities and skills He placed in our lives; the Maker and the person can celebrate accomplishments together. As you celebrate your accomplishment today, also take time to celebrate God's goodness to you for creating you the way He did. "Rejoice in the Lord always. I will say it again: Rejoice!" (Phil. 4:4).

Quiet Family Prayer

What did you do to celebrate your accomplishment? God is pleased when you fulfill your potential and make accomplishments as you learn and grow. Thank Him for giving you the ability to do what you can do.

Quiet Times

Younger Kids: Read 1 Corinthians 9:24. Today you get the prize for a job well done! Ask God to help you continue to do your best in all things so that you are pleasing to Him and can achieve things others may not want to put forth the effort to do.

Older Kids: Read 1 Corinthians 9:24. Very rarely do we do our absolute best at something; it depends on our motivation. Now that you have been successful, are you going to rest—or are you already looking for the next challenge? Ask God what He wants you to do to continue to build on your successes.

Read: Daniel 9:13

Quick Start

Where is your emergency preparedness kit located? Can you name the items that are in it?

Quest

When a disaster takes place—a massive flood, tornado, hurricane, or wild fires—people often wonder what God has to do with it. Some think God should have stopped it from causing such damage; others think God caused it because people are no longer serving Him. In the Bible, God often allowed disasters to happen so that His people would turn away from other gods and turn back to Him for help and guidance. Only rarely did God deliberately cause devastation (the Great Flood during the time of Noah, Sodom and Gomorrah, Egyptian plagues); even then, it was after repeated warnings to the people to repent or face His judgment. Sometimes we can blame God for bad things that happen, but really we should be looking to Him for help and guidance in the midst of the disaster. We should also look for ways to help others in their time of need and share God's love with them. It is during times of devastation that people need to know God's love the most.

Quiet Family Prayer

Disasters are almost never good news; there is much pain and suffering. But God is there and His people can make a real difference in the situation to bring healing and comfort. Ask God to send the right people, resources, supplies, and protection so that lives will be changed by those who show His love to them.

Quiet Times

Younger Kids: Read Psalm 31:3. A rock and a fortress are secure, solid, and safe. That is what God is like for those who trust in Him. Ask God to help those facing disaster that they may be comforted.

Older Kids: Read Psalm 31:3. Have you ever needed God to be a rock or a fortress for you? Ask God to help you turn to Him quickly in challenging times that you will be at peace and feel the security He can give.

SICKNESS

Read: Exodus 15:26

Quick Start

Being sick is never fun. What is the worst part about being sick?

Quest

One of the things Jesus did most during His three years of ministry on the earth was to heal the sick or lame and free those in spiritual bondage. In fact, when John the Baptist's disciples asked Jesus if He was truly the Messiah, Jesus told them to go back to John and say, "The blind receive their sight, the lame walk, those with skin diseases are healed, the deaf hear, the dead are raised, and the poor are told the good news" (Luke 7:22). Sometimes sickness comes upon us for no reason; sometimes it is our body telling us we need some rest. Even though we take the medicine doctors prescribe to us, we know that it is God who brings the healing. Sick times are great times to spend reading the Bible, praying, listening to Christian music, and trusting that God will bring your body back to wholeness in His time. We put our lives and our bodies in God's hands for His use and purposes and have faith that He will always do what is best.

Quiet Family Prayer

Sickness is sometimes devastating; sometimes it is a warning our body gives us. Use times of sickness to slow down, seek God, and let Him guide us to read His Word or pray for others. Ask God for healing and to use your sick time wisely.

Quiet Times

Younger Kids: Read James 5:16. We pray because we believe God will listen to us. God created us and can heal our bodies in His time and in His way. Tell God what you would like Him to do and watch as He responds to your prayers.

Older Kids: Read James 5:16. Sickness can really get in the way of important things, but sometimes sickness helps us focus on what is really important too. Listen to what God may want to say to you at this time; ask Him if there is anything you need to learn as well.

SAD TIMES

Read: Psalm 34:18

Quick Start

How do actors cry so easily for a play or a movie when it is all make-believe?

Quest

God wanted us to have joy in our lives, but sometimes sad things happen. We may have to move to a new place; we may experience the loss of something or someone we love; we may get bullied at school; or we have to face the consequences of our bad decisions. Whatever it is, God knows and He says that He will ever leave us or forsake us (Heb. 13:5). There is no one who knows how to heal a broken heart like Jesus; when we are crushed in spirit, God wraps His loving arms around us and reminds us of His unfailing love for us. God does not always change the situation, but He does walk with us through it until we are okay. He puts His people around us to encourage us and help us along the way. He sends His spirit to lift us up when we are weak and strengthen us when we don't think we can even face the next day. He knows about sad things, because He had to watch His own Son be beaten, scourged, mocked, and crucified on a cross. Christ suffered for us and can understand what we are feeling; now He walks with us to help us stand on solid ground once more.

Quiet Family Prayer

Sad times will come; so will disappointments. God knows our hearts and will lift us up when we are downcast. Ask God to restore to you the joy He provides even in the midst of sad times.

Quiet Times

Younger Kids: Read Psalm 51:12. Even in sad times, we can celebrate the good things God has done for us. Ask God to help you keep your eyes on Him rather than the things that make you sad.

Older Kids: Read Psalm 51:12. Joy does not always come in the circumstances of life, but it can come in our salvation. Knowing God loves us, saves us, protects us, guides us, strengthens us, and cares for us will help free us from our sadness.

A WEDDING

Read: Matthew 19:5

Quick Start

Do you remember a time when you became separated from your mom or dad and thought you were lost?

Quest

Some people can hardly wait to get out on their own and start their life apart from their parents. Others don't know if they can manage very well without their parents' cooking, laundry services, and compassion, car repairs, financial help, and wise counsel. Sometimes we look for a wife that is similar to our mother, or a husband that is similar to our father, because that is the closest example of what a husband or wife has been for us. Leaving home and being joined to another person to form your own home can be very exciting and very intimidating at the same time; wise parents will encourage you to become less dependent upon them and more dependent upon your spouse. Wise parents will help a new couple build their own home so it will be strong enough to weather the storms that may come. Becoming "one flesh" with your spouse is both an event and a process, but it is necessary and will prepare for your own children, who will see what a mother and a father are supposed to be. Let the adventure begin!

Quiet Family Prayer

From the creation of the very first man and woman, God had marriage in mind. He wanted to use families to show His great love for His people. Ask God to bless this marriage and to become the center of their new home together.

Quiet Times

Younger Kids: Weddings can be very fun, boring, exciting, and tiring all at the same time. What was your favorite part? Ask God to bless the couple who were married and to help them as they make their new home together.

Older Kids: Read Ephesians 5:25, 28. Love, submission, respect—what do all of these mean to you? If a wife and a husband both honor and respect one another with Christ, and keep Him in the center of their marriage, their home will reflect His love. Pray God will guide and protect this new marriage in the days to come.

GAME DAY

Read: Philippians 4:13; Colossians 3:23; 1 Corinthians 9:24

Quick Start

Have you ever played on a team that never won a game all season or played in a tournament where you didn't win one game? Did that really make you a "loser"?

Quest

Winning or losing does not affect how God sees you. He looks at your heart, not at the scoreboard. Did you play your best? Did you represent Him well in the game? Did you play to win, or did you fool around out there? Coaches will respect an athlete who always plays their best and is a person with good character and integrity more than a player who shows off their talent at the expense of their team. How you perform in a game sometimes reflects how you live your life. Are you doing your best to represent God well at school, at home, with your friends? Every day is Game Day with God; He wants to be able to trust us to do what we are gifted and talented to do, so that we can support all the other team players out there.

Quiet Family Prayer

What do you think would be some great things to pray for today? How about safety, good sportsmanship, fun, good character? Ask God to help each player represent Him well today.

Quiet Times

Younger Kids: Read Colossians 3:23 again. Ask God to help you always do your best because you know He is watching you and is pleased when you do your best.

Older Kids: Read Colossians 3:23 again. How can you do things as if you were doing it for the Lord? Thank Him for giving you the wisdom and strength to work your best at all times.

HALLOWEEN

Read: Corinthians 13:14

Quick Start

Are you afraid of ghosts? Do you have a favorite ghost story?

Quest

The older translations of the Bible called the Spirit of God the "Holy Ghost"; that means the words *ghost* and *spirit* are the same. In the Bible, the only *Ghost* God sent was not only friendly, but our best friend who truly cares for us and protects us. This same Holy *Spirit* is what unifies all believers together and unites us in Christ. The Holy Ghost is nothing to be afraid of; in fact, He loves us dearly and applies God's blessings and grace to our life every day. He is a gift sent by God when Jesus returned to heaven; He is our friend and best supporter (Acts 2:38). You might not believe in ghosts, but you can believe in the Holy Ghost who watches over you and even helps you to pray when you don't know what to say. So with the Holy Ghost on your side, you can accomplish everything God wants you to do. Because the Spirit of God does not have a body, He is able to be with every person around the world who belongs to God. What a great encouragement that is to us!

Quiet Family Prayer

Talk for a minute about the difference between all-powerful God and the presence of His Spirit in your lives and home. Thank God for His Holy Spirit that protects, guides, teaches, and helps us whenever we call upon Him.

Quiet Times

Younger Kids: Read Joshua 1:9. Remember that we never have to be afraid when God is with us. Thank God for His love, His protection, and His mighty angels that watch over His people.

Older Kids: Read Joshua 1:9. Is there anything that you are afraid of or that worries you? Use this verse as a promise God makes to you. Thank Him for His mighty arm of protection over you, and put your confidence in Him.

Read: Mark 16:14–20

Quick Start

If you had to get an important message to someone who lived on the other side of the world, what would be the three quickest ways you would transmit the message?

Quest

Christ did not leave us with an easy task, but He did give us a very important task: to take the gospel to every person on the earth. Matthew records Jesus saying, "Go, therefore, and make disciples . . ." (Matt. 28:19). But Mark is more specific, saying that every person needs to be given the chance to respond to the Good News so they can repent of their sins, believe in Christ, and have a relationship with their heavenly Father. Too often we leave the task of sharing the gospel to the professionals like pastors, ministers, and missionaries; but this command was for you, for me, for everyone who is a believer in Christ. Do your neighbors know about Jesus? Do your classmates? How about your coach or your relatives? Can you share the gospel on your social-networking sites? Jesus said, "The one who has My commands and keeps them is the one who loves Me" (John 14:21). If you share the Good News with others, you show your love for them as well.

Quiet Family Prayer

Go around the room and name as many countries as you can. Pick three countries to pray for today. Ask God to send people to share the gospel to the people in those countries. Ask Him to bless and care for any missionaries who are already there.

Quiet Times

Younger Kids: Read Matthew 28:18–20. Jesus tells us to tell others about Him and to live our lives so others would want to know Him too. Ask God to help you tell someone about Him this week.

Older Kids: Read Matthew 28:18–20. Who was it who first told you about Jesus? Ask God to give you a chance to share your faith in God with a friend or acquaintance this week. Pray now for God to give you the right opportunity and the right words to say.

NAME DAY

Read: Genesis 17:5, 15; 32:28; Revelation 2:17

Quick Start

What do you like best about your name? Do you know what your name means? If you had to choose another name for yourself, what would it be?

Quest

Sometimes God gave people new names to better reflect what He was going to do in their life. For Abram, God changed his name to Abraham and for his wife Sarai, to Sarah because God was starting something new through them. Similarly, God changed Jacob's name to Israel, as his sons would establish the twelve tribes of Israel. Often names were given with a promise or a hope that the meaning of the name would describe the character the person would have when they grew up. Sometimes a name doesn't have a very special meaning, but you can give it great meaning by how you live your life. When people hear your name, they will remember how God used you in a mighty way and forever associate God's blessing and strength with your name. We carry with us the name of Christ when we call ourselves Christians; we need to always remember to honor His name in how we act and in what we say wherever we are.

Quiet Family Prayer

Take a moment to say each person's full name aloud. Each person should say the meanings of their name. Ask God to bless each person by name and to use them to be a blessing to others as they live their life to honor Him.

Quiet Times

Younger Kids: Your name is very special. You will create a reputation for your name by how you act. Whenever people hear your name they will think of you. Ask God to help you live in such a way that everyone will have a good thought when your name is mentioned.

Older Kids: Read Genesis 12:2. When did Abraham's name become great? Only after he obeyed God. What do you think it would take for God to make your name great among people? Ask God to help you honor Him so that He can bless you.

BOXING DAY

Read: James 1:17; 1 Peter 4:10

Quick Start

The day after a big celebration (Christmas) can be quite a letdown. What can you do to make this day special and one to remember?

Quest

Boxing Day (the day after Christmas) is celebrated in many countries around the world and is also called the Day of Goodwill, St. Stephen's Day, the Day of the Wren, and even the second Christmas Day. Like many holidays, it is deteriorating into a shopping spree with Boxing Day Sales for stores to clear their inventory. But it used to be a day for people to gather with their friends and family after Christmas and celebrate the season together. Some believe it began with masters allowing their servants to return home after Christmas carrying boxes of food and Christmas bonuses for their family. Some countries will have special sport competitions (college basketball, European football, prize fights) on this day each year. Many families have begun their own traditions for using this day to be a blessing to others who are less fortunate. After all the Christmas wrapping paper is put away, and the tree looks bare with unwrapped presents, consider for a moment how good God has been to you and your family. Remember the gifts God has given to us are not meant to be hoarded but to be shared with others around us.

Quiet Family Prayer

Ask God to show you how to be a blessing to someone else or to another family today. What does He want you to do to encourage others at this time of year?

Quiet Times

Younger Kids: Read Matthew 22:39. Why do you think God commands us to love our neighbors? What can you do this week to show love to your neighbors? Thank God for your neighbors tonight.

Older Kids: Read Matthew 22:39. This can be a very challenging command. Read Luke 6:35. Even more challenging. Ask God tonight to show you how you can do this in the next week.

GRADUATION

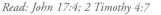

Read: John 17:4; 2 Timothy 4:7

Quick Start

What significant accomplishments can your family members name that they have achieved so far?

Quest

As Saul, he was a great hindrance; as the apostle Paul, he was a great contributor to God's kingdom. After Christ reoriented his life, Paul could reflect and know that he had done everything he could to please his Lord and to serve God faithfully. Finishing well is important because it brings a great deal of satisfaction for all the hard work it took to get there. It is great to celebrate achievements and successes and to reward yourself for a job well done. Take time to mark the occasion: take a picture, hang something on a wall or put it on a shelf, throw a party, hang out with your friends and family. You are to be congratulated on succeeding where others have failed or did not finish. Thank God and others for helping you make it to the end and being there for you when it was tough going. After you take a breath, think about what the next challenge might be in your life—the next mountain to climb, the next goal to achieve, the next opportunity to grow. But today, just have fun and enjoy the moment!

Quiet Family Prayer

Thank God for providing the stamina, wisdom, and strength to finish the race well. Ask His blessing upon the graduate today that he or she would use their life and training for His glory.

Quiet Times

Younger Kids: Read Luke 2:52. Graduating means you have learned all that the school wanted you to learn. Are you learning all that God wants you to learn too? Ask God to help you be wise both in knowledge and in favor with Him.

Older Kids: Read Luke 2:52. Graduation often means you have grown up and are ready to face new challenges in life. This can be scary and exciting. We may finish school, but we never stop learning about God who helps us navigate through life. Turn to Psalm 25:4–5 and pray these verses for yourself.

WAR

Read: 1 Timothy 6:12; 2 Timothy 4:7

Quick Start

Do you have any relatives or friends who have fought in a war? If you were conscripted (drafted) to fight for your country, in which of the military branches would you want to serve?

Quest

War always has a very heavy cost financially, emotionally, psychologically, and in lives lost. Many times irreparable damage is done to nations and to its citizens. The Bible talks of God's people fighting in many battles, particularly in the Old Testament, as they relocated to the Promised Land after living in exile as slaves. The Syrians, Assyrians, Babylonians, and Persians, all had their turn at conquering the Promised Land, even into the days of Jesus, where they endured Roman occupation of their lands. Some things are certainly worth fighting for; some things are not. Paul reminds us that we should be fighting the "good fight." It is the kind of fight that is more important than any other battle you will face, because it has to do with your eternal life. It won't matter how many battles you fight in on earth if you have not won the battle for your faith—which results in salvation. Put on your spiritual armor (Eph. 6:11), face your enemy, and walk forward with Christ.

Quiet Family Prayer

There is a time for war and a time for peace. Though we fight spiritual battles all the time, we are to be peacemakers as God's people. Ask God to show you how to be a peacemaker and to be faithful to pray for those who will be going to war on behalf of their country.

Quiet Times

Younger Kids: Read 2 Chronicles 20:17. It would be an amazing thing to see God fight for you. But this is His promise to us too. Thank God for taking care of your enemies when you call out to Him.

Older Kids: Read Proverbs 21:31. What do you think this verse means? Are there battles you are facing that you need the Lord to guide you through or fight on your behalf? You always get the victory when you let the Lord guide you.

A FAMILY ENGAGEMENT

Read: Matthew 19:4–6

Quick Start

An engagement ring is a promise—it does not mean a person is married, only that they have promised to marry in the coming days. Will your engagement time be stressed, all-consuming, and all about you—or will it be fun and relaxed, focusing on friends and family who will be your support after the wedding day is over?

Quest

Too often engagements are all about planning a wedding day instead of planning a life together. The wedding day will come and go and you will have pictures and videos to remember it. But unless attention is paid to all the days after, you will have a very bumpy first few years together. The Bible offers many clues as to how a husband and wife should relate to one another, how to pray with one another, how to serve one another, and how to create a God-honoring home together. Congratulations on your engagement, and may God bless the home and marriage you will be forming together with His help and guidance.

Quiet Family Prayer

Take time to thank God for inventing marriage and for answering your prayers to provide a godly spouse for your child. Ask God's blessing and wisdom in the coming days that everything would be in place for them to start their new life together well.

Quiet Times

Younger Kids: Read Ephesians 5:31. What do you think it means that two people become "one"? The only way this can really happen is if God helps their hearts and minds to agree together and let Him be in the center of their marriage. Take a minute to pray for the two people who are engaged that they would honor God in their relationship.

Older Kids: Read Mark 10:8. It has been God's plan all along for a man and wife to form their own marriage and their own family. Ask God to help you stay pure in your own life so that when it comes time for you to be engaged, you will have nothing to be ashamed of or regret.

NEW YEAR'S EVE

Read: Isaiah 43:18–19

Quick Start

Would you prefer to have an antique car or a brand-new car? Antique furniture or brand-new furniture? Antique toys or brand-new toys?

Quest

When you think about it, walking into an antique store can be very depressing, if you consider everything in there was once owned by people who are presumed dead. Everything in the store was once brand-new. Having antiques in your home is a way to connect with the past and a way to remember family members who lived long ago. Some people actually prefer to live in the past and resist all the "new-fangled contraptions" in the stores each year. God has worked mightily in the past, but His plans include working mightily in the days ahead as well. We need to respect and honor the past, but not let it keep us from experiencing the wonder of new things God wants to do in the coming days. Past struggles and fears can be conquered, and we can be liberated from the excuses that have always held us back from serving God. God is interested in taking the old and making it new, fresh, exciting, and challenging so that we would have an abundant and joyful life in the future.

Quiet Family Prayer

Ask God to forgive you for any sins or failings you have had in the past year. Ask Him to guide you into His Word so that you will be able to discern His will for your family and gain the answer you will need for the challenges you will face in the coming year.

Quiet Times

Younger Kids: Read 1 Samuel 2:21, 26, and 3:19. Take a minute to ask God to help you grow in Him in the coming year so all you do and say will be pleasing to Him.

Older Kids: Read 1 Samuel 2:26. In what three ways does the Bible say Samuel grew? You may have stopped growing taller, but you can never stop growing in relationship with God and with others. Ask God to help you grow in Him this next year and in your relationship with others.

NEW YEAR'S DAY

Read: Leviticus 26:9–12

Quick Start

How many New Year's resolutions have you kept?

Quest

Every once in a while, we have to get rid of the dust that has accumulated on curtains, walls, cupboards, etc., or clean out the storage areas of our homes to make room for new things. It always feels good when you are finished, but it can also be a lot of work. Each new year brings with it the anticipation of what God is going to do in our families. We may not have any idea what may come our way, but God does. Psalm 20:7 says many people trust in their own strength and securities, but we will trust in the name of our God. We should always be grateful that He gives us one more year to serve Him and to worship Him and to make a difference in people's lives. Ask God to help you make the most of this coming year and to reveal to your family what is on His heart for you to do to impact the lives of others with the gospel of love.

Quiet Family Prayer

Thank God for all that He has done in your family in the past year, and ask God for wisdom as you enter into a new year. Ask for His help to guide your family to follow and honor Him every step of the way.

Quiet Times

Younger Kids: Read 2 Corinthians 5:17. By staying close to God, you will be able to handle whatever this year brings—good, bad, and sad things. Ask God to help you stay close to Him this year so it will be one of the best ones ever.

Older Kids: Read 2 Corinthians 5:17. Just as a new year brings many possibilities, so does our new life in Christ. When we are "born again," we are given a new chance to live for God. Ask God tonight to help you live this year for Him so that your life will make a difference in God's kingdom.

Read: Psalm 139:13

Quick Start
What is your earliest memory?

Quest
God is the giver of life, regardless of how it comes about. He did not create the world in Genesis and then sit back and watch everything happen on its own; He is still very much involved in His creation. A pregnancy is a time of fascination and wonder as a baby miraculously grows and forms in the womb. Each time the baby turns around or a little foot kicks from the inside, we wonder what the child will be like. Sometimes fears arise, like contemplating the sort of world the child will inherit. But God knows all these things, including what the world will be like; just as He is here for us now, He will be there to walk with your child in the days to come. A new life brings new possibilities, new opportunities, new challenges, and new joys we never could have imagined. Pray now that the child will come to know God early in life and seek to live a life that is pleasing to his or her Creator.

Quiet Family Prayer
Thank God for the miracle of a baby; pray for His protection as the baby continues to grow and develop. Ask God to prepare the mother for the new life coming into the home.

Quiet Times
Younger Kids: Read Jeremiah 1:5. God formed us inside our mothers and gave us personalities, talents, and abilities that we could use to bring joy to Him. Thank God tonight for how He created you and thank God for all the great things you will be able to do to bring Him glory as you grow up.

Older Kids: Read Jeremiah 1:5. God had a plan to use Jeremiah from before he was even born. God has plans for each person He creates. What do you imagine God planned to do through your life? Can you see how the talents and spiritual gifts He has given you can be used for His glory? Thank Him for these things and ask Him to show you what He has in mind for you to do this week.

(Un)Answered Prayer

Read: John 14:13

Quick Start

Have you ever prayed to God and felt like He did not answer the prayer like you wanted Him to?

Quest

Some say that God always answers prayer: sometimes yes, sometimes no, and sometimes wait. But Jesus says He will do whatever we ask in His name! So that means we should always get a "yes," right? The key is to know what praying "in His name" means. It means we pray according to what Christ wants to accomplish in, through, and around us. When we ask Christ what we should pray, He begins to show us what He is doing and what He wants to accomplish, so that when He answers the prayer, we know we have been a part of His activity. Before you start praying, ask Jesus what you should pray; ask who you need to pray for; and ask Him what it is He wants to do through you to impact people around you. Then watch as He brings about everything He directed you to pray for. It is an exciting way to walk and work with God. This is how a Master and a servant work together in the kingdom of God. What does Jesus want you to pray for today?

Quiet Family Prayer

Thank God for answering your prayers and for showing His vast love for you and your family. Ask Him to show you some ways you can show your love for Him this week.

Quiet Times

Younger Kids: Read 1 Thessalonians 5:18. Think about all the times you have prayed and God answered your prayers. Take time to thank God for answering your prayers.

Older Kids: Read Colossians 4:2. What do you think it means to "pray with thanksgiving"? Tonight when you pray to God, remember to thank Him for His answers that will come—it shows you trust He knows what you need and will respond in your best interests.

DISObjectPOINTMENTS

Read: John 14:27

Quick Start

What has been your greatest disappointment or most difficult day so far?

Quest

Jesus was not just being nice when He told us that our hearts did not have to be troubled or afraid. He wasn't patting us on the head saying, "There, there, everything will be okay." He was making us a promise. He also said, "I have told you these things so that in Me you may have peace. You will have suffering in this world. Be courageous! I have conquered the world" (John 16:33). The promise is that He is stronger than whatever disappointment we are facing in our lives, and that we can have peace in the midst of it because we have trust and faith in Him—not in the present circumstances. Peace in our hearts comes from His Spirit's presence living in us. It comes from the assurance that even when what we see with our eyes is disappointing, we know God is working in all things for our good (Rom. 8:28). God's love for us is never failing and He will not let us down.

Quiet Family Prayer

Take a few moments to praise and thank God for all that He has done for you. Tell Him that you trust Him, and that you know He loves you—and that you will be looking to see how He is going to work everything out for your good in the days to come.

Quiet Times

Younger Kids: Talk with your mother or father about your disappointments, and about how you are feeling about them right now. Remember, God sees and knows what you are going through. Take out your Bible and read John 14:16. Thank God that He promises to stay with you during the rough times.

Older Kids: Read John 14:16. Jesus prayed for you! He wanted His Father to give you the same kind of Comforter that He had during the tough times He faced on the earth. You can be confident that He will not only be with you but will guide you through tough and challenging times. Thank Him tonight for how He will see you through this disappointing time in your life.

Tom Blackaby holds a BEd, MDiv, and DMin and has served as an associate pastor of music/youth/education in four churches in three countries and as senior pastor of North Sea Baptist Church in Stavanger, Norway, for seven years. He was the National Worship Consultant for the Canadian National Baptist Convention and currently serves as International Director for Blackaby Ministries International. Tom leads conferences/seminars and speaks in the areas of men's ministry, worship, prayer, experiencing God, revival, the God-centered family, and spiritual leadership. Tom has authored or coauthored:

- *The Man God Uses* (and *The Student God Uses* version)
- *Anointed to Be God's Servants: Lessons from the Life of Paul and His Companions*
- *The Blackaby Study Bible*
- *Encounters with God Daily Bible*
- *The Family God Uses* (trade book and workbook)
- *Experiencing God's Love in the Church*
- *The Commands of Christ*
- *Sammy Experiences God* (children's book)
- *7 Steps to Knowing and Doing the Will of God for Teens*
- *Experiencing God at Home*
- *Experiencing God at Home Family Devotional*

Tom and Kim have three great kids: Erin, Matt (both in college), and Conor (high school) and they live near Vancouver, BC, Canada.

Rick Osborne is a best-selling author and coauthor of a great number of books all dedicated to the biblical concept of making disciples at home and in the church. Rick has authored or coauthored:

- *Teaching Your Child How to Pray*
- *The Parent's Guide to the Spiritual Growth of Children*
- *801 Questions Children Ask about God*
- *The Boy's Bible*
- *A Perfect Pet for Peyton: The 5 Love Languages for Kids* (coauthored with Dr. Gary Chapman)
- *Sammy Experiences God* (coauthor with Tom Blackaby).

His production *The Singing Bible* (SingingBible.com) is hailed as one of the best collections of Christian children's songs ever. For more information you can find Rick online at Rick-Osborne.com.

NOTES

For the Whole Family!

EXPERIENCING

GOD

AT HOME

Welcome

TOM & RICHARD
BLACKABY

Experiencing God at Home takes a fresh path back into the rich roots of Henry Blackaby's world-renowned *Experiencing God* writings to connect what happens in our homes to what happens in our churches.

Every WORD Matters™
BHPublishingGroup.com

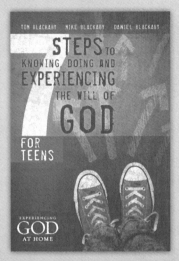

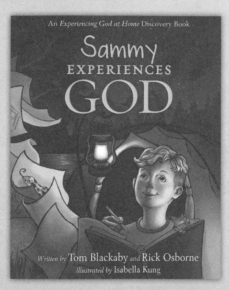

For teachers and librarians everywhere —L.N. & F.D.

If You Take a Mouse to School

If You Take a

BY **Laura Numeroff**

ILLUSTRATED BY **Felicia Bond**

Laura Geringer Books
An Imprint of HarperCollins*Publishers*

is a registered trademark of HarperCollins Publishers

If You Take a Mouse to School
Text copyright © 2002 by Laura Numeroff
Illustrations copyright © 2002 by Felicia Bond
Manufactured in China. All rights reserved.
www.harpercollinschildrens.com

Library of Congress Cataloging-in-Publication Data
Numeroff, Laura Joffe.
    If you take a mouse to school / by Laura Numeroff ; illustrated by Felicia Bond.
        p.   cm.
    Summary: Follows a boy and his mouse through a busy day at school.
    ISBN-10: 0-06-134957-7 — ISBN-13: 978-0-06-134957-7
    [1. Schools—Fiction.   2. Mice—Fiction.]   I. Bond, Felicia, ill.   II. Title.
PZ7.N964Ii   2002   00-067280
[E]—dc21   CIP
                                                                                AC

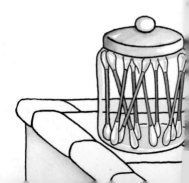

Mouse to School

If you take a mouse to school,

he'll ask you for your lunchbox.

When you give him your lunchbox,
he'll want a sandwich—

and a snack for later.
Then he'll need a notebook
and some pencils.

He'll probably want to share your backpack, too.

When you get to school,
he'll put his things
in your locker
and take a look around.

He might do a little math,

and spell a word or two.

He'll even try a science experiment!

Then he'll need to wash up.

You'll have to take him to the bathroom.

Once he's nice and clean,

he'll be ready for his lunch.

On the way to the lunchroom,
he'll see some building blocks.

He'll build a little mouse house

and make some furniture out of clay.

Then he'll need some books
for his bookshelf.
He'll start by writing
one of his own,
so he'll need a lot of paper.

He'll probably use up all your pencils.

When he's finished,

he'll want to read his book to you.

Then he'll want to take it home.
So he'll put it in your lunchbox,

and tuck it in a safe place.

When the bell rings,
he'll run out to wait for the bus.

While he's waiting,
he'll play a quick game of soccer.

Then he'll ask you to
shoot a few baskets,

and do a little skateboarding.

When he stops to catch his breath,
he'll want to eat his snack.

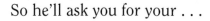

So he'll ask you for your . . .

lunchbox.

And chances are,

if he asks you for your lunchbox,

you'll have to take him

back to school.